YOUR BEST
HEALTH CARE
NOW

Get Doctor Discounts,
Save with Better Health Insurance,
Find Affordable Prescriptions

FRANK LALLI

TOUCHSTONE

New York   London   Toronto   Sydney   New Delhi

TOUCHSTONE
An Imprint of Simon & Schuster, Inc.
1230 Avenue of the Americas
New York, NY 10020

First Touchstone hardcover edition September 2016

TOUCHSTONE and colophon are registered trademarks of Simon & Schuster, Inc.

For information about special discounts for bulk purchases, please contact Simon & Schuster Special Sales at 1-866-506-1949 or business@simonandschuster.com.

The Simon & Schuster Speakers Bureau can bring authors to your live event. For more information or to book an event, contact the Simon & Schuster Speakers Bureau at 1-866-248-3049 or visit our website at www.simonspeakers.com.

Manufactured in the United States of America

1   3   5   7   9   10   8   6   4   2

Library of Congress Cataloging-in-Publication Data

Names: Lalli, Frank, author.
Title: Your best health care now : get doctor discounts, save with better health insurance, find affordable prescriptions / by Frank Lalli.
Description: New York : Simon & Schuster, 2016. | "A Touchstone Book."
Identifiers: LCCN 2016011242 | ISBN 9781501132865 (hardback)
Subjects: LCSH: Medical care, Cost of. | Health education—Research. | Medical economics. | BISAC: HEALTH & FITNESS / Health Care Issues. | BUSINESS & ECONOMICS / Personal Finance / General. | BUSINESS & ECONOMICS / Consumer Behavior.
Classification: LCC RA410 .L35 2016 | DDC 338.4/73621—dc23
LC record available at https://lccn.loc.gov/2016011242

ISBN 978-1-5011-3286-5
ISBN 978-1-5011-3290-2 (ebook)

To Carole,
who told me to write this book
to help others find affordable care.

Contents

1. **How to Use This Book:** How I Became a Health Care Detective, and How You Can, Too   1

2. **Get the Health Care You Deserve:** A Guideline for Patients   11

3. **America's Health Care Is Actually Better Than Ever:** What You Need to Know About the Affordable Care Act   29

4. **Ten Essential Health Care Benefits You Are Entitled to Get:** What You Are Guaranteed—and What to Watch Out For   39

5. **The Smart Way to Shop for Health Insurance:** Pinpointing the True Cost—and Value—of Any Plan   55

6. **How to Keep the Doctor and Hospital You Like:** And Navigating Other Open Enrollment Challenges   69

7. **Watch Out for Big Medicare Surprises:** Ten Mistakes Everyone Over Sixty-Five Should Avoid   83

8. **Confounding Billing Codes and Other Bizarre Obstacles:** Why Understanding Medical Codes Is Key to Figuring Out Costs   103

9. **Pink Confusion:** When Should Women Get Screened for Breast Cancer?   115

10. **Don't Let Dental Insurance Bite You:** How to Be Your Own Best Advocate in the Dentist's Chair   134

11. **The Pluses and Minuses of Health Savings Accounts:** What You Save—and Might End Up Paying—with an HSA ... 141

12. **The Smart Way to Book a Doctor Visit:** And Get a Discount, Too ... 147

13. **Don't Cough in the Doctor's Office Unless You Really Mean It!:** Tips to Avoid Sneaky Fees ... 156

14. **Stop Paying Twice as Much for Your Drugs:** Why Prescription Drugs Are So Pricey ... 172

15. **Seventeen Ways to Save Money on Drugs:** Easy Ways to Work with Your Doctor, Your Insurer, Your Pharmacy, and Others to Get the Best Prices ... 197

16. **The Wonder Drug Racket:** Secrets to Getting a Costly Specialty Drug at a Price That Won't Bust You ... 211

17. **What to Do When the Doctor Suggests a Costly Procedure:** Don't Get Blindsided by a Budget-Bashing Bill ... 218

18. **If You Go to the Hospital, Don't Pay the Bill:** Nine Ways to Save Money at the Hospital ... 228

19. **If You Get Bad Medical News:** Follow This Positive Action Plan ... 239

20. **Rules for Life:** The Three Keys to Becoming a Health Care Detective and Getting Your Best Care—Now ... 279

The Health Care Detective Glossary in Plain English ... 291

Easy-to-Find Resources ... 311

Acknowledgments ... 317

Index ... 323

CHAPTER 1

How to Use This Book

How I Became a Health Care Detective, and How You Can, Too

No one should be surprised to get cancer. More than half of us will be diagnosed with the disease in our lifetimes. Still, when I got hit with it, I was stunned.

I got the phone call so many of us have learned to dread in November 2008 while I was at a high point in my career. I was the editor in chief of Reader's Digest International, managing the company's fifty worldwide editions in twenty-two languages, and I had just helped launch a *Reader's Digest* magazine for mainland China. At a kickoff lunch in Beijing, our select group of executives was warned to avoid politics. But after several rounds of toasts, the Chinese team leader demanded my opinion of the U.S. presidential campaign. I surprised him and the other older Communist Party leaders there by boldly predicting that the young black candidate, Barack Hussein Obama—obviously a person of color—would become America's next president; days later, I gained immeasurable stature with the Chinese when I was proven right.

The magazine launch was a historic accomplishment for our company. DeWitt Wallace's once virulently anti-Communist magazine was now on sale in Red China. Population: 1.3 billion.

I loved the challenge of my job and the travel. I would fly

from London to Beijing for a business lunch and fly back the same day, holding meetings in the car to and from the airports. Surely, I thought, the occasional shortness of breath I had first felt walking downhill from London's Piccadilly Circus had something to do with flying around the world three times in ten months. It couldn't be anything more than that; after all, I was only sixty-six and jogging four miles a day. Still, I was concerned enough to see our family doctor, an excellent internist. He said I was anemic, probably because of the demands of my job. But he wanted me to see an oncologist "out of caution" to rule out anything serious.

The oncologist was upbeat. He ran a series of tests, including a spinal tap—again to rule out anything serious. He said he would call in a few days with the results.

I got his call in my favorite hotel room in London overlooking St. James's Place—a block from lovely St. James's Park, where I jogged around the lake after work as regal white swans floated by. I felt fine.

The oncologist, Raymond Pastore, a normally jolly fellow, didn't sound upbeat. Slowly I realized that he was telling me that, sorry, his tests had confirmed that I had a relatively rare form of blood cancer called multiple myeloma. The walls of the room closed in on me. I was trapped and utterly alone. I had just gotten a death sentence three thousand miles away from my wife, Carole, and my family, back home in New York.

"This is deadly serious," I heard myself saying. There was a pause, and Dr. Pastore said, "It is serious. But it is not necessarily deadly. We can treat this cancer and get it under control."

And we did.

My doctors assured me that I was in a "smoldering" presymptomatic phase that could last for God knows how long. But the disease would inevitably cross the line to "active." Then I'd have to confront my cancer by enduring months of debilitating chemotherapy, followed by a lifetime of drug "maintenance." A pill a day to keep the cancer away.

My cancer became active eighteen months later, and if I had not undergone chemo, I could have died within a year. Since the chemo, my maintenance drugs have kept my cancer in check for the past six years. Aside from getting on a first-name basis with more doctors than I want to shake a checkbook at, I've lived rather normally. My wife, Carole, our two daughters, son-in-law, and two adorable grandsons—not to mention me—are very grateful for that. If I drive carefully, don't try to break up fights in the subway, and don't play with guns, I should live to my eighties. What more could anyone ask?

Except there is a problem. The wonder drugs that are keeping me alive are insanely expensive. The pill I take each day now costs $809.52. If I had to pay that retail price—which works out to about $17,000 a month, or $204,000 a year—the pill would keep me alive long enough to file for bankruptcy. After more than fifty years of working and saving, I would have to choose between going broke or deciding to stop taking my medicine.

Still, I have been luckier than others. I have pills that control my cancer. Not everyone can say that.

In addition, my old employer, Time Inc., picked up my drug costs for the first few years. The most I had to pay for all of my medications, including my cancer pill, was $1,000 a year. But then in November 2012, the company announced a drastic cut in its health care benefits. Time Inc. would no longer cap employees' annual drug costs. Suddenly, beginning a month later in January 2013, there would be no limit on how much my out-of-pocket drug expenses might be. No limit. Not even for cancer drugs.

I assumed my familiar MO: I started working the story. With my old company no longer capping my costs, how could I get quality affordable health care to prolong my life? My first priority was to figure out what I would have to pay in 2013 for my maintenance drug, Revlimid, which I had been taking for years—and which cost $571 a day retail.

Sound simple? It wasn't. Depending on whom I talked to, I rarely got the same story twice. Various company staffers told me my Revlimid would cost me anywhere from $240 a year to $17,000.

Over a couple of weeks of relentless phoning, I filled my reporter's notebook with quotations from seventy people at sixteen different institutions. And in the end, I pinned down the cost: it turned out to be a manageable $60 a month, or $2 a pill, not $571.

But my two-week ordeal trying to navigate the health care system was so surreal that my wife urged me to write about how I became my own Health Care Detective for the *New York Times*. My op-ed article drew an immediate response. Soon I was poring over a stack of letters from readers who were going through similar and even worse experiences trying to find affordable care. The more I learned about our broken health care system, the more Carole told me to write a practical book about how regular people can become their own Health Care Detectives, get the care they deserve, and maybe save a few dollars, too.

Unless people get easy-to-follow guidance, how could the average person—someone without journalism skills, which include tenacity and a shameless willingness to be a nuisance; someone perhaps with scant Internet savvy and maybe only limited time—how could such a person find his or her way through such a system? My answer is: You can do it. I knew I could help people navigate our broken system, just as I had shown people how to master our personal finance system when I was editor of *Money* magazine.

Should America have a health care system that forces people to make seventy calls to find out what their lifesaving prescription will cost? Should insurance companies be allowed to refuse to put their prices in writing? Should doctors and hospitals be allowed to refuse to tell you their prices, let alone post them? And should we have a system that can leave you paying $2 a day for medicine or $571, depending on which person you reach on the phone and believe?

Of course not. But that's the system we have. That's the American way of health care.

One of my mother Ann's four sisters, Aunt Josephine, had a favorite saying: "God helps those who help themselves." I never liked that idea, because it made God the ultimate front-runner. But if Aunt Josephine could see today's health care system, she'd be saying, "I told you so. You have to take care of yourself."

I have learned how to take care of myself. As I sit here writing this, I am not paying $809.52 a day for my new cancer drug, Pomalyst, an amazing drug for newly relapsed myeloma patients like me. In fact, I am not paying a dime for it. My Pomalyst is being supplied to me free of charge for 2016 at least, but not by any of the sources you might imagine. Not by the government out of compassion, not by the drugmaker to avoid press attacks about profiteering on the sickest among us, and not by my very profitable supplemental health insurer. And certainly not by my old friends at my former employer, who once promised editors like me and others generous health benefits for life, but ended up handing us limited lump sums and wishing us luck shopping for our own insurance.

I'm getting my pill free because, literally out of self-preservation, I have figured out who to ask, what to ask, and what to do to get my best health care at the best price, including how to get my exorbitantly priced cancer drug free of charge.

Since my diagnosis in 2008, world-renowned doctors and surgeons have treated me at three of the country's top hospitals. At every turn, I have received some of the finest care this country's medical system offers—and I have gotten it for a lot less than people pay normally. For instance, after some negotiation, an acclaimed surgeon I wanted to operate on my back reduced his fee by 75 percent.

Everything I did, *you* can do. That's why I wrote this book. I believe I can help you become a Health Care Detective and master the skills to do three important things:

Navigate our country's sadly dysfunctional health care system, get better care than you have now, and save money.

If you want affordable health care—and who doesn't?—my book will help you:

- whether you are considering a regular checkup or a complicated surgery;
- whether your doctors want you to take low-cost generics or are suggesting the newest costly brand-name drugs advertised on the nightly news;
- whether your employer offers decent health insurance or you have to shop for coverage on your own;
- whether you've just enrolled in Obamacare and are worried about rising premiums and high deductibles that are increasing faster than your wages; and
- whether you're on Medicare and still getting surprised by costly bills.

No matter what your medical conditions or questions might be, you'll find useful guidance here. This book is not a drawn-out discussion of our national health policy. It is not a polemic. It's not theoretical. It's a practical guide to help you get better health care.

This book begins where those policy books end. Yes, our nation's health care system is broken, and Obamacare won't fix most of what's wrong with it. Okay, now what? My findings will show you what to do today to get the first-rate and affordable health care you deserve.

My advice is based on the reality that American health care is like a Middle Eastern bazaar. Everyone should start with the presumption that the price of nearly every service in our fee-for-service system is negotiable or probably beatable. For example, the best medicine at the best price is often under the counter and out of sight—until you ask the right questions. Then it's yours, maybe even for free. Recently, one of my doctors handed me $1,080 worth of a new nonaddictive pain medicine for free; all I did was ask for it.

No matter how professional your medical providers might be, they are also merchants trying to make a living. Indeed, a good living. They sell the same medical services on a sliding scale, depending on patient volume. It's not unusual, for example, for a doctor to sign contracts for his services with twenty or more insurance plans featuring twenty or more different sets of prices, depending on the number of patients the plans figure to deliver to his waiting room. The doctor's prices for identical services range from his deepest-volume discounts to the government in return for a parade of Medicare and Medicaid patients, to stratospheric retail heights for the uninsured stragglers who—very unfortunately—don't realize they probably could get a better price by asking for one, just like they do when they buy a car.

Remember the last time you were in a physician's waiting room, or perhaps at a hospital? There's a good chance someone sitting near you was about to get the same care as you did at one-quarter to one-half of your cost. This book will help you become a favored patient.

With all due respect to physicians, patients need to take doctors off some lofty perch and talk to them eye to eye. Dr. Marcus Welby—the small screen's kindly personification of doctor knows best played by actor Robert Young—is as long gone as the TV test pattern. You should think of your doctors as your well-informed health care partners. If you have a primary care doctor, you should trust that he or she knows a lot about your health. But studies show that physicians commonly start talking about eighteen seconds after a patient begins describing his health condition. And, in many cases, doctors move on to the next patient after only eight minutes, especially in hospitals, where they are increasingly being pressured to treat more patients more quickly.

Here's a typical experience that an old friend had last year with a top hospital dermatologist she's been seeing for thirty years: "I trusted him totally until last year, when he rushed through my appointment though I was having tests for squamous cell skin cancers, which often come back positive. He was reluctant to biopsy other spots. He looked at my well-dotted skin and said, 'You want me to biopsy all those?'

"I pointed out that three of the six he'd done were cancerous. But he insisted I'd made a five-minute appointment and refused to listen when I said that I'd called ahead and specified that I needed him to check my entire body. After he'd rushed off, I told his assistant that if I hadn't gone to him all those years, I'd think he was the worst doctor I'd ever seen."

Care like that is all too common and never acceptable. Given the high cost of medical services, plus the proliferation of health plans at work and on the Obama exchanges with high copays, coinsurance, and deductibles, patients get the best care at reasonable costs only when they demand that their doctors work with them as transparent partners and communicate fully.

Beyond that, not only *can* you negotiate with your new partner physicians about your care and its costs, you *should* negotiate. Your doctor has a sworn responsibility to protect your health. And I believe strongly that he also has a moral imperative to help protect your financial well-being. This book will tell you how to establish a relationship with your medical providers based on mutual respect, so that together you can make the best possible shared decisions about how to get the care you need—at a fair and affordable price.

HOW TO READ THIS BOOK

You're welcome to read every word of my book, cover to cover. But I think that relatively few people besides my wife, my editors, and me will actually do that. This is a consumer guide. It is organized to escort you through the health care system and point out the wise decisions you can make each step of the way, depending on your priorities. You'll find chapters describing exactly how to find your right-priced insurance plan; what you should do *before* you walk into a doctor's office for a checkup; what to do during an exam; the questions to ask when your doctor suggests a costly procedure and so on; and smart advice about how to handle a baffling and bloated hospital bill. (Hint: Don't pay it too fast.)

I suggest that you go to the chapters devoted to the most pressing health care issues you're facing. For example, if you're trying to find your best health insurance option, flip to chapter 5, "The Smart Way to Shop for Health Insurance." Digging deeper, if you're worried that your health plan might drop your doctor, go to chapter 6, "How to Keep the Doctor and Hospital You Like." Confused by Medicare? See chapter 7, "Watch Out for Big Medicare Surprises." Or if you're sick of surprise doctor bills, look at chapter 13, "Don't Cough in the Doctor's Office Unless You Really Mean It!"

On the other hand, if you're concerned about the high costs of drugs—and who isn't—turn to chapter 15, "Seventeen Ways to Save Money on Drugs." Also read chapter 16, "The Wonder Drug Racket."

Or if you or a loved one has gotten a troubling diagnosis, go to my very helpful chapter 19, "If You Get Bad Medical News."

And finally, be sure to read uplifting chapter 20, "Rules for Life."

Along the way, if you come across any medical, insurance, or bureaucratic terms that you might not understand fully, turn to our glossary for plain-English definitions.

The guidance throughout this book is meant to address the common health care issues people like you face, and then help you resolve them by following the straightforward advice you'll find here from front to back.

At its core, this book is grounded in my personal experiences and guided by my passion to inform and help my readers. I am not only a patient; I am an award-winning journalist who has long been guided by my motto as the editor of *Money* magazine: Our Readers Above All. Since my cancer diagnosis, health care has become my news beat, and helping others find affordable care has become my passion. Researching this book while also reporting about health care for the *New York Times*, *Parade* magazine, *Reader's Digest*, the *Boston Globe*, *AARP the Magazine*, and National Public Radio's Robin Hood Radio, I have interviewed more than three hundred doctors, medical experts, and policy makers, as well as scores of ordinary people with stories to tell. Then, guided particularly by my years at *Money*, I have distilled my findings into a series of simple tips that you can use to turn yourself into an effective Health Care Detective.

All you need, beyond my book, is a phone, the Internet, a notebook, and a little skepticism about what any one person in the system might tell you. Our health care system, as broken as it is, can still serve you well, if you make it serve you.

Here's my promise to you: My book will help you get better health care—and save you hundreds, if not thousands, of dollars.

CHAPTER 2

———— • ————

Get the Health Care
You Deserve

A Guideline for Patients

"If you're walking out of a doctor's office," said Dr. Allan "Chip" Teel, "and you can't think of anyone to thank—not the receptionist who greeted you, the nurse who took your vital signs, or the doctor who treated you—you might want to find another physician."

Dr. Teel, a board certified family doctor in Maine, is an associate of the Lown Institute, a Massachusetts-based think tank dedicated to strengthening the relationship between patients and physicians. Institute doctors believe that the closer you are to your physician, the better your care will be—with fewer needless and costly tests, procedures, referrals to specialists, and prescriptions.

When I began writing this book a few years ago, I thought experts who argued that Americans were being harmed by too much unnecessary care and medicine had it backward. I thought the big problem wasn't overutilization of health care but underutilization, which is why we needed the Affordable Care Act to help tens of millions of people to afford to see a doctor, sometimes for the first time.

But as I worked on this book, interviewing more doctors and reading studies, my opinion shifted. I still think underutilization is a huge problem. And so is overutilization, which might be inflating the nation's health care costs by around one-third, or $1 trillion (with a *t*), each year, as some experts estimate.

I have come to agree with the core belief of the Lown Institute (rhymes with *down*), an independent nonprofit organization with a growing network of five thousand participating providers. Like the Lown members, I think that millions of people are deprived of necessary care each year, while millions of others are harmed by unnecessary, ineffective, and sometimes unwanted medical treatments.

Renowned cardiologist Dr. Bernard Lown, a Nobel Peace Prize winner, founded the Boston-based institute in 2012 and made its mission as pointed as a scalpel: To convince medical providers to give their patients only the care they need, based on the best scientific evidence.

Lown's motto for providers is: "Do as much as possible *for* the patient, and do as little as possible *to* the patient." Makes sense to me.

But exactly what standard of care do patients deserve? I decided to collaborate with the Institute to spell this out. Not just the care you normally get, or probably expect, or settle for too often—but the level of personal care you deserve.

Later in this book, we'll deal with how to navigate the health care system, including how to find the best plan, pay the least money for quality procedures, and avoid surprise medical bills. But let's start here by establishing a few guidelines about what you need to do to get the health care you deserve—now.

SHOULD YOU GET AN ANNUAL EXAM?

An increasingly persuasive number of experts say that people without symptoms or chronic conditions can safely skip one or two annual exams. The Lown doctors I interviewed tended to agree, but only for people up to age fifty. They drew a bright line there. They say people over fifty should get full physical examinations every year.

"It's true that there isn't a whit of evidence that annual exams prolong lives," said Dr. Michael Fine, a family doctor and the former director of the Rhode Island Department of Health, "but I always learn something valuable."

The doctors pointed to three substantial benefits of annual exams.

First, regular visits strengthen the personal bond between the patient and the doctor. Lown's doctors stressed that the visits help patients and physicians learn to trust one another, so they can have open and honest conversations when they face big decisions, such as whether or not to have an operation or try a new medicine with potentially severe side effects. "Patients need to know that the doctor cares about them," said Dr. Katie Grimm, a palliative care doctor in Buffalo, New York. She said she often spends an hour getting familiar with new patients.

Dr. Patrick Lee, medical director of the Lynn Community Health Center in Massachusetts, underscored that point by quoting Teddy Roosevelt: "Nobody cares how much you know until they know how much you care."

Second, patients who come in for regular checkups get invaluable preventive care. For example, Dr. Fine said that colon cancer could be virtually eradicated if everyone over fifty got regular colonoscopies. "Colon cancer is a preventable disease," he said. "And it rarely affects people under fifty."

He added that HIV-AIDS could also be eliminated nationwide by screening all sexually active men and women, and then stabilizing those infected to control the transmission of the disease. "The screening, which is voluntary, costs about thirty dollars," he said, "compared with the four-hundred-thousand-dollar lifetime cost of treating someone with the full-blown disease." Because of an emphasis on screening, Rhode Island reported only seventy-five new cases of HIV in 2014 out of a population of one million.

And third, the regular visits help doctors to eliminate extra unnecessary and wasteful care. The doctors stressed that their regular patients never walk into their offices as strangers, perhaps needing a battery of largely useless and costly tests just to get started.

"If I don't know you, and you walk in sick," explained Dr. Fine, "we're starting at zero. But if I know you, chances are I have your problem diagnosed before you walk in." (For more on the debate over annual checkups and my advice, go to chapter 13, "Don't Cough in the Doctor's Office Unless You Really Mean It!")

HOW LONG SHOULD YOU WAIT FOR AN APPOINTMENT?

The most important point is this: If you have a serious symptom, the doctor should see you *immediately*.

Emergencies aside, you should not need to wait more than two or three weeks for a checkup with a general practitioner and no more than two months to see a specialist. However, people on Medicare and Medicaid in particular can run into long delays based on the hundreds of dollars more the physician can collect by keeping private patients at the head of the line.

Whatever the reason, don't accept long delays without badgering the doctor's office with daily calls, as I do, to see if a slot has opened. Or if your primary doctor refers you to an elusive specialist for, say, your crippling back pain or a possible serious concussion, don't hesitate to ask your primary to help you get the earliest possible appointment.

Doctors tend to refer their patients within informal networks of specialists and other providers. And the mutually beneficial referrals are reciprocated. The more a doctor recommends a particular specialist, the more likely the specialist might be to return the favor. Keep that in mind the next time you run into a delay seeing a provider your doctor recommended. Tell your doctor about your difficulty booking the visit and ask her to call for you.

One call from your doctor should open the specialist's door, as you'll see in Maggie's story in chapter 9, "Pink Confusion: When Should Women Get Screened for Breast Cancer?"

The Lesson. I believe strongly that a doctor who refers you to another has an obligation to help you actually see that physician. Do not hesitate to ask your doctor to intercede for you.

HOW LONG SHOULD YOU HAVE TO WAIT IN THE WAITING ROOM?

Lown doctors differed on this question, from no more than five minutes to twenty-five at most. But all of them said the staff should apologize and keep you informed about any delay.

"I handed out coupons for coffee," said Dr. Fine, who tended to run late. "That worked out for the patients and the coffee shop across the street."

He also remembers being a bit too efficient when he took over his first practice from a revered rural physician famous for his two-hour waits. "I cut my wait times to fifteen minutes, and the patients went into an uproar," he said. "They had come to count on the other doctor's much longer waits to catch up with their neighbors. They didn't want to see me as much as they wanted to socialize."

"When you finally see the doctor," said Dr. Lee, "he should shake your hand and explain exactly why you had to wait, even if his reception team has already done that."

Many primary physicians book twenty to twenty-five patients a day, which works out to about twenty-five minutes per patient in a long day. They figure that some simple ten-minute visits will allow them to spend up to forty-five with others. But emergencies do disrupt the best of offices—and overbooking plagues the worst.

As a general rule, the older patients are, the more likely they will be to put up with long waiting times. "In my experience, members of Greatest Generation especially are too forgiving toward disrespectful doctors," said Lown Institute president Vikas Saini, a cardiologist, who swore to me that he stayed on schedule 70 percent of the time.

No matter what your age, if you find yourself sitting next to a couple of people who are also booked for your time, seriously consider not waiting around for an hour or two to see who wins the lottery to see that doctor first. Find a physician who does not overbook on the assumption that up to one-third of the patients won't show up—and if they all walk in along with you, that's your hard luck. So sad, too bad.

Recently, after waiting more than an hour for her dermatologist, my wife Carole went up to the receptionist and said as politely as she could, "I can't wait any longer. I'm leaving. Please tell the doctor that my time is as valuable as his is." The receptionist stood up and implored her not to leave: "I'm sure he can see you in five minutes."

A nurse immediately led my wife into an examination room. Sure enough, the doctor walked in five minutes later and apologized for the "emergency delay." Since this was a follow-up visit to check on a negative biopsy, the doctor needed only three minutes to see that the biopsy wound looked fine. Then, despite her seventy-five-minute wait for three minutes of care, the doctor couldn't resist pointing out that the follow-up visit was included in his original bill.

"You know," he said, "this one is on the house." As if he deserved to be paid for his extremely discourteous treatment.

Even with that mistreatment, my wife was more fortunate than Patricia Cyr was. In her book *A Patient's Perspective: Tips for Your Doctor Visits and More*, Cyr recalls being ushered into an examination room at around noon. The doctor asked her to take off her clothes, put on a paper gown, and wait. He said he'd be right back.

After around a half hour, she needed a restroom. Cyr put her clothes back on and headed down the hall. She heard several people laughing and talking in a room at the far end of the hallway. When she looked in, she saw the doctor and his staff sitting around a table eating lunch.

Showing extraordinary patience, Cyr returned to the examination room, got back into the flimsy gown, and waited for the doctor to finish his lunch. He didn't see her until around one o'clock, well over two hours late.

"It was very obvious to me that when he told me to put on the gown, he knew he'd be spending nearly a full hour down the hall eating lunch," said Cyr. "I thought it was very rude of him." Chalk up Cyr as a master of understatement.

My Teaneck, New Jersey, high-school pal Sybil Sage would never do that. She fights back. Sybil, one of the trail-blazing female TV comedy writers (*The Mary Taylor Moore Show, Rhoda, Maude*), told me that after many experiences, she's up to her nose with doctors keeping her waiting:

"One doctor that really pissed me off was Beverly Hills plastic surgeon Harry Glassman. I sat in his waiting room and got to stare at a famous movie star who looked great waiting with me. But after close to an hour, I went to the desk and said, 'If I'm not taken next, I'm getting a T-shirt that says, *I got my nose from Harry Glassman.*'"

Sybil doesn't like her nose. Apparently Dr. Glassman doesn't either. He saw her next.

"There should be a group called Patients Without Patience," Sybil added. "We all vow to leave if the doctor doesn't see us in twenty minutes."

Who knows? Maybe patients marching in with Patients Without Patience T-shirts would work. If your doctor regularly runs late, you don't have much to lose trying that, beyond the $20 to make the T-shirt.

Here's my (more serious) advice: Promise yourself that you'll never again wait for a doctor for more than a half hour. The next time an assistant says the doctor is running late for whatever reason, say that you can only wait until a specific time, such as a quarter to one. Faced with a deadline, chances are the staff will find a way to fit you in. But if you're still waiting at a quarter to one, do what my wife did. Tell the person in charge at the front desk politely but firmly that your time is valuable and that you are leaving.

Then leave—and don't look back. Find another doctor with similar qualifications, but one who treats his patients with the respect they deserve.

HOW MUCH FACE TIME
SHOULD YOU GET WITH THE DOCTOR?

Dr. Saini said flatly, "You can't do a proper annual physical exam in twenty minutes." He thinks the examining doctor needs a minimum of forty-five minutes with the patient. Lown doctors are committed to getting the patient's full medical history, listening to the patient describe his health without interrupting, and performing a hands-on exam to check the patient's vital signs.

Dr. Lee goes a step further. He asks his patients to describe their most important goals for the next few years, such as seeing a granddaughter graduate or completing a training program to get a better job. Then he asks them to write down two or three things they can do to help meet those goals, such as quitting smoking or exercising more. They then both sign the paper. "My patients walk out of my office with a signed contract in their own words," said Dr. Lee. "It works. People improve their health habits."

The extended time Lown doctors spend one-on-one contrasts sharply with common practice, particularly in hospitals, where doctors often spend no more than eight to ten minutes with patients. Lown doctors argue that too many of those doctors interrupt their patients' descriptions of their conditions and then try to fill the gaps in their knowledge by ordering wasteful lab tests and costly procedures as well as needless prescriptions.

Dr. Saini added bluntly, "Too many doctors substitute testing for the time they should be spending with their patients, getting to know them and figuring out their conditions."

According to Dr. Teel, "Generally, lab tests lead to the correct diagnosis only five percent of the time." He explained, "You get eighty-five percent of the diagnosis from your patient's medical history and ten percent from your physical exam. Tests should be a last resort. They are no substitute for a proper exam."

By the way, although Lown doctors agree that the patient's detailed health history is critical, they differ on how best to obtain the information. Dr. Lee relies on multipage questionnaires that can take patients up to two hours to complete. The questionnaires are detailed enough to probe sensitive subjects that patients are often reluctant to discuss, such as depression or addiction.

But Dr. Fine told me: "I hate the questionnaires. I want to hear the patients' stories in their own words face-to-face. They talk. I listen. Then I toss in lots of pesky questions, sometimes about their sex lives or spousal violence. I want to hear it all."

Words to remember: Oliver Sacks, the brilliant neurologist and author who died in 2015, was a Lown doctor in spirit. He believed strongly that you couldn't understand disease unless you understood the person. And like Lown doctors, he worried that this basic truth was being papered over with scans, tests, and procedures.

He wrote: "To restore the human subject at the centre—the suffering, afflicted, fighting, human subject—we must deepen a case history to a narrative or tale."

WHAT IF YOU WANT MORE CARE
THAN THE DOCTOR SAYS YOU NEED?

This is one of the areas that tests the bonds between patients and doctors. Generally, Lown doctors will listen carefully to the patient's request, say, for a Magnetic Resonance Imaging (MRI) scan of a knee sprain. "After listening, I will tell the patient he is wasting his time and money," said Dr. Fine.

And if he insists? "If I don't think the request will do any harm, chances are I might go along to maintain our relationship," Dr. Fine said.

"Fact is, in my experience, ninety percent of my recommendations are done without true conviction, so there's room for compromise."

But Dr. Fine stressed this: "Every time the patient's request presents a potential risk, I say no. For example, I never write prescriptions for unnecessary narcotic medicines."

HOW SHOULD YOUR DOCTOR FOLLOW UP?

Many doctors do not follow up with patients after a visit because they are not paid to do it. But the Lown doctors I interviewed consider following up an essential medical service. Their nurses or other staffers, sometimes called "health coaches," phone all patients within two or three days to check on how they feel and whether they are following instructions and taking their medicines. And if a patient has had a procedure, like an epidural or a colonoscopy, a staffer normally calls the next day.

Dr. Fine goes beyond that. Aside from follow-up calls, he sends his patients letters after each checkup describing their health in detail. He said, "They get that letter from me even if they are normal."

When the office has lab results, nurses call with good news. The doctor delivers bad news.

"I invite the patient, along with a spouse or friend, to come in and see me," said Dr. Fine. "I keep the visit as honest and positive as possible by pivoting to specific steps we should take to address the problem."

He added, "The patient leaves my office with a positive plan of action and knowing that I am here to take care of him."

Dr. Fine also worries about patients who check on their own lab results electronically in a patient portal. Often they don't understand the medical terms and misinterpret the results. Worse, they run the risk of being shocked by a stark description of a dreaded diagnosis.

"A patient portal," said Dr. Fine, "can be a very lonely place to be to get bad news."

My Advice. Unless you are confident that you can understand a lab report and are prepared for some possible bad news, I suggest that you rely on your doctor's office to explain the results to you. Always ask when you can expect the doctor to give you the results. Then, if you don't hear from the office by that day, call.

In my experience, the worst I've had to deal with were a day or two of delays that my doctors blamed on the lab. I've sometimes waited anxiously, especially for my latest blood cancer counts. Even then, I've preferred to have my doctors report any significant results to me rather than risking that I would misread the results and turn my anxiety into a panic attack of unfounded fears.

Right now a hospital tests my blood every Monday and sends the results to my primary care doctor, my oncologist, my myeloma specialist, and me. We're monitoring how much my powerful new drug, Pomalyst—a combination anticancer agent and immune system suppressant—is inhibiting the proliferation of my blood tumors (a good thing), but also debilitating my immune system (a bad thing).

My New York oncologist, Dr. Pastore, and I compare notes on this balancing act regularly by phone and email as the lab numbers slide this way and that. So far, so good.

SHOULD YOUR DOCTOR GIVE YOU HER HOME PHONE AND EMAIL ADDRESS?

Lown doctors' preferences vary. Dr. Teel gives his regulars his home number. "I get a couple of calls in the middle of the night a year," he said. "If anything, patients might be more reluctant to call me at home than they should."

Other Lown doctors told me they rely on email that they and their staffers try to answer within twenty-four hours.

As Dr. Teel put it: "A doctor's office should not be surrounded by a stone wall."

I have gotten all the access I've needed either through the doctor's home phone or email. For example, the first time I visited Dr. Kenneth Anderson, the acclaimed multiple myeloma specialist at Dana-Farber Cancer Institute in Boston, he said, "You are my patient. Here is my email address."

My New York primary care doctor, John Rodman—a family friend and my medical "quarterback"—gave me his home phone long ago and has urged me to call him, or even come to his home, when I needed him. But as Dr. Teel noted, if anything, having John's home number has made me hesitant to bother him. And that's not the smartest thing I did in 2015.

A deep crimson rash appeared on the inside of my right thigh that then seemed to spread to the left side of my chest above my heart, where a pacemaker was inserted years ago to help my system tolerate my drug Revlimid. I also felt lousy. When John examined me in his office, he thought I might have been infected by an insect bite. If so, I should feel better by Saturday. But if I did not, he said I should come to his home Saturday, and he would examine me there.

I didn't feel any better on Saturday and the rash near my pacemaker was redder, but I couldn't bring myself to bother John at home. I told myself, "You don't feel any *worse*; you'll be fine."

By Monday, when I saw him in his office, the pacemaker area was a deep, angry red. He rushed me to NewYork-Presbyterian Hospital. One possibility was that a lead wire from the pacemaker to my heart had become infected. The doctors there—including my cardiologist, the surgeon who inserted the pacemaker, and an infectious disease specialist—were more or less baffled the first day until my blood tests revealed that I had a festering case of Lyme disease. All I needed was a round of the antibiotic doxycycline to knock it out.

Of course, I could have saved myself a couple of days of grief if I had seen John at home on Saturday. Which is a point he has made to me several times since.

SHOULD DOCTORS POST THEIR PRICES?

Fact is, extremely few doctors post their prices in their offices or online. Several of the doctors I interviewed—whom I consider good guys—told me they wished they saw a way to do it. They explained that they accept roughly twenty or thirty different health insurances, so depending on how much each carrier paid, they actually have twenty or thirty different prices for each of their services. Therefore, they said, posting prices makes no sense.

Here's where I part with them. Doctors actually have one price—the asking price for each of their services. They award discounts of 15 percent to 75 percent off that price, depending on the volume of patients the insurance sources figure to deliver. I believe doctors should post their asking prices. "There's a big game going on," one physician conceded. "The more the insurance companies, Medicare, and Medicaid squeeze their reimbursement rates, the more doctors jack up their asking prices." Obviously, that's a game better played in secret.

Over a glass or two at a wine bar, a respected specialist not associated with Lown offered an unvarnished reason for not posting his prices. "That would be aggravating," he told me. "The minute I posted my prices, some guy down the road would undercut me."

Which is precisely why I'd like to see all medical providers compelled by law and ethics to post their prices and create a transparent marketplace for patients to shop for the best health care at the fairest prices.

CAN YOU ASK YOUR DOCTOR FOR A DISCOUNT?

Medical costs are a lot like airline tickets. They range widely and are negotiable. So, yes, you can ask for a discount, especially if you are paying cash because you have a high-deductible health plan; people with insurance are not legally obligated to use it. Or perhaps you don't have insurance at all. Or you simply can't afford the full fee. One study showed that more than 60 percent of patients who asked for discounts got them.

As you'd imagine, patients have to raise the issue. And they should do it before the examination begins, if possible, face-to-face with the doctor. Once they earnestly describe their financial circumstances, some doctors routinely cut their rates in half or even ask for as little as 10 percent. In rare cases, they might manage to provide the care for free.

Dr. Fine recalled that when he was practicing in dirt-poor eastern Tennessee, a teacher with no health insurance walked unsteadily into his office. From the patient's severe lack of balance, Dr. Fine knew he needed an MRI of his brain stem immediately. He also knew the low-paid teacher didn't have the hundreds of dollars to pay for it.

"I called around to some friends with MRI equipment," said Dr. Fine, "and I made it happen for free."

He added: "I believe that people who go into the medical profession have an ethical core to help patients as much as they can."

The Lown Institute has no policy on doctor discounts. But Dr. Fine said, "I say to the patient, 'Just pay me what you can afford.' Sometimes that's five dollars. That's okay, because I'm building a relationship with that person and his family and friends. In a year or so, he might have a job with great health insurance. Believe me, it all works out."

My Advice. If you are facing a medical bill you truly can't afford, consider this idea: Whether or not your doctor is among the 90 percent of physicians who accept Medicare patients, offer to pay the low Medicare rate. And if the provider accepts Medicaid, offer the even lower Medicaid rate.

Or go see Dr. Fine.

SHOULD DOCTORS GIVE YOU COPIES OF YOUR MEDICAL RECORDS?

The Lown doctors said that your medical records are your property, and providers should give them to you promptly when you ask for them. Under the 1996 federal Health Insurance Portability and Accountability Act (HIPAA), insurers and providers should send copies of your medical and billing records within thirty days. In some states, including California, New York, and Texas, they must send them in as little as five days. Generally, they can charge "reasonable costs" for copying and mailing records but cannot bill you for retrieving them.

But be warned, many doctors might keep you waiting a lot longer for two reasons. First, busy office staffers struggling with daily pressures often give rounding up records a low priority. In addition, some doctors sense that many patients request their records to help themselves find another provider; the sooner the patients get their records, the sooner they are former patients.

If you run into delays getting your records, become insistent. It once took me nearly two months to get my records from a respected specialist. I began calling the office every day until I finally connected with a staffer who either was tired of me or felt sorry for me. I'll never know which. But I got my records the next day.

WHAT'S THE RIGHT WAY TO BREAK UP WITH YOUR DOCTOR?

There might be fifty ways to leave a lover, but basically there are three scenarios to consider when you think your doctor is no longer giving you the time, attention, or perhaps the expertise you need.

Scenario One: You and the Doctor Barely Have a Relationship. You don't necessarily owe her an explanation about why you are moving on to a new physician. Simply send her a medical-records release request signed by your new doctor.

Scenario Two: You and Your Doctor Had a Reasonably Good Relationship, but You've Decided to Switch to a New Provider. As with other similar breakups in your life, you owe him a concise "Doctor John" letter. It should be marked "Personal," so you're sure it will get to him. And, no, you can't get by just by sending an email!

Thank him for his past care, but detail clearly why you are breaking up. Although it's too late for you, your criticism might spur him to make changes that will help his other patients. Don't forget to wish him well; you want to leave on the best possible terms, if for no other reason than you or your next doctor may someday want to ask him a question about your history.

And include a medical-records release request from your new doctor.

Scenario Three: You Two Once Had a Great Relationship, but It Has Gone Sour Lately, for More Than One Reason. Ask for a "last appointment" visit, and show up with carefully prepared notes. First, thank her for the care you used to get. But then turn to your list of the ways the doctor has disappointed you. Perhaps she used to spend thirty solid minutes with you, and now she barely sees you face-to-face for ten. Or her office has repeatedly messed up your prescription refills, forcing you to make extra trips to the pharmacist and also causing a delay or two in taking your medicine. Be as specific as possible.

Then stop talking and listen to what your doctor says. Perhaps she has just increased her staff to free herself to spend more time with her patients, and she's replaced the aid who tended to mix up prescriptions. If you are impressed by what she says, make another appointment.

On the other hand, if she doesn't say anything that satisfies you, thank her again and leave.

Then follow up with a handwritten thank-you card expressing your gratitude for the many things she did to keep you healthy in the past. Even when physicians are getting dumped, Dr. Lee said, "Handwritten thank-you notes mean a lot to us doctors."

And, of course, include a medical-records release request from your new doctor.

In the chapters that follow, we'll dive into specific aspects of health care that you need to understand to get better care and save more. For example, you'll learn whether the highly touted health savings accounts are a good bet for you or a ticking bomb you ought to avoid. Also, you'll see the critical factors to consider when you or a loved one is choosing between original Medicare and the popular Medicare Advantage plans. Plus, you'll learn the smart questions you should always ask to get the prescriptions you need at the lowest possible prices.

But first, let's turn to the Affordable Care Act. Whether you realize it or not, the sweeping law is influencing every aspect of your health care, no matter how you get your insurance coverage. And whether it's repealed, replaced, reformed, or left largely unchanged, the law will continue to affect you and your family for the foreseeable future.

CHAPTER 3

America's Health Care
Is Actually Better Than Ever

What You Need to Know About
the Affordable Care Act

One of Kathryn and David Schanfield's persistent nightmares about their vivacious and intelligent daughter, Abigail, has finally come to an end. The University of Minnesota graduate was born in 1991 with congenital toxoplasmosis, a wicked infectious disease that has forced her in and out of hospitals her entire life. She had her first surgery to imbed a shunt in her brain at ten months, followed by a series of shunt replacements and two eye operations.

Adding to the family's worries, Abby's parents feared constantly that her mounting medical costs would one day smash through their insurer's payout limits and crush them and their small manufacturing business with six-figure hospital bills.

"What would we have done?" Abby's mother said to me. "We didn't know. We would have lost everything." (See chapter 14 for a drugmaker's alarming attempt to hike the price of a drug that controls Abby's life-threatening disease by 5,000 percent, from $13.50 to $750 a tablet.)

Today the Affordable Care Act is helping the Schanfields of Minneapolis—and countless millions of others:

- The law phased out both the annual and lifetime limits on how much insurers would pay for covered medical bills.
- It mandates that insurers must cover everybody regardless of their medical history, including the seventeen million children like Abby with health issues. Before the ACA, insurers routinely rejected around one-third of the people shopping for insurance on their own.
- Insurers also can no longer charge people with preexisting conditions extra; before the ACA, insurers demanded as much as $2,000 a month more in premiums alone.
- Insurers can't charge women extra either, including women of childbearing age, who sometimes had to pay 50 percent more than men.
- Plan members can renew each year; insurers can no longer drop people who get sick.
- The law allows three million sons and daughters to remain on their parents' policies until age twenty-six.

On top of all that, the law greatly improved the quality of insurance being sold to individuals and families like the Schanfields by requiring that all health care plans offered through Obamacare and by large employers cover ten "essential health benefits." I will explain the essential benefits in detail in the next chapter.

Before we can dive into the hints and tips for saving you money on your health care costs, you need to understand the fundamentals of your health care options today. Health care rules are a moving target, but I'll try to keep what I tell you as timely as possible. As I write this, here's what you need to know about the Affordable Care Act (aka the ACA, or more commonly, Obamacare).

FORGET WHAT YOU *THINK* YOU KNOW
ABOUT OBAMACARE

Do you love it or loathe it? Or maybe you're somewhere in the middle, like me. As you'll see, I believe it's a positive but imperfect health care reform. That said, we've all heard too much misinformation about Obamacare. No matter what you think of the sweeping law that President Obama jammed through Congress in 2010 without a single Republican vote, you need to understand three things:

- **The Reform Law Is Here to Stay.** It might be improved by Congress in the next few years. But there's little chance it will be repealed before 2020, at the earliest.
- **It Is Improving Health Insurance.** How? Particularly by setting higher uniform standards, which, in turn, force insurers and employers to upgrade the coverage they offer.
- **It Is Achieving Its Primary Goal of Providing Health Insurance to the Uninsured at Largely Affordable Prices After Sizable Subsidies.** Only around 10 percent of Americans were left uninsured in 2016, down from nearly 19 percent three years earlier.

Those aren't just numbers. They measure lives. Before the ACA began reducing our masses of uninsured, including 200,000 cancer patients, experts estimated that the lack of health insurance contributed to 123 deaths a day—or 5 people an hour—largely among the working poor. US Congressman G. K. Butterfield Jr. (D-NC), chairman of the Congressional Black Caucus, said bluntly, "People are dying while lawmakers play political games."

Today most people get health insurance through work. Roughly 150 million Americans are covered by their employers. Another 125 million are insured by government programs such as Medicaid (72 million), Medicare (50 million), and the Veterans Administration (VA) (9 million).

By contrast, around 12 million people were signed up for Obamacare in 2016. More than 60 percent of them were uninsured before they signed up. Of that 12 million, around 9 million were enrolled in the thirty-eight states that use the federal marketplace HealthCare.gov, and 3 million had come in through the twelve exchanges run by individual states and the District of Columbia. In addition, another 7 million working poor earning slightly above the poverty line were enrolled in Medicaid in half the states that accepted the federal government's 100 percent funding for the entire expansion; in 2020 the feds will pay 90 percent and ask the states to pick up the remaining 10 percent.

Whether you are impressed by those 19 million enrollment numbers or not, you cannot escape its reach. Increasingly, nearly everyone you know will be affected by the reform of our health care system.

OBAMACARE 101: HOW THE LAW WORKS

Obamacare is a three-legged stool—or, depending on your point of view, a three-legged monster. The reform law needs its three legs to provide more than 90 percent of Americans access to affordable quality health coverage as a human right, not a privilege.

First, the law said that insurers must offer decent health plans at reasonable prices to everyone, despite the person's medical condition, health history, gender, or age. And so must all employers with fifty or more full-time workers clocking at least thirty hours a week; that's what's commonly called the "employer mandate."

Second, the law said every citizen must get health insurance or pay a fine, including the young and the healthy who might think they don't need insurance; that's called the "individual mandate." The fine—or "shared-responsibility payment," as the government's jargon-meisters dubbed it—began in 2014 at either a relatively modest $95 a year or 1 percent of your annual income, whichever was greater. But in 2016 it jumped sharply to $695 or 2.5 percent of household income—again, whichever is greater. In addition, as the regulations read today, if your health plan at work covers only you, you could be fined for up to two dependents if, say, your mate or child or other dependents do not get health coverage.

And third, the law provides generous subsidies to individuals and to families making up to $97,000 who buy Obamacare health plans through the law's online marketplace. Essentially, the federal government is stepping into the traditional role of employers for the working class and middle class and subsidizing about 75 percent of the cost of their Obamacare insurance available on the exchanges.

So to oversimplify, insurers must cover all comers, including the sickly. Obviously, that requirement puts insurers at risk. To mitigate that risk, the law greatly expanded the pool of insurance customers by requiring every citizen to get coverage, including the young and healthy. A vast number of the young, as well as many others, might not need much care in any given year, but the insurance carriers selling Obamacare need their premium money every year to remain solvent and profitable.

And the government is kicking in billions in subsidies in the form of tax credits to ensure that the poor and working families can afford the Obamacare health plans. Roughly 85 percent of the people buying Obamacare insurance on the state exchanges in 2016 were collecting generous subsidies, which allowed most of them to pay only around $100 a month in premiums for quality coverage. In addition, more than half of those collecting premium subsidies are also getting valuable federal cost-sharing assistance.

THE SUPREME COURT HAS SPOKEN,
BUT CRITICS KEEP BARKING

Republican lawmakers will continue to insist that the country cannot afford this sprawling entitlement, and that they will come up with a much better system once they control the White House and Congress. I'll outline popular right-leaning ideas in chapter 14. Meantime, Republicans have voted fruitlessly more than sixty times to gut President Obama's signature legislative achievement, including the repeal they got through Congress in 2016—which the president vetoed immediately.

In addition, conservatives have repeatedly attacked the constitutionality of the entitlement program in the courts, including the individual mandate, but they have only dented it, at best. Led by Chief Justice John Roberts, the Supreme Court has ruled that health care is a universal right, not a privilege only for those who can afford it.

The conservatives' cleanest victory was in *Burwell v. Hobby Lobby Stores Inc.*, in 2014. In a 5-to-4 decision along ideological lines, the court ruled that closely held corporations that follow deep religious principles can refuse to pay for specific contraceptives for their workers. This is the first time the court has ruled that for-profit corporations have religious rights. The court followed up in 2015 by ordering the Obama administration not to force some nonprofit religious organizations and churches to cover contraceptives for its employees until the courts sort out the church case.

Also, in *National Federation of Independent Businesses v. Sebelius*, conservative Chief Justice Roberts led a 5-to-4 ruling that allowed the fifty states to choose whether to expand Medicaid. That ruling has prevented an estimated 5 million poorest of the poor in half the states—disproportionately red and southern—from getting health coverage. However, in that same 2012 case, Roberts and the four liberal justices upheld the constitutionality of the individual mandate—one of the law's crucial three legs.

Then in 2015 Justice Roberts again led a 6-to-3 drubbing of what many experts considered the right's last best chance to upend the law through the courts. In *King v. Burwell*, the plaintiff (who had access to government care himself) failed to persuade all but the three most conservative justices that one funky four-word phrase in the nine-hundred-page law—"established by the state"—prohibited the federal government from continuing to provide subsidies to the thirty-four states, virtually all led by Republican governors, that had not set up their own state exchanges. The *New York Times* editorial page dismissed *King* as "a cynically manufactured and meritless argument" that would have stripped away the health coverage of 6.4 million Americans.

Justice Roberts ruled: "A fair reading of legislation demands a fair understanding of the legislative plan"—in this case, to provide subsidies nationwide to help the poor and middle class afford ACA health insurance, many for the first time in their lives.

The late conservative justice Antonin Scalia, who was angry about Roberts again saving Obamacare, used the abbreviation for the Supreme Court to sarcastically say in his *King* dissent, "We should start calling this law SCOTUScare." Roberts laughed off the remark.

The defeats don't mean that conservatives will stop trying to "repeal and replace" Obamacare. Following the *King* ruling, many leading Republicans repeated that poll-tested pledge in their requests for campaign contributions. But political experts on the right and left say the Republican Party remains far from a consensus on a law to replace Obamacare. For example, if the court had sided with the conservatives in the *King* case and stopped the subsidies to millions, experts say the Republicans would have splintered and been blamed for the chaos—as well as for the ugly stories that would have surfaced, including broadcast coverage of people who could no longer afford their chemo and had gone home to die.

Or as Joseph Antos of the right-leaning think tank the American Enterprise Institute (AEI) conceded, Republican leaders would have been "the dog who caught the car."

None of this will stop the barking on the right, however. Antos's AEI, for example, wants to end the tax deductions employers receive for providing health coverage and use that money to subsidize a scaled-down version of Obamacare with ideas such as these:

- Ending the tax deductions would give many bosses a strong reason to stop supporting health care for their workers.
- Government subsidies would go only to people making around two times the poverty rate rather than four times under Obamacare.
- People would lose their protections for preexisting conditions if their coverage ever lapsed—say, for example, if they were laid off. Millions could be affected, since 129 million people under sixty-five have preexisting conditions. The unlucky ones would end up back in those old high-cost, high-risk pools, facing premiums of $7,000 or more a month and deductibles as high as $25,000.
- People could again choose cheap "consumer-directed" plans with few essential benefits, and again risk getting hit with big surprise medical bills that could wipe them out.
- Insurers would be allowed to sell policies across state lines, allowing the companies to create national plans based on the laws of the state with the fewest patient protections.

Listen to Executive Director Ron Pollack of Families USA, a consumer advocate group in Washington, DC, who has devoted his career to securing affordable health care for all. "The Affordable Care Act is here to stay," he said emphatically. "And it will get strengthened. The coverage it provides now is a floor, not a ceiling."

The reform law came along just in time for many working families. Historically, employers have provided health insurance to Americans as a benefit to attract and hold the best workers— and as a cheaper alternative than giving workers raises. But executives began rethinking the wisdom of providing coverage in the 1990s, when health costs started soaring. As per capita health costs nearly doubled in the ten years before the ACA became law, many companies capped how much they were willing to pay for health insurance and began dumping the rising costs onto the workers. According to the Henry J. Kaiser Family Foundation, a policy research organization, from 2010 to 2015, premiums rose more than twice as fast as wages (24 percent to 10 percent), and deductibles soared nearly seven times as much as raises (an eye-popping 67 percent to 10 percent). As a consequence, workers got bloodied. The Milliman Medical Index, which tracks health costs, shows that over the same five-year period, total health care costs for a typical family covered at work rose 43 percent to $24,671, while the employers' share of those costs rose only 32 percent.

What's worse, many truly unlucky souls have seen their coverage at work disappear altogether. CEOs grappling with the country's slow-growth economy continue to look for increasingly desperate measures to drive down costs and boost profits (as well as collect their executive bonuses), such as no longer covering spouses, early retirees, and anyone eligible for Medicare.

But thanks to the ACA reforms for individuals and small groups, there is good news for many workers. If your family income is up to $50,000 or so, and your boss pushes you or your dependents into Obamacare, you might end up better off. As I've mentioned, the federal government is providing generous sliding-scale subsidies to people earning all the way up to four times the poverty rate—including individuals making up to $47,080 a year in 2016 and families earning up to $97,000.

On average, families enrolled in Obamacare collected around $5,500 in subsidies in 2014, and 75 percent of them polled by the Gallup organization said they were satisfied with their health care costs. That's a higher number than the 61 percent of all insured respondents who said they were satisfied with their health costs, including those covered at work.

One of Obamacare's best provisions is that the coverage comes complete with annual hard-dollar caps on your *combined* out-of-pocket medical and drug expenses of about $6,400 for individuals and $12,800 for families.

In addition, in 2016 California's health insurance exchange, called Covered California, became the first state exchange to cap what consumers have to pay for expensive medications each month. Most people buying insurance through Covered California will have their specialty-drug costs capped at $250 per month per prescription.

Thanks to the reform law, people are getting the coverage that only lucky employees of major corporations enjoyed in the past. Indeed, one survey showed that 98 percent of health plans sold to individuals in 2013 did not meet the new ACA health plan standards.

"The idea of the law was to lift the quality of individual and small-group coverage to the same level as the coverage of large groups," said Claire McAndrew, senior health policy analyst at Families USA. "Everyone deserves quality health insurance."

CHAPTER 4

Ten Essential Health Care Benefits You Are Entitled to Get

What You Are Guaranteed— and What to Watch Out For

One of the main goals of the Affordable Care Act is to deliver ten essential health benefits to nearly every citizen who gets health insurance. All health plans sold in the ACA state marketplaces must incorporate each of the benefits. In addition, they set a standard for comprehensive coverage for all insurers.

Having said that, one of the first things you need to understand is that the essential benefits vary from state to state, depending on whether local insurance standards currently meet or exceed the federal government's goals. Also, large companies and corporations tend to self-insure workers, giving the executives the freedom to shape their own rules. Usually, however, big companies provide coverage that reflects the essential benefits.

All in all, if you have health insurance, your coverage should address these ten essential health benefits. Before you enroll in any insurance plan, measure its benefits against these ACA standards. Ideally, you want the most generous version of all ten.

THE TEN ESSENTIAL BENEFITS UNDER THE ACA

Ambulatory Patient Service. This is the most common form of health care, often called outpatient care. You walk into a doctor's office or medical facility with anything from a bruise to bronchitis, get treated, and walk out the same day. Virtually all health insurance plans provide this coverage, and members are commonly charged around a $20 to $45 copayment per visit. But a specialist could bill you double or triple that amount. A little oddly, this category also covers home health services and hospice care, and some health plans might limit the benefits to short periods.

Tip. The nation's roughly five thousand walk-in clinics, sometimes staffed only by nurses, often charge less than your copay for basics such as treating a bad cold or vaccinations. Check your nearby clinic's services and prices before you run to the doctor for a minor condition.

But don't run to a so-called convenient care clinic for every little sniffle; those charges add up, too. Harvard Medical School researchers concluded that people it studied wasted money getting treated at clinics for conditions they would typically have treated on their own, like waiting out a sore throat or low-grade fever.

Emergency Care in and out of Network. You go to a hospital emergency room with a sudden and serious condition, such as the symptoms of a heart attack or stroke. The emergency visit is widely covered, and people pay anywhere from $100 to $250.

Tip. Under Obamacare health plans, emergency room patients do not need to get preauthorization, and they cannot be charged extra for landing in an out-of-network ER.

Hospitalization. You are injured or become so sick that you are admitted to a hospital or skilled nursing facility for what's called inpatient care. As too many families know, with hospitals charging the uninsured around $2,000 or more per day just for room and board, here's where bills can soar. One day in a hospital can easily cost $5,000 to $10,000. I'm not joking. As I've mentioned, under the reform law, ACA health plans cap your maximum annual out-of-pocket expenses (excluding premiums) at an estimated $6,400 for an individual and $12,800 for a family. Those hard-dollar caps cover not only doctor and hospital bills but also drug costs—a significant benefit.

But there is a big *but*. The caps apply only to hospitals and other providers that are in your plan's network. If you go outside of your network for care from providers who do not have service contracts with your insurer, you might have to pay anywhere from, say, 30 percent to 100 percent of the bill.

Tip. Ask your insurer for the most current list of your plan's network doctors and hospitals that you are likely to need, and then stay "in network" if you possibly can. For example, assuming you are up to it, get to the hospital on your own rather than calling an ambulance that might deliver you out of network and out of luck. Also, if you might need skilled nursing, check to see if your plan limits its coverage—commonly up to around forty-five days.

Maternity and Newborn Care. Under the ACA, individual and small-group insurers must provide prenatal care at no extra cost, as well as cover childbirth and infant care for up to thirty days, depending on state standards. In addition, beginning in 2016, insurers must cover screening for depression in women during pregnancy and after birth. An estimated one in seven new mothers experience marked depression.

Traditionally, more than 90 percent of private plans sold to individuals before the ACA excluded maternity coverage. Others demanded an extra $1,000 a month for a year or two before childbirth.

Want to bet whether male or female executives at insurance

companies have historically had the last word on writing maternity benefits? During the Obamacare debates, when Arizona Republican Senator Jon Kyl said that, as a man, he didn't need maternity coverage, Senator Debbie Stabenow (D-MI) shot back, "Yes, but your mother probably did."

In addition in 2016, there were efforts in some states, including New York, to allow women who become pregnant to apply for Obamacare coverage immediately rather than having to wait until they gave birth or for the fall open enrollment period. Like childbirth, pregnancy would become what the ACA calls, with no irony at all, a "life event."

In addition, as I've noted, a child can be added to your family plan and remain covered until age twenty-six.

Tip. With many hospitals charging anywhere from $5,000 to $45,000 for a normal vaginal delivery, many new parents with insurance will continue to go home with $3,000 to $5,000 in bills, along with their priceless baby. So it's smart to nail down costs in writing with hospitals and birthing centers in your plan's network well before you have a child. Then budget for surprises. *Twins?!*

Mental Health and Substance Abuse Services, Including Behavioral Health Treatment. Not only does the reform law provide this relatively rare coverage, it offers services for a wide range of problems, including depression, drinking, and domestic violence. Plan members may be billed around $45 per session.

The Department of Health and Human Services estimates that nearly one in five Americans has a diagnosable mental illness. Yet around 40 percent of them were not getting treated before the ACA included mental illness as an essential benefit. As a result, millions of newly insured patients are pouring into mental health clinics, causing extensive backlogs.

Tip. This benefit varies widely state by state, often depending on whether you live in a Democratic blue state, where insurance standards tend to be more generous, or in a Republican red state. So if you or a loved one needs help, get the details from your insurer as soon as possible. Unfortunately you might have to deal with delays of up to two months before you get into a clinic, and then possibly face annual limits. In Utah, for instance, ACA plan members are generally covered for a maximum of eight visits a year with a behavioral therapist. Limiting care for people with mental problems is stupid public policy, in my opinion. But it's also the norm in many states, despite the ACA.

Rehabilitative and Habilitative Services. In short, rehabilitative care helps you recover skills, and habilitative care helps you develop them.

If you are injured or become ill, many health plans cover rehabilitation therapies to relieve pain and help you regain your ability to speak, walk, or work. The plans usually include equipment such as canes, knee braces, walkers, and wheelchairs.

Traditionally, however, few health plans addressed the reform law's requirement for habilitative service meant to overcome long-term problems such as maintaining physical abilities in the face of a debilitating disease like the degenerative neurological disorder multiple sclerosis. The new rules also cover speech therapy to help children develop the skills to speak at appropriate age levels.

Depending on your plan, you might pay anywhere from $20 for an outpatient visit to 20 percent or more coinsurance for inpatient therapy at a hospital. Plans also commonly limit sessions to, say, around thirty a year.

Tip. If you have the option, it's safer to choose plans with fixed dollar costs for services, called a copay, rather than those that impose a coinsurance percentage—anywhere from 20 percent to 80 percent—of what the provider charges. With fixed copays, you can budget more confidently and sometimes save hundreds of dollars, too.

Laboratory Services. With the essential benefits, insurers cover routine tests such as breast cancer screenings, prostate exams, and Pap smears as preventive care at no extra charge.

Tip. Ask your doctor whether each test he suggests is preventive or diagnostic, and why it is necessary. Unlike preventive procedures, you will nearly always have to pay something for a diagnostic lab test. Costs can range from a manageable $45 copay for a simple blood test to a 20 percent or more coinsurance for a $3,500 Magnetic Resonance Imaging scan—and, remember, that's *after* you have paid your annual deductible. Ouch!

Preventive and Wellness Services as Well as Chronic Disease Management. Many experts believe this benefit holds the key to curbing the nation's rising medical costs. The idea is to get people to see doctors and make healthier choices *before* they develop chronic diseases and run up bills at hospitals. Chronic disease accounts for nearly 90 percent of our health care costs. Partly to combat those costs, the new law greatly expands what is considered preventive care: tests and services generally available to you at no extra cost. For instance, prenatal care is considered preventive. In addition, you are allowed a free "wellness visit" with your doctor once a year to discuss your health and agree on the specific steps you can take to improve it, like losing weight, drinking less, quitting smoking, and exercising more.

In all, the law instructs insurers to provide the exhaustive list of fifty free screenings and services recommended by the United States Preventive Services Task Force. The USPSTF is an independent panel of experts in prevention and evidence-based medicine. The task force, formed in 1984, works to improve the health of Americans by making recommendations about preventive services such as screenings, counseling services, and preventive medications.

The task force's list includes aspirin with a prescription for men forty-five and up and women fifty-five and older to help prevent cardiovascular disease, cholesterol screening for men thirty-five and up and women forty-five and older, and obesity screening for everyone, beginning with children at age six. (Go to www.uspreventiveservicestaskforce.org for the entire list.)

Tip. With the essential benefits, your next colonoscopy should be a little less of an ordeal. Under the reform law, colonoscopies are classified as a preventive service. With an exchange plan, you cannot be billed for a routine colonoscopy—even if the doctor finds and removes polyps. Polyps, which are tiny masses that form on the colon lining or rectum, can be serious. One in five can develop into cancer eventually if they are not removed.

Despite the risk that polyps present, most company plans and even Medicare do not cover removing them at no cost. While the plans classify a routine colonoscopy as a free preventive service, the doctor could bill you hundreds of dollars extra if he removes a polyp. Once he finds a polyp, he considers the procedure diagnostic, not preventive. With a company plan, you could well be billed a percentage (often a coinsurance of around 20 percent) of the entire procedure, plus the usual office visit fee or the much higher hospital "facility" charges for, say, "renting" the operating room.

Doctors often charge the uninsured anywhere from just under $1,000 to well over $3,000 for a routine colonoscopy, plus up to $1,000 for removing polyps. And don't think it couldn't happen to you or someone close to you: studies show that doctors find polyps when screening 25 percent of men and 15 percent of women.

Prescription Drugs. As noted earlier, Obamacare plans sold on the exchange currently cap your combined out-of-pocket medical and drug costs at around $6,400 a year for individuals and $12,800 for families. That's a significant benefit for people with cancer and other serious illnesses. Although Americans, on average, spend about $800 a year on prescriptions, people who need wonder drugs can face bills ranging from $100,000 to

$700,000 or more a year. And those costs are soaring. According to a drug industry study, the number of Americans with medication costs over $100,000 tripled in one year to 139,000 in 2014.

Fortunately, many company health plans cap how much their workers have to pay for drugs, sometimes at around $1,000 or $2,000 a year. But, unfortunately, a significant number do not provide such a safety net.

You might be surprised to hear that Medicare Part D drug plans also do not cap drug costs. All Part D beneficiaries must keep paying—even the oldest and sickest who reach the program's "catastrophic" care. All patients, without exception, are responsible for 5 percent of their drug costs *after* their out-of-pocket costs exceed Part D's so-called catastrophic limit of $4,850. As one Medicare helpline staffer told me, rather jollily, "You keep paying forever, even if your costs top a hundred thousand dollars, or a million, for that matter." (For more on catastrophic care, see chapter 7, "Watch Out for Big Medicare Surprises.")

Tip. Check with your Human Resources Department and your insurer as soon as possible to learn what your exact medical and drug out-of-pocket limits are, assuming you have any. At the very least, you need to understand your risks.

Pediatric Care for Children up to Nineteen, Including Oral and Vision Care. In addition to allowing children up to age twenty-six to remain on their parents' policies, the new essential benefits cover children's basic dental and vision services. Health plans can now help protect children up to age nineteen against lifelong health problems by covering teeth cleaning twice a year, X-rays, filings, and necessary orthodontia at no extra cost. Children also are entitled to an eye exam and one pair of glasses or contact lenses a year.

Tip. Take full advantage of these new benefits for your kids, who might have been getting by without the dental and vision care they need. Few small-company plans offered these benefits until now. A recent government survey found that in 2013 roughly 95 percent of small-group plans did not cover child dental checkups, 40 percent did not cover eye tests, and 92 percent did not cover eyeglasses. And when dental or vision was offered as an option, members generally had to pay an extra $40 to $80 per month for a family plan. How do you spell rrrrrip-off?

WATCH OUT FOR RELENTLESSLY RISING COSTS AT WORK

Someone has to pay for those enhanced benefits, and at many companies that someone is you. Almost surely, the next upbeat-sounding open enrollment letter you get from HR will try to mask your company's latest efforts to shift more costs onto you. Since 2006, the total amount of health care costs that employers pay rose around 50 percent. That's a big number. But the share that workers pay doubled. My old employer set a cap on benefit payouts back in 2001 and has been pushing costs onto its workers and retirees since then. IBM began doing it in 1993, and so it goes.

Obviously, company executives don't broadcast shifting health costs onto their workers and retirees, though one executive I worked with kept boasting, "I saved the company from the retirees." Normally, they communicate much of the "cost sharing" as obscurely as they can.

So brace yourself if you see any of this increasingly common insurance jargon. It translates to this: Your boss is looking to jar open your wallet even wider, or perhaps even bar you from enrolling:

- If you see **"unitized pricing,"** that means you'll now pay for each of your dependents rather than getting a lower family rate. A recent national survey conducted by the insurance broker Aon Hewitt showed that only 5 percent of companies use unitized pricing now, but half of those polled expect to switch to it in the next three to five years. If you get unitized, you'll feel it. Health care benefits consultant Russ Blakely of Chattanooga, Tennessee, said that if you've been paying $400 a month for your family, expect to pay $450.

- **"Reference-based pricing"** means your employer is among the 10 percent of large companies capping how much you'll get reimbursed for certain services, especially those with prices that vary widely, such as MRIs or radiology. For example, the website Clear Health Costs (www.clearhealthcosts.com) reported in 2015 that people in the New York area could pay from $400 to $1,200 for a lower back MRI or $50 to $1,050 for a simple mammogram. Only 10 percent of companies providing health insurance have imposed reference pricing, but studies show that nearly 60 percent plan to introduce it soon.

- **"More efficient provider network"** means a narrow network. You'll have fewer doctors and hospitals that you can go to without paying extra for getting care outside of your plan's provider network.

- **"Wellness or healthy living incentives"** means your employer is asking you to take specific steps to improve your health, such as quitting smoking, in hopes of reducing the cost of covering you. Commonly, workers get rewarded with bonuses for taking the action but are sometimes penalized harshly if they don't. In all, around 35 percent of corporations have these programs.

Some employers, usually larger corporations, are asking workers to fill out health questionnaires and then join programs to lose weight or manage their diabetes, for example. And an estimated one in twenty large employers paid incentive bonuses of around $500 to $1,000 in 2015 to workers who followed through. But some companies penalized those who did not cooperate by raising their premium costs—or sometimes going so far as to prohibit them from enrolling in the company health plans.

As unfair as this sounds, it is all apparently legal: Judges in 2016 were ruling that barring workers who did not submit health questionnaires did not violate the Americans with Disabilities Act, which prohibits employers from discriminating against workers with severe health conditions.

In addition, the Affordable Care Act allows employers to use so-called financial incentives of up to 30 percent of the firm's cost of coverage—which can amount to thousands of dollars' worth of rewards or penalties. According to the Kaiser Foundation, around half of the large companies that offer wellness programs use carrots and sticks on workers, including some that apparently regard their workers as herds that need prodding.

- **"Consumer-directed health plan"** is just a friendly-sounding term for high-deductible insurance. Around 15 percent of all companies—and one-third of big corporations—were giving their workers no choice by 2015; they were only offering high-deductible plans. And another 40 percent of companies expected to do that soon, too.

  Bosses are pushing consumer-directed plans in large part because they are often upward of 20 percent cheaper to provide than traditional plans. Big companies, including Wells Fargo, JPMorgan Chase & Co., Honeywell International, and General Electric, are saving hundreds of millions by offering only high-deductible plans.

  In all, one out of every five people had high-deductible health insurance in 2015.

  Your boss might be so eager to shift you out of traditional coverage that he'll offer you up to $2,000 in "seed money" for enrolling. Still, even with a company contribution—or should I say bribe—the plan's high deductible will likely force you to pay for most, if not all, of your health costs out of your own pocket. The Kaiser Family Foundation (KFF) reported that one out of five workers with an individual plan at work in 2015 had an average deductible of $2,000 or more. In addition, more than 40 percent of all companies saddle their workers with deductibles of $1,000 or more. And 60 percent of small companies do that, too.

My Advice. Don't fall for HR's upbeat-sounding benefits letters. If you see a term you don't understand, or one that seems new, call HR and stay on the line until you get a straight answer. When Time Inc. stopped capping drug costs at $1,000 a year while I was taking a $140,000-a-year pill, the first HR staffer I reached tried to assure me that the change wouldn't affect me. But I pushed until I got the truth and then did all I could to protect myself. And as I've said, everything I did, you can do, too.

ARE AFFORDABLE CARE ACT HEALTH PLANS ACTUALLY AFFORDABLE?

When I began researching this book in 2013, I felt confident that Obamacare coverage would be affordable. I also thought the plan's expanded preventive services would keep people healthier and eventually hold down medical costs. Now I'm not so sure.

The ACA plans are costlier than I first thought for three main reasons:

Skyrocketing Costs. First, America's ever-rising health costs—already the highest in the industrialized world—are swamping whatever savings the extra preventive services might be providing so far. Although the increases are down from the annual double-digit pace of the past, health care costs are still rising at three times the rate of inflation. Powered prominently by runaway pharmaceutical prices, health care costs rose 6.8 percent in 2015 and were on track to climb an additional 6.5 percent in 2016.

Comprehensive Coverage Comes with a Price. The consensus among more than a dozen experts I've interviewed on this point is that the law's higher standards add around 4 percent to premium costs, depending on how robust or lean your state's health insurance standards were originally. In other words, two-thirds of the average 6 percent premium increase in 2015 could be traced to the law's comprehensive coverage.

It's worth noting that the 4 percent estimate is only a fraction of the alarmist "rate shock" talk you hear from Obamacare's long-standing critics. Or as Anthony Wright, executive director of Health Access California, a consumer group, has put it:

"Would you pay ten percent more for fifty percent more medical coverage? Would that be a premium increase or a health care discount?"

A Wider, Sicker Pool of Insured. Third, and most importantly, by 2016, Obamacare plans were attracting older and therefore sicklier people than many insurance industry experts had predicted. Remember, under the ACA, insurers must accept everyone, and they are prohibited from charging a penny more because of a person's illness or disability. People with health issues who were rejected in the past are enrolling and getting long-delayed treatment.

As a result, health insurers are raising their premium prices aggressively to cover their higher medical claims and trimming their provider networks to cap premiums—and, of course, help the companies make a profit. Also, fewer than 28 percent of the people who enrolled in Obamacare plans from 2014 to 2016 were between eighteen and thirty-four years old. Insurance executives had hoped that those healthy young adults would make up around 35 percent of Obamacare members and pump in more than enough monthly premium cash to cover the older members' costs.

In 2015, optimistic insurers increased premiums 5.4 percent, on average. But by 2016, in one state after another, insurers demanded premium rate increases of 20 percent to 40 percent—and more. Blue Cross and Blue Shield plans, for example, asked regulators for increases of 31 percent in Oklahoma, 36 percent in Tennessee, and 54 percent in Minnesota.

Thanks to the ACA, increases of 10 percent or more are subject to review. But get this: after a careful review, the Oregon insurance commissioner, who was worried about the solvency of Obamacare plans, told some carriers to raise their 2016 rates beyond what they had proposed. A company called Health Net, for example, had asked for an average of 9 percent and got 34.8 percent, while Oregon's nonprofit Health Co-op wanted 5.3 percent and got a 19.9 percent increase. It's worth noting that a disturbing total of twelve of the nation's twenty-three nonprofit co-ops had shut down by 2016 after losing hundreds of millions largely by setting premiums too low to cover the tsunamis of costs set off by their older and sicker members.

Obamacare supporters are quick to note that around 85 percent of the people enrolling qualify for the government's generous premium subsidies and that, in fact, around two-thirds of them ended up paying only about $100 a month in 2015.

That's a fair point. But premiums are only one part of the health plans' costs. Various studies in 2016 showed that:

- drug costs in many ACA plans often cost twice as much as average employee plans;
- ACA plans offer 40 percent fewer specialists; and
- only a fraction of ACA doctors are actually accepting new patients.

What's more, the deductibles on these plans—the amount you pay before your insurer kicks in a dime—tell another grim story. They are largely out of sight.

When I helped our younger daughter shop for a 2016 Obamacare plan in New York, I was surprised to see so-called affordable "silver" plans with $2,000 deductibles, $5,000 to

$11,000 out-of-pocket maximums, $400 premiums before subsidies—and no out-of-network benefits. We ended up with a "gold" plan. It has a higher premium and no out-of-network benefits, but at least it features a more reasonable $600 deductible and a worst-case $2,000 out-of-pocket max, which my daughter could absorb.

Studies show that when people face daunting out-of-pocket costs, they reduce their spending by 10 percent to 15 percent. But not necessarily by shopping for cheaper care or doing the right things. Most of them stop going to the doctor. They don't even go in for free preventive care. Nor do they see a doctor for serious medical conditions that require regular care.

And that behavior hurts not only the people who turn away from doctors and instead often turn to God in prayer, as polls show, ignoring symptoms and risking serious chronic illness, but it harms everyone by driving up health care costs in the long run.

With premium costs spiking, plus the other plan deficiencies, it's no surprise that the public was turning against Obamacare by 2016. Early in the year, a Kaiser Family Foundation tracking poll showed that 46 percent of Americans had an unfavorable opinion of the law, compared with 40 percent who viewed it favorably.

I wish Obamacare health plans were more affordable and were "driving the cost curve down," as President Obama repeatedly promised when he campaigned for its passage back in 2010.

But as a consumer advocate, I do not oppose the ACA. Beyond raising the country's standard of care, by 2016, the reform law was providing health care to roughly twenty million people who had been largely uninsured and undertreated. That group includes millions of people in the thirty-one states that choose to expand Medicaid for individuals making up to $16,000 and families earning $30,000—people like Joycelyn Archibald of Hackensack, New Jersey, who has her diabetes under control after a lifetime of going uninsured and untreated. This country is made up of millions of Joycelyn Archibalds who deserve decent health care as a human right, including the three to four million working poor without insurance in the twenty or so largely red states that refuse to expand Medicaid.

Yet the good intentions of the law aside, no one can say for sure today whether the ACA will end up being affordable enough (without taxpayer subsidies) to survive as this country's best possible health care safety net. Independent experts say we finally will get the answers in 2018 or so, when the law is fully implemented and entrenched in society. So within a very few years, this country should have the facts to decide whether to keep Obamacare, or thoroughly rethink it to address its flaws, or replace it with a politically conservative alternative, or discard it and switch to a single-payer system like the "Medicare for All" plan proposed by Vermont Senator Bernie Sanders. (See the box "Medicare for All, by the Numbers," on page 191.)

Meanwhile, most of us will continue to sign up for insurance at work, where the choices are getting both costlier and trickier. Fortunately, there is a smart way to size up health plans, as the next chapter explains. And, take note, the monthly premium cost—which most people focus on—is far from the most important factor.

CHAPTER 5

The Smart Way to Shop for Health Insurance

Pinpointing the True Cost—
and Value—of Any Plan

A couple I know, who don't want to be identified, claimed for years that they had great health insurance. They loved the fact that the plan had no premium charges and therefore didn't cost them a dime upfront. "That works for us," the wife said happily and often.

And the health plan did work for them, until the husband came down with a mysterious illness that baffled the doctors in his plan's limited network. One physician whom the couple was counting on for a diagnosis spent months ordering costly tests and then said, "I'm sorry, there is nothing I can do for you."

Without a referral to the right specialist, the husband ended up spending more than a year and a lot of money bouncing from one ineffective provider to another: from doctors, to chiropractors, to acupuncturists. He didn't get diagnosed until he signed up for a better plan, with premium costs and a skilled physician who steered him to the right specialist at a major teaching hospital. The specialist knew immediately that he was suffering from inclusion body myositis (IBM), a rare autoimmune disease that leads to severe weakness of the arm and leg muscles.

"We wasted two years when I could have been getting treated," the husband told me.

As that story illustrates, the most common mistake people make shopping for health insurance is focusing on the plans' premiums rather than on the overall cost and quality of the insurance. It's only logical that when insurers collect little or no money from customers up front through premiums, they look to control costs by reducing benefits and their provider networks. In the end, the plan's limitations can cost you no limit of headaches and expenses.

Here's what to do. When you shop for your next health plan, set aside the premium number and, instead, pin down the plan's "actuarial value."

Anything "actuarial" sounds complicated. But it's just a fancy insider term for a critical piece of information you need: What percent of your medical expenses will your health plan actually pay?

Do you know what percent of your health plan's standard stack of medical bills your insurer expects to pay? You should, because your insurer figures you'll end up paying everything beyond that actuarial percentage. Does your insurer figure to cover 60 percent of your bills? If so, that will leave you with 40 percent of the costs. Or does the plan expect to cover 70 percent, 80 percent, or 90 percent?

Trust me, your insurer has very precise estimates for every plan it sells. The percentage your insurer expects to cover is your plan's actuarial value—your best window into how much your insurance will shell out to cover your bills, and how much you're likely to pay out of your own pocket. Most commonly, your plan's actuarial value will be about 80 percent, which means experienced insurance executives calculate that the plan members—including you—are going to pay the remaining 20 percent. We'll discuss more specifics about how to determine this actuarial value on page 59.

The plan's actuarial value is also a window into the premiums you'll be asked to pay. The higher the actuarial value— therefore the more the insurer expects to pay—the higher your premiums will be. Somebody has to pay those doctor bills.

According to Lynn Quincy, a health reform expert at Consumers Union, the policy division of *Consumer Reports*, your insurance plan's actuarial value reflects the plan's "relative generosity." The more "generous" the plan is, the less you're likely to pay out of your pocket for medical services—but the higher your monthly premiums will be.

Keep in mind, at the end of the day, your insurer and you are going to pay the doctor bills. Therefore, assume that if your insurance company's "generous" plan is covering a lot of your actual medical services, your insurer will demand more from you in monthly premiums. And vice versa. The less it collects from you up front, the lower the share of your health care bills the company expects to pay—after your copays or coinsurance for your medical services, as well as your annual off-the-top deductible.

Also, take an especially close look at your deductible. That's the amount you must pay for medical services before your insurer kicks in a dime. Plans with low or no premiums almost always have high deductibles, often upward of $2,000 to $4,000. I've even heard of deductibles of up to $30,000.

In addition, low-premium plans can end up with coverage largely in name only—as the couple discovered when they needed a savvy specialist.

In many cases, the only care people get for their low premiums is preventive care. If they are lucky enough to stay healthy and out of the doctor's office, not to mention the hospital, they might tell friends for years that they have great, affordable health insurance. But sooner or later, when many of those people get sick, they sadly realize that they are stuck with doctor bills that their insurance company won't pay and the family can't afford.

Around two-thirds of the people who are driven into bankruptcy each year because of medical bills have health insurance policies. But it's "Swiss cheese insurance," as Families USA executive director Ron Pollack called it: "The insurance is full of costly holes."

On average each year, medical bills drive around 650,000 American households into bankruptcy—including around 400,000 families with health insurance who were often stunned to learn their plans did not cover their chemotherapy, diabetes, newborn child's life-threatening illness, and countless other bad breaks.

The Obama administration claimed in an official filing that people with ACA coverage will "no longer face bankruptcy when they have health insurance." That should be largely true—but only if you stay in your plan's network of hospitals and doctors.

Before you go shopping for health insurance, try to calculate what your total medical bills might be next year. Start with last year's total bills. Then think about whether you're likely to need less care or more. Did you address any nagging health issues? Are you coughing because of a cold? Or have you been coughing for a month? What's your blood pressure? Do you get short of breath? Dizzy?

Let's assume you feel fine. Still add up to 33 percent to last year's total as a cushion. Believe me, stuff happens.

With that projected total in mind, ask yourself what percent of it you could comfortably afford. If your bills might reach, say, $10,000, could you get along with an insurance plan that carries an actuarial value of 60, meaning that experienced insurance executives figure you might have to pay 40 percent of your doctor bills next year? That would be around $4,000 in copays, coinsurance, and that dreaded deductible. Plus your premiums, of course.

As a general rule, you should stay away from insurance plans with actuarial values as low as 60. Having to face 40 percent of any hospital bill would be a nightmare for most people. On the other hand, if your plan has an actuarial value approaching 90 percent, ask yourself if you can afford the plan's inevitably high monthly premiums? You are looking for a balance. For most people, plans with actuarial values at around 70 to 80 percent offer reasonable coverage and affordable premiums after subsidies as well as manageable cost sharing.

FIND OUT THE ACTUARIAL VALUE OF YOUR PLAN

Your Human Resources Department and insurer should tell you the actuarial values of any plan they are offering and then discuss your options depending on your budget. But be prepared. It won't always be easy to get the information. You might have to prod the person on the other end of the phone. He or she can get the information for you. Insist on it.

In sharp contrast, you'll have no trouble getting actuarial information if you're shopping for Obamacare insurance in the government's online marketplace. All ACA health plans sold in your state are rated side by side according to their actuarial value. That allows consumers to compare plans on the computer screen much as they do when they shop for airline tickets and hotels online.

The exchange offers four levels of coverage, each with metal names that reflect the plan's projected "generosity." The ratings range from a low of a 60 percent payout rate for bronze plans; 70 percent, silver; 80, gold; and 90, platinum.

By 2015, the greatest number of people buying Obamacare insurance were settling for silver-level plans covering around 70 percent of their medical costs. By comparison, people lucky enough to have employer-provided insurance had more generous plans covering around 82 percent of their costs.

People under thirty also can buy a "catastrophic" 57 percent "tin" plan. But I strongly recommend against that. I think these so-called tin plans are unacceptably risky for young people with presumably modest salaries and negligible savings. No question, young people tend to be healthy. But assuming you are the parent of one of those "invincibles," ask yourself what would happen if your twenty- or thirty-something tore an ankle ligament while being attacked by a rabid alley cat. (I swear that actually happened in our family.) Or contracted debilitating Lyme disease, or got pregnant, or got into a car accident—and landed in the hospital for just about any reason.

These days, emergency room treatment for a *sprained* ankle can run $15,000. Again, no joke. And childbirth, without complications, often costs $35,000 to $45,000 and maybe more in the San Francisco Bay Area and other affluent areas. If you don't know how your children would pay nearly half of bills like those, urge them to invest in insurance with an affordable deductible and a reasonable out-of-pocket cap.

You probably will be protecting yourself as well, since, from my experience and perhaps yours, our kids tend to turn to us when they get into money trouble. When our youngest calls and opens with an especially upbeat "Hi, Dad!" I know I'm about to get tapped, and I chip in every time.

I think parents should talk to their "invincibles" about helping the entire family avoid a potential financial nightmare due to a serious medical emergency. If you get through to them, your children will get an immediate health benefit, and so will you: You'll sleep better.

ARE YOU UNDERINSURED?

A tremendous amount of attention has been focused on the open question of whether the ACA will reduce the total number of uninsured from about thirty million today to its goal of fewer than twenty million. But relatively little has been written about the law's comparatively safe bet to greatly benefit the additional thirty-one million people with insurance who are *under*insured.

A large percentage of those thirty-one million are workers who are covered on the job but have health plans with deductibles that exceed 5 percent of their income or total out-of-pockets costs that eat up more than 10 percent of their income. Here's what you need to know to figure out whether your health care coverage is adequate, and how you might upgrade—perhaps at little or no additional cost.

You might have heard that if you are covered at work, you are not eligible for the ACA's government subsidies if you decide to drop your company's insurance and buy a health plan on your state exchange. While that is true for people with decent coverage, it's not the whole story for the underinsured.

Under the law, companies with fifty or more full-time workers must provide decent and affordable health insurance that meets the new federal standards or pay a fine of around $2,000 to $3,000 per employee a year, beginning in 2016. That provision is commonly called the employer mandate. If your boss's coverage fails to meet the ACA standards, you might want to consider dropping it and applying for a subsidized plan on the online exchange.

Health coverage at companies with fifty or more workers must meet the following standards to be acceptable under the reform law:

Your Employer's Health Insurance Must Be Affordable.
Your monthly premiums at work, which have doubled on average in the past ten years, cannot exceed 9.6 percent of your individual income. For example, if you are making $35,000 and paying a penny more than $280 in monthly premiums, you should look into applying for subsidized Obamacare coverage on your state exchange.

Your Employer's Insurance Cannot Stick You with Too Many Medical Bills. As long as you stay within your plan's network of doctors and hospitals, your boss's health plan must be designed to pay at least 60 percent of the average worker's total drug and medical bills. If it fails to meet the 60 percent standard, you can go to the exchange and shop for subsidized coverage.

"YOU AREN'T GOING TO WRITE ABOUT THIS, ARE YOU?"

How much health insurance customers can suffer and how matter-of-factly it is accepted as a cost of doing business was driven home to me at the Medicare Congress Convention a few years ago. I got a look at how thoroughly fraud and abuse are woven into the health insurance business, and therefore how it's driving up your costs by 10 percent or more.

Around eighty people gathered to hear a senior attorney from the powerful Washington, DC, firm of Arnold and Porter warn them to "get ready" for crackdowns from the Department of Justice (DOJ) and the Office of the Inspector General (OIG). Most of them were senior officers of health insurance companies. "DOJ is putting a target on you," he told the executives bluntly.

I was the only journalist in the room.

The lawyer warned the executives to focus on possible violations of the century-old False Claims Act of 1863 by their employees either "cherry-picking" plan members or "upcoding" medical bills to collect higher reimbursements from the government. He said the insurers should appoint "compliance czars" to police their firms. And he urged them to drill down to the staffers handling the billing claims to make sure "that no one is being incentivized with bonus money" by a supervisor to upcode or otherwise inflate the bills, which would ultimately be reimbursed by the government's Centers for Medicare and Medicaid Services (CMS).

He added that most False Claims Act cases are triggered by company whistle-blowers who see questionable conduct and first complain within the firm—but then get fired. Or as the lawyer put it: "HR mishandles the [whistle-blower's] firing."

Then the fired employee goes to authorities. The lawyer said that the overworked federal investigators "need a spur" like a whistle-blower complaint to open a case.

He stressed that False Claims cases can drag on for five years. "It's a loser for everybody," he said, "because you have to pay my fees," which he estimated at $3 million to $4 million. But he added, "That's better than paying a hundred times that in fines and penalties if you lose."

He closed with a pitch to the executives to keep Arnold and Porter and him in mind to defend against prosecution. The white-collar defense lawyer, who once was a DOJ prosecutor, added, "I am the poster child of the revolving door in government."

He got a nice round of applause.

As he was preparing to leave, I introduced myself. "I didn't realize there were any reporters here," he said. He seemed alarmed. "You're not going to write about this, are you?"

I told him that whatever I did, I would not use his name. I said that for two reasons. I felt sorry for him for foolishly speaking so candidly at a public forum about the health insurance industry's false billing problem. But more than that, the lone white-collar defender is merely a by-product of our broken health care system, where 10 percent of every Medicare dollar we spend goes up in the smoke and mirrors of everyday fraud and abuse.

Your Boss's Plan Must Provide Decent Health Care. Here the regulations get fuzzy. The line between decent and indecent coverage is like the Supreme Court's old pornography standard for indecent images: The people running the state exchanges will know it when they see it. Anyway, that's the hope.

Under the reform law, your employer health plan should address Obamacare's essential health benefits—everything from maternity, child medical care, prescriptions, mental health therapies, and more, as I spelled out in chapter 4, "Ten Essential Health Care Benefits You Are Entitled to Get."

Also, watch out for this loophole: companies can become exempt from the ACA by taking on the financial responsibility of insuring themselves—and then go on to offer their workers the skimpiest of health plans. Generally, these minimum essential coverage (MEC) plans cover only up to 60 percent of health costs and have numerous coverage gaps.

California's consumer advocate Health Access pushed for a law to bar such "junk" coverage in 2015. As Health Access described them, these subminimum company health plans cover:

- diabetes testing but not insulin or other treatment;
- cancer testing but not surgery, radiation, or chemotherapy;
- oral health evaluations but no teeth cleanings or fillings; and
- vitamin supplements but not prescription drugs.

In short, beyond prevention-only coverage, the plans do not cover doctor care, hospitals, emergency rooms, and ambulances, as well as X-rays and MRIs.

However, if a worker accepts this plan, perhaps because the low premiums are all he can afford, the employer cannot be penalized for offering substandard coverage.

Your employer might tell you that if you sign up, you no longer have to worry about penalties for not having insurance under the individual mandate. That's true. However, your employer probably won't go on to warn you that you are also signing away your option of going to the exchange and collecting federal tax subsidies to help you afford far better Obamacare insurance.

In 2015, employers did not face penalties for offering such MEC coverage. The most likely employers to exploit the MEC loophole have transient low-wage workforces and are often in the agricultural, fast-food, lodging, and janitorial fields.

Health Access stressed that the Internal Revenue Service could close this loophole nationally with one new rule.

So if you believe that the health plan offered at work is substandard because of its high cost or low benefits, don't hesitate to act. Go to your state exchange through HealthCare.gov, or call 1-800-318-2596 and ask for an "eligibility determination" of the insurance you are being offered.

The exchange's trained counselors, called "navigators," can help determine whether you qualify for ACA coverage and subsidies, which can range up to thousands of dollars a year, depending on your income. The lower your income, the higher the subsidies. It is possible, for example, for a family of four making $40,000 and paying around $1,000 a month in premiums to buy solid coverage for $165 a month after subsidies. If you'd like quick estimates of your premium costs after subsidies, go to HealthCare.gov or the Kaiser Family Foundation Website (www.kff.org).

In 2016, more than eight out of ten of the 11 million people who bought plans on the exchanges qualified for premium subsidies—including families earning up to $97,000 a year. On average, the subsidies slashed their premiums by around two-thirds.

In addition, as I've noted, more than half of Obamacare members also qualified for medical cost-sharing subsidies. That group included people earning up to 250 percent of the national poverty level—individuals making up to $29,425 and families earning up to $60,625.

What's more, depending on your income and dependents,

staffers at the exchange can tell you whether you are eligible for Medicaid or the Children's Health Insurance Program (CHIP) for children under nineteen. If you qualify, you can sign up for Medicaid at any time. The government estimates that around three million people who inquired about Obamacare in the initial enrollment period in 2013 ended up getting Medicaid.

And remember, you cannot be rejected because of your medical condition, even, for instance, if you walk in the door scheduled for surgery.

If the authorities rule that your employer insurance is "credible," you could still decide to drop it and buy an exchange plan during the next open enrollment period beginning the following November 1. You might consider that, for instance, to get superior maternity or child care benefits. But if you make that switch, you will not be allowed to collect any company or federal subsidies. As a result, dropping coverage that exchange authorities consider credible rarely makes financial sense.

And here's a reminder to Medicare beneficiaries: If you are enrolled in Medicare or another government program, you have credible coverage. That means you do not need to buy more insurance to comply with the law; in fact, you are not eligible to buy Obamacare insurance on the exchange. Remember that if a salesman ever tries to talk you into, say, a Medicare supplement, Medigap, or Advantage plan because of Obamacare rules and regs or other double-talk, hang up on him. He's at best misinformed or, at worst, a fraudster.

DIAL *M* FOR MARKETING MISCHIEF: PHONE-Y INSURANCE SERVICE

A few years ago, in my latest stint at *Reader's Digest*, I worked on an important program with a multibillion-dollar Medicare Advantage advertiser. *Reader's Digest* and the carrier had teamed up to sell co-branded health plans to the *Digest*'s millions of readers. My job was to produce the editorial content supporting the plans, including the print advertising and a series of glossy healthy-lifestyle magazines that plan members got for enrolling at no extra charge.

I was also asked to create the members' welcoming booklet outlining the basic plan and highlighting its benefits. Since no outline, no matter how carefully prepared, can cover every question a member might have, I included the insurer's helpline phone number on nearly every other page.

The marketing team said they liked the booklet very much. But just as we were about to send it to the printer, my phone rang. It was the senior staffer I had worked with most closely, and he had a question.

Marketer: Can we take out all the helpline phone numbers?

Me: Why would we do that? If our members have a question, they won't know how to reach us.

Marketer: Some people in marketing have research showing that members who call the hotline are more likely to drop their plans than people who don't call. So they're saying we should take out the phone numbers.

Me: You're saying that rather than improving your helpline so more members get the answers they need and hang up satisfied, we should frustrate members who have questions by making it difficult for them to reach us. That's not customer service. That's a *dis*-service. Tell the people in marketing that the phone numbers are staying in.

And the phone numbers stayed in. But the request raised a question in my mind about the big health insurance company. What sort of corporate culture allows people with so little regard for their customers to reach senior marketing positions? Rather than analyzing why their customers were calling, or improving the helpline, or truly wanting to help their members, their instinct was to let their customers suffer in silence.

---•---

CHAPTER 6

How to Keep the Doctor and Hospital You Like

And Navigating Other Open Enrollment Challenges

I remember having coffee in New York's historic Algonquin Hotel with health insurance whistle-blower Wendell Potter as he lamented that President Obama had campaigned for the Affordable Care Act by promising that people would be able to keep their insurance with the doctors and hospital they liked.

"People around him should have known better," Potter told me. "I thought that was nonsense and that those words would haunt him."

As the former Cigna public relations executive and the author of *Deadly Spin: An Insurance Company Insider Speaks Out on How Corporate PR Is Killing Health Care and Deceiving Americans*, explained it, insurers constantly alter their plans by adding and dropping doctors and hospitals from the plan networks as they hunt for the best providers who'll accept the lowest payments.

Critics blame Obamacare for provider churn. But the fact is, provider churn is a routine industry practice. President Obama should have known that the ACA would not reverse that basic business strategy.

Furthermore, under pressure from rising medical costs,

many insurers are reducing the number of doctors and hospitals in their networks drastically.

As a result, there is a good chance that a doctor or hospital you like might disappear from your plan's network, no matter what health insurance you're buying—including Obamacare plans.

For example, United HealthCare, the nation's largest health insurer, dropped the Yale University Medical Group from all of its networks in Connecticut in 2014—as part of a 10 percent reduction in providers nationwide. Many of United's plan members lost their favorite doctors virtually overnight.

In addition, insurance companies are shedding providers from their Obamacare plans. For instance, Anthem Blue Cross lowered its ACA plan premiums by 25 percent for its largely working-class and middle-class customers on the New Hampshire exchange in 2014 by sharply restricting the network serving them. Anthem's move touched off a furor because the insurer excluded ten of the state's twenty-six hospitals. To make matters worse, Anthem was the only company selling insurance on that state's exchange.

Insurance companies insist that tighter networks help them keep a lid on premiums by driving plan members to less expensive doctors and hospitals that nonetheless provide quality care.

But as networks tighten, the costs of going to a doctor or hospital that's not in your plan's network often rise, sometimes by as much as 40 percent to 100 percent. New York State is a case in point. None of the more than fifty health plans sold on New York's online exchange in 2016 offered any out-of-network coverage, including the top-tier platinum plans that charge around $600 a month in premiums. That means if you are in a network hospital and under the care of a network doctor but get treated by an out-of-network physician or specialist or surgeon (perhaps while you are unconscious), you might be liable for 100 percent of that out-of-network care.

Furthermore, if you get hit with out-of-network charges in an ACA plan, not a penny of that money counts against your out-of-pocket maximum of up to $12,800 for a family. A bill to protect patients in that jam in the California legislature stalled on the last day of the 2015 session in the face of heavy health industry lobbying. What a surprise!

Even when your hospital is in your network, your health plan might cover only certain procedures, such as trauma care. So shop carefully.

WHAT YOU SHOULD DO BEFORE SIGNING UP FOR A HEALTH PLAN

The best way to keep the doctor and hospital you like is to become a diligent Health Care Detective:

Start by Asking Detailed Questions About the Health Plan's Provider Network. Don't rely on the plan's fine-print summary; figure it was written by company lawyers to protect the insurer, not the customers. Read it, of course. But also call the insurance company and get an informed staffer on the line; if the call center staffer you reach is fumbling for scripts and reading them word for word, hang up, and phone again—or politely insist on speaking to a supervisor.

Look Ahead. Once you're talking to a smart-sounding staffer, ask that person to walk you through exactly which doctors, specialists, and hospitals are included in the plan network *for the coming year.* Are your favorite doctors and hospital in your plan's network? Even if they are, ask whether there will be limits on approved-doctor visits, as well as rehab treatments, or other therapies. And make sure each of your prescriptions is on the plan's approved list, called the formulary.

Don't Take a Staffer's Word for It. Get It in Writing. Ask for the important details in writing, either through the mail or online. Unfortunately, talk is cheap. Misinformation is expensive.

But as I learned, getting quotes in writing can be difficult. When I first tried to find out what my $571-a-day Revlimid would cost me, a young staffer at CVS/Caremark named Rebecca finally assured me that my cost would be a manageable $60 a month. She said she and her supervisor were "absolutely sure."

Then I asked the key question, though I suspected that what I was about to request was against company policy. I asked her whether she would put the quote in writing. To my surprise, she immediately said yes. Minutes later, she sent me an email confirming the $60 quote.

A couple of weeks later, I started worrying that CVS/Caremark might have fired Rebecca for putting the quote in writing, despite the fact that it was the correct price. I called Rebecca's number repeatedly but couldn't reach her. Finally, she answered.

I said, "Are you okay? I was afraid you might have been fired for putting the sixty-dollar quote in writing."

And, as I suspected, she confirmed that she had indeed made a mistake and been reprimanded.

"Oh, everything is fine," she said. "It was a mistake on my part to put anything in writing. My supervisor told me it was a learning experience for me."

In other words, if you want to continue to work for CVS/Caremark, don't ever again put a quote in writing for a customer.

Still, remember, I got the quote and got it in writing by asking for it. And you should be able to do that, too. Be insistent.

Finally, If You Insist on Focusing on Low Premiums, Watch Out for What You Are Surrendering. Be particularly careful if you're getting an incredibly low premium. If you're not giving the insurer much money each month, the company needs to withhold something from you to reduce its costs and make its target profit of 5 percent or more. What the company is excluding, such as limiting substance abuse support sessions, might not be important to you. No harm, no foul. On the other hand, the company might be taking away your doctor or hospital. Could you live without him or her? Or the esteemed teaching hospital fifteen minutes away? You might have to decide if that's worth a low monthly premium.

HOW TO SHOP FOR HEALTH CARE

Every fall, as you head into the rite of passage known as open enrollment—aka Health Insurance Hell—you need to prepare yourself for unwelcome surprises. And some might be whoppers. Perhaps your boss urges you to have that knee replacement or heart operation you've been considering in a hospital in Istanbul. Or your company caps the amount you'll get reimbursed for common medical services, such as an X-ray or MRI. Or your employer hands you a little money and tells you to buy your own health insurance. Even if your company continues to provide insurance, it might surprise you by refusing to cover your dependents—or by forcing you to pay a lot more to insure them.

Still, despite the surprises and turmoil, if you understand your options and shop wisely, you can find your best health insurance for the coming year and maybe save money, too.

If You Get Your Insurance Through Work

Overseas Medical Travel. A small but growing number of self-insured companies of all sizes are offering their employees the option of having major operations, such as coronary artery bypass surgery and hip or knee replacements, at vetted hospitals overseas from Puerto Rico to Thailand. More than a million Americans leave the country for medical care every year. The trend isn't as crazy as it might sound, because you can save thousands of dollars. Typically, a self-insured employer will cover every penny of the worker's costs and might even throw in a bonus of around $5,000. Even with the expense of the operation and a bonus, the company usually ends up paying only half of what it would have cost here.

Workers who get treated abroad might walk away as satisfied as Wayne Wright of Marshall, Texas. "My wife thought I was crazy," said Wright. But he went ahead with a double knee replacement in the Cayman Islands under a medical travel option offered by his employer, and he saved more than $6,000. "I didn't pay a penny out of pocket, including airfare and the resort hotel. We got treated like royalty. And my knees feel great."

Patients Beyond Borders CEO Josef Woodman said that a number of factors are driving global medical travel, including this country's aging baby boomers, who need advanced care such as cardiovascular and orthopedic surgeries. Such care is expensive here, but is often covered abroad 100 percent by their employers. Woodman's company publishes books and other consumer information about medical travel.

Woodman said the global trend began a decade ago when the Joint Commission on Accreditation of Healthcare Organizations (JCAHO) began vetting hospitals abroad, including a pioneering Cleveland Clinic affiliate in Abu Dhabi. The agency, now known as the Joint Commission, began in 1951 with thirty-seven hospitals worldwide, which it judged by the same standards as its US counterparts. Today it accredits more than 600.

"Americans have many choices among trustworthy, quality, affordable hospitals," said Woodman, who went on to tick off top-rated facilities in India, Thailand, Singapore, Turkey, and Belgium—and closer to home in Mexico, Colombia, and Costa Rica.

Plus, the savings for patients, especially for the increasing number who face high deductibles, can be huge. "The savings could be anywhere from forty percent to, say, eighty percent in India, or perhaps as high as ninety percent in Malaysia," he said.

He noted, however, that most Americans stay within a four-hour plane ride.

Industry experts estimate that half of global patients go for restorative dental care, such as dental implants, dentures, bridgework, and crowns. Another 15 percent get cosmetic surgery. Most of the rest seek more serious treatments for heart disease, cancer, orthopedic problems, or obesity.

Woodman added this extra come-on: "The hospitals are newer and therefore have better ventilation systems, and that lowers the risk of hospital-borne infections."

If you're adventurous and interested in global medical travel, tell management or call a medical travel specialist. Companion Global Healthcare, for example, can arrange operations at many overseas hospitals, including several that are affiliated with top US hospitals, including Johns Hopkins and the Mayo Clinic.

Domestic Medical Travel. Major corporations, including Lowe's, Walmart, and Boeing, have struck deals with a number of prestigious hospitals here at home as well.

At the Cleveland Clinic, for example, workers at participating companies can elect to undergo cardiac procedures at virtually no cost. The participating companies receive discounts of up to 20 percent or so off the hospitals' prevailing rates, and their employees are often back at work sooner and with fewer complications.

Dr. Joseph Cacchione, head of the Cleveland Clinic's operations and strategy initiative, said its five-year program with Lowe's has been especially successful. The clinic handles about 30 percent of the company's cardiac surgery patients from across the country in Cleveland with no copays or deductibles, no matter how complicated the operations, including heart valve and cardiac bypass surgeries.

In addition, the company covers all of the patient's travel and lodging, and provides a stipend for food.

Lowe's has found that the program saves it money, partly

because the clinic estimates that about 10 percent to 15 percent of the patients who are told they need heart surgery actually don't need it. "There is a huge cost avoidance savings," said Dr. Cacchione.

PepsiCo has a similar arrangement—featuring cash incentive bonuses for its 250,000 workers—with Johns Hopkins Hospital for various conditions, including joint replacements. Other companies have programs with the Mayo Clinic and other leading hospitals.

In addition, sometimes patients can get the care within driving distance from the main hospital or one of its satellites. Cleveland Clinic, for example, soon plans to double its satellite facilities to twenty around the country.

Again, if you're interested in domestic medical care at some of the nation's best hospitals, speak up at work.

Risky Business. Under the lure of "consumer choice," more large companies will shift the risk of high health care costs onto millions of their unlucky workers in 2016. The companies will stop providing health coverage directly and instead give their workers a set sum of money to buy their own health insurance online from among a group of diverse insurers in "private exchanges" run by benefits consultants such as Aon Hewitt and Mercer Insurance Group.

Employers save by capping how much they spend subsidizing their workers' health care. The workers also can save by choosing less expensive coverage with higher deductibles—though they then run the risk of getting hit with ruinous medical bills if they get sick.

The worker's risk is real. Medical bills remain the leading cause of family bankruptcies. Jamie Court, president of the independent nonprofit Consumer Watchdog, said, "Instead of providing a pretty secure boat, these companies are offering workers life vests and forcing them to weather the health care storms on their own."

Health Savings Accounts. More companies also are choosing to save up to 20 percent of their health costs by shifting workers from their standard group health coverage to health savings accounts (HSAs). A new high of 16 percent of companies surveyed by Aon Hewitt will provide tax-advantaged HSAs as their only insurance option in 2016. Many companies still offering group health plans will try to induce workers to switch to HSAs with so-called seed money bonuses of $1,000 or more.

Even with inducements, don't jump into these savings accounts. The problem is that before you can open an HSA, you must enroll in a high-deductible health plan. One company I researched was pushing an HSA that came with a deductible of $3,000 per person, or $12,000 for a family of four. "People were signing up to save money without comprehending that deductible," one company executive told me.

If you're young, well paid, and stay healthy, you can sock away thousands in those portable accounts tax free each year.

But if you get sick, or stumble into an ER with, say, a compound broken wrist, your out-of-pocket expenses could wipe out your HSA balance—and maybe you, too.

Bottom line: Experts say that as long as you have a choice, you should stick with traditional group health coverage with reasonable deductibles and out-of-pocket maximums. (For a full examination of HSAs, go to chapter 11, "The Pluses and Minuses of Health Savings Accounts.")

Push to Obamacare. Under the ACA's company mandate, workplaces with fifty or more full-time employees were required to offer decent health plans to their workers beginning in 2016 or face an annual penalty of around $2,000 per worker. Many companies rushed to upgrade their plans.

But others exploited loopholes in the law. For example, employers do not have to provide insurance—or pay penalties—for workers who make so little that they qualify for

Medicaid and enroll in the jointly funded federal and state program. Some companies began identifying those workers and encouraging them to enroll.

Still other companies skirted the ACA by self-insuring their workers and then trimming their group health coverage. Some offered workers "raises" of $300 or more a month to help them buy Obamacare insurance on the online public exchanges at HealthCare.gov. However, a study by business consultant ADP showed that even after some small employers paid two-thirds or more of health plan costs, only around one-third of workers making about $20,000 signed up for the Obamacare insurance. Why? They said they couldn't afford the health plans.

Doctor Knows Best. Some employers are increasing their workers' insurance options by signing up independent networks of physicians like One to One in Chattanooga, Tennessee. Workers who go to One to One doctors are charged low copays. The doctors then try to drive down the employers' costs by monitoring the sickliest workers closely. Staffers, for instance, call high-risk patients a couple of times a month to make sure they're taking their meds. "It's like having a nurse in the family," said one supporter. At the end of the year, any health care savings are split between the employer and the doctors.

Doctor-directed outfits like One to One are springing up around the country.

Reimbursement Caps. Well over 10 percent of companies capped the amounts they pay in 2016 for anything from MRIs to serious procedures like bariatric surgery for weight loss. The limits on reimbursement are meant to force workers to shop for less expensive providers—often, thankfully, with the help of advocates that the company brings on board to advise workers at no extra cost.

Milwaukee-based Patient Care, for example, identifies at least three quality options for workers seeking costly care. Patient Care saved a New Jersey worker who needed a pelvic MRI thousands of dollars in 2016 by presenting him with options from a low of $810 up to $3,841.

"With health care so increasingly complicated, expensive, and frustrating," said Patient Care CEO Jane Cooper, "everybody needs an advocate."

My Advice. If your company begins implementing reimbursement caps, tell your supervisor, or the boss, about advocacy outfits such as Patient Care, to save you and the company chunks of money.

Family Trouble. More companies will refuse to cover spouses who are eligible for health insurance elsewhere. And in a perverse twist on the 2015 Supreme Court's decision upholding same-sex marriage, experts fear some companies will stop covering domestic partners unless the couples formally marry.

Take This Step and Call Me if You Get Sicker. Increasingly insurers are looking for ways to control the expense of specialty drugs that turn deadly diseases like rare hereditary illnesses into chronic conditions—but at a cost of upward of $100,000 a year per patient. So ask if any health plans you're considering impose "step therapy." With step therapy, your plan will not automatically cover expensive prescriptions you and your doctor think you need. No matter how sick you feel, you might be required to try older, less expensive treatments first. Even after that initial treatment fails, you and your doctor will need to get prior approval from the insurer's doctors before it will cover the high-priced drugs you may then desperately need.

Employee benefits adviser Russ Blakely said, "You don't want to be required to suffer while you get sicker before you get the cure."

If You Get Your Insurance Through Obamacare

Wild Prices. Amid the blare of alarmist headlines, you may not know that Obamacare premiums, on average, increased well below double digits nationally for 2016. But the rates varied wildly. Many insurers asked regulators for double-digit premium increases, including some of over 60 percent.

And it wasn't only Obamacare premiums that rose; the cost of private health plans for individuals increased across the board as well.

In some states, carriers increased premiums of their individual policies more than for Obamacare. In Florida, for instance, United HealthCare proposed raising Obamacare premiums by 18 percent. That's a big number. Still, the carriers wanted to raise premiums for its individual plans sold through brokers by up to 31 percent and hike other individual plans by 60 percent.

While Obamacare premium rates continue to rise—and sometimes soar—year after year, remember that a vast majority of Obamacare members do not get hit so badly. The federal government picks up most of the increases, since more than 85 percent of Obamacare members collect generous federal premium subsidies—ultimately provided by taxpayers. Critics on the right deplore this "wealth transfer," while progressives applaud it.

My Advice. If you have ACA insurance, promise yourself that you will shop carefully for next year's plan, even if you love your current plan and your participating doctors and hospitals. Network doctors, specialists, and hospitals come and go each year. Don't assume they will be part of next year's plan or that your prescriptions will still be on the approved list. Instead, shop the HealthCare.gov marketplace like a Health Care Detective to find your best combination of benefits, total costs, and government subsidies for the coming year.

Ditch COBRA. For thirty years, untold millions of laid-off workers have been thankful to have COBRA (Consolidated

Omnibus Budget Reconciliation Act) health coverage, which allowed them to keep their old employer's insurance for more than a year—though at full price. But now experts say that many COBRA candidates will be better off with Obamacare, especially if their suddenly low incomes qualify them for federal subsidies. And you don't have to wait for the open enrollment period. Getting laid off and losing your insurance makes you eligible immediately to apply for Obamacare coverage—as well as the law's premium and cost-sharing subsidies.

If You Get Your Insurance Through Medicare

Paying Up. The fact that Social Security payments did not increase for 2016 turned out to be good news for the 70 percent of Medicare beneficiaries who pay their Part B doctor premiums through their Social Security deductions. By law, in years when there is no cost-of-living (COLA) increase, people paying through deductions do not have to pay a penny more in Part B premiums than they paid the year before—in this case, $104.90. However, the other 30 percent got socked with premiums of $121.80 and up, depending on their incomes.

That 30 percent includes well-off people, who presumably can afford to pay more. But it also includes all newly eligible beneficiaries, though an estimated 1.8 million of them are living on less than $23,500 a year.

Joe Baker, president of the nonprofit Medicare Rights Center, urges beneficiaries struggling with health costs to call 1-800-Medicare and ask about the Medicare Savings Program (MSP). Only one-third of those eligible are actually enrolled in the four MSP programs that amount to an umbrella of assistance for low-income people with high medical bills.

Paying Attention. Part D prescription insurers constantly shuffle drugs on and off their lists of approved medications, while also often ratcheting up the cost of specialty medicines. Consequently, half of Part D beneficiaries would save money by changing plans each year. But unfortunately, only about 10 percent actually switch.

Do yourself a favor. Find your best Part D plan at Plan Finder on Medicare.gov or call 1-800-Medicare for help shopping.

Dis-Advantages. More than three in ten Medicare beneficiaries are enrolled in Advantage plans created by private insurers such as Humana and Aetna, rather than in the government's original Medicare. Typically, Advantage plans feature low premiums, all-in-one medical and drug coverage, and extras such as gym memberships and twenty-four-hour nurse helplines. But most Advantage plans offer very limited provider networks, often concentrated in one geographic area, as you'll see more clearly in the next chapter.

———•———

CHAPTER 7

Watch Out for Big Medicare Surprises

Ten Mistakes Everyone Over Sixty-Five Should Avoid

Part D appeal: Ms. F. of NJ, severe Crohn's disease. Enrolled in new Part D plan. New plan refused coverage of her prescription. Reduced dose to half, all she could afford. Significant weight problem, GI issues. Rights Center appealed to an administrative law judge and won. She got reimbursed. However, her well-being was compromised by an eight-month struggle to get her medicine.

Those are the notes from a typical successful Medicare Rights Center case that underscore the theme of this chapter: Sooner or later you're in for a big surprise like Ms. F. from NJ unless you learn how to avoid them.

When it comes to Medicare, seniors fall into two camps: the half who admit that they don't understand much about the program—and the rest, who are kidding themselves.

There's a cartoon of a guru on a mountaintop saying, "I can explain the meaning of life, but I wouldn't dare try to explain Medicare."

If you are planning to sign up for the federal government's

Medicare program during the annual open enrollment period, from October 15 to December 7, or even if you're one of the fifty million already enrolled, you need to learn more about the surprises you face to get all the services and savings you deserve.

The nonprofit national Medicare Rights Center, which fields about fifteen thousand consumer calls a year, is a good barometer of the levels of confusion surrounding Medicare. The calls divide roughly in thirds among people seeking help with:

- affording health care and billing issues;
- Medicare denials and the appeals process, especially with Medicare Advantage plans, as opposed to the original Medicare;
- the number one complaint, transitioning into Medicare with a smooth coordination of benefits—which should be much easier than it is.

It is striking that one of the most confusing aspects of a fifty-year-old program is when and how to sign up for it. But that's our first surprise.

Surprise 1: You Must Enroll On Time or Face Huge Penalties

Signing up can be simple. Once you begin collecting Social Security benefits, you will automatically be enrolled into Medicare Part A for hospitalization insurance, Part B for doctor's services, and Part D for drug coverage on your sixty-fifth birthday. No sweat. You can use the government health plan—or delay indefinitely—without penalty.

But if you're still working at age 65 or older and not classified as a "retiree," the fun begins, as a New York senior called Mr. S. by the Right Center learned.

Mr. S. had comprehensive health insurance through his employer, a major pharmaceutical maker, so he kept that good coverage for a year after he retired at age seventy. A few months before his employer plan ended, he called Social Security to enroll in Part B.

Surprise: He had missed an obscure but important deadline. Though he had signed up for Part A when he turned sixty-five, he had declined Part B because his employer plan was covering his doctor bills. That's okay. But in the last few months, he had missed his "special enrollment period" for Part B. No one had told him that when a worker's status changes to retiree, he or she has an eight-month window called a special enrollment period to sign up for Part B. Now, with that window closed, Mr. S would have to wait until January 1 to sign up for coverage that would not begin until July 1.

All in all, he faced nearly a half year without insurance for doctors' services as well as a hefty lifetime late-enrollment penalty on his Part B premium.

Those late penalties add up. If you miss your enrollment deadline, as Mr. S. did, and later decide you want Medicare after all, you will have to pay an extra 1 percent in premiums for every month you were late. Let's say you enroll exactly twelve months late for Part B; you'll pay an extra 10 percent in premiums each month for the rest of your life.

Enrolling late in Part D costs even more. For every twelve months you're late, you pay an extra 12 percent per month for life. Five years late for each? You'd pay 50 percent more for Part B premiums and 60 percent more for Part D.

And, depending on your tardiness, there are no limits on how high those late penalties can climb.

Be especially careful if you have an Obamacare health plan and are approaching sixty-five. When you become eligible for Medicare, you must cancel your exchange coverage; you are no longer eligible for Obamacare. Also, enroll in Medicare immediately. If you fail to enroll in Medicare on time, you could get hit with higher health care costs, gaps in your coverage, disrupted access to needed care, and penalties. For more details, go to the Medicare Rights Center's Medicare Interactive (MI) website.

By the way, why doesn't the Department of Health and Human Services give Obamacare members a timely notice about exactly what to do as they near Medicare eligibility? Is that too much to ask?

My Advice. Forget about trying to grasp every nuance of these transition rules and be wary of trusting someone in your HR department—assuming your company hasn't eliminated HR to cut costs. The Rights Center reported, "The confusion around Medicare transitions cannot be overstated." I agree. I read one fat paragraph from experts on these rules four times— *slowly*—and still didn't understand it all.

Instead, keep it simple. If you're not enrolled in Medicare through Social Security for any reason when you approach sixty-five, call your local Social Security office and find out the first date that you can sign up. Typically, you can enroll beginning three months before your sixty-five birth month and no later than three months after that month. Again, you don't have to begin using and paying for Medicare services through Social Security deductions, but you must enroll to avoid any chance of facing those stiff late penalties.

Surprise 2: Medicare Is Far from Free

Experts say that Medicare covers only around 60 percent of the average beneficiary's medical costs after you count all the so-called cost-sharing: the $104.90 or more Part B monthly doctor premium, $1,228 Part A hospital deductible, copays, coinsurance, and so on. As a consequence, in 2016 over one-quarter of Social Security checks go to pay medical bills. Those bills are especially tough on the one-half of all Medicare beneficiaries living on less than $2,000 a month. "Elderly people choosing between food and medicine call us all the time," said Joe Baker.

Fortunately, there is federal medical and drug assistance available to people with incomes of around $300 to $400 a week and meager assets of about $7,000—plus many state and local drug-assistance plans for families earning up to $75,000.

But unfortunately, as I've noted, only about one-third of those eligible for Medicare assistance—through the Medicare Savings Program—are enrolled.

My Advice. If you think you might qualify for assistance, call 1-800-Medicare. If you meet certain financial conditions, the Savings Programs might pay your Medicare Part A hospital and Part B doctor insurance, plus deductibles, coinsurance, and copayments. Also, if you are struggling financially, don't wait for the open enrollment period to contact your state Medicaid office. Instead, call immediately to see whether you are eligible to enroll in either Medicare or Medicaid, or both.

Surprise 3: If You Don't Know the Billing Code for an
Upcoming Medical Service, You're Out of Luck—
Medicare Will Not Tell You How Much It Might Cost You

In our for-profit, fee-for-service health system, there are several sets of codes of letters and numbers that cover virtually every medical service imaginable. The codes help providers describe their services and bill for them accurately. Generally, hospitals bill with International Classification of Diseases (ICD) codes, while doctors use Current Procedural Terminology (CPT) codes.

If your doctor does not tell you the code for, say, the particular MRI or type of hip surgery she is recommending, you will have trouble comparison shopping. If you don't have a precise billing code, Medicare will not tell you what you might end up paying—even if you can describe the procedure in plain English. (For a case study of this surprise, see chapter 8: "Confounding Billing Codes and Other Bizarre Obstacles.")

My Advice. You might be able to find the CPT code at two websites that track medical costs by their billing codes. Go to either the Clear Health Costs or Healthcare Bluebook websites and simply enter the name of the procedure. Up will pop the CPT code as well as prevailing prices. Beyond your efforts, I suggest that if your doctor flatly refuses to give you a billing code for the service or procedure he's suggesting, find a doctor who will.

Surprise 4: There Are No Limits on How Much You Can Be Charged for Drugs in a Medicare Part D Drug Plan

Few of the thirty-six million people enrolled in Medicare's Part D prescription plans realize that if they qualify for catastrophic care in 2016—the government's least costly coverage for people who have racked up more than $4,850 in drug costs—they still must pay 5 percent of all their additional drug costs for the rest of the year. Result: The oldest and most chronically ill among us often pay the most for their medicine.

The Kaiser Family Foundation reports that many seniors taking just one expensive drug for arthritis, hepatitis C, multiple sclerosis, or cancer will still spend between $4,000 and $12,000 in 2016.

Since the patients must typically pick up 25 percent to 33 percent of the cost of their top-tier medication, sometimes plus a deductible, they fall into Medicare's costly coverage gap, called the "donut hole," within the first months of the year by racking up $3,310 in costs. Then, while in the gap, they are responsible for 45 percent of the cost of brand-name drugs and 65 percent for generally less expensive generics.

In a blink, their spending moves upward of $4,850 as they climb out of the gap and into the catastrophic care trap. Then, with catastrophic care, they are billed for 5 percent of their drug costs—with no annual or lifetime limit.

Do the math. If your drug costs, say, $10,000 a month, as some wonder drugs do, you're on the hook for $500 in catastrophic costs—every month.

KFF singled out my old blood-cancer fighter, Revlimid, as

the most costly drug it studied. It estimated that a senior on Revlimid spends a median of $11,538 a year, meaning that half of the patients pay more and half pay less.

Gleevec, a drug used to treat leukemia and other cancers, came in second at $8,503 a year, followed by Zytiga, for advanced prostate cancer, at $7,227. Medicare beneficiaries on drugs for multiple sclerosis or hepatitis C spend a median of $6,000 to $7,000 a year.

And here's the kicker: These sick people are shelling out 50 percent to 60 percent of that money after they go onto catastrophic care. For many families, that is indeed catastrophic.

My Advice. If you are living on $300 to $400 a month and struggling with health costs, call 1-800-Medicare and ask about the Medicare Savings Programs. Depending on your level of eligibility, the programs can cover virtually all of your hospital, doctor, and drug costs.

Also, if you have a limited income and resources, you might be eligible for Extra Help through Social Security. That program might pay some or all of your prescription drug costs. You can apply online at www.socialsecurity.gov/extrahelp or call Social Security at 1-800-772-1213 (TTY users, 1-800-325-0778). Social Security representatives are available Monday through Friday, from 7:00 a.m. to 7:00 p.m.

If you are over fifty-five, you might qualify for an array of government and private assistance programs covering health care and drug costs. To find out if you're eligible, go to the website BenefitsCheckUp, from the nonprofit National Council on Aging, at www.benefitscheckup.org. Enter your financial profile and see what might be available to you.

In addition, you can seek a private nonprofit foundation grant, particularly if your income is too high for government assistance. Nonprofit organizations sometimes award lump-sum grants that cover a needy patient's entire prescription costs. Check the Patient Access Network (PAN) Foundation at www.panfoundation.org for a list of programs, arranged by diagnosis. You can apply by yourself or ask your doctor's office or specialty pharmacist for help. To find a participating pharmacy, call 1-800-806-7501.

Surprise 5: You Need to Check Your Medicare Part D Plan Carefully Each Year, Even if You Like Your Plan

Medicare Part D providers constantly change their plans. The prices of drugs on the providers' approved lists, or formularies, keep climbing—and sometimes your drug may vanish altogether. And guess what—the premiums increase, too.

For example, the Kaiser Family Foundation and researchers at Georgetown University reported that, on average, enrollees in stand-alone Medicare Part D drug plans faced 13 percent premium increases for 2016. Yet around nine in ten Part D members don't bother to shop for plans with lower prices for their drugs during Medicare's open enrollment period from October 15 to December 7.

Why not? Because people assume that sorting through the twenty or so plans available to them will be a chore. But actually, the folks at the Centers for Medicare and Medicaid Services have made shopping for Part D plans easy. Just make a list of the medicines you take—including the exact dosages. And that's assuming you haven't already made that list to show your doctor every time you see her.

Now with the list in hand, you have two choices. You can call 1-800-Medicare, and a CMS representative will search the plans available to you and then mail your top choices in roughly three business days. Or you can go to www.medicare.gov and enter your prescriptions into the Medicare Plan Finder I mentioned earlier. Your top options will pop up on your computer screen, where you can compare them side by side.

Still, convenience aside, it's best to be careful before you make your final selection. Check any key information with your top provider, such as whether a costly prescription you're taking is indeed covered; or whether your favorite doctor, hospital, or pharmacy is indeed in the plan's network.

Shopping this carefully might take an occasionally frustrating hour or maybe two, depending on wait times and computer gremlins. But I consider that a worthwhile investment to end up with the best drug coverage you can find for the next eventful year of your life.

My Advice. Do yourself a big favor: never purchase—or renew—a Part D plan before making sure that all of your medicines are covered and that your costs are as reasonable as possible.

Surprise 6: Spending a Night in the Hospital Doesn't Mean You Were "in" the Hospital

It seems reasonable for hospitals to observe you for a day or two before deciding whether you need to be formally admitted for care as an inpatient. But critics say that some hospitals are holding Medicare patients for up to a week or so in "outpatient observation status" and then billing them as outpatients under Medicare's more expensive Part B doctor plans rather than under Part A hospitalization. That inpatient abuse has cost some patients tens of thousands of dollars.

In addition, Medicare beneficiaries must be classified as inpatients for at least three midnights to qualify for skilled nursing rehabilitation care after they are released. Observation days do not count toward nursing care. All told, if you are not admitted, your hospital costs go up, and you're not eligible for skilled nursing.

My Advice. After one night in a hospital, ask your doctor politely but pointedly about whether you have been admitted as an inpatient. If you don't get a straight answer, including when you might be admitted, ask for the hospital's "discharge planner." That person often works in what's called the "utilization review department." Just throwing around insider terms like that should get you some attention.

Bottom line: Don't assume anything. You're either "in" the hospital as an admitted patient, or you are not.

Surprise 7: *Advantage Plans Look Good, but They Can End Up Going Bad*

Sad but true, a sizable number of the seventeen million people enrolled in Medicare Advantage plans don't actually understand how sharply the plans differ from original Medicare until something goes wrong. Then many of them, who account for one-third of all Medicare beneficiaries, can end up getting stung by surprises.

The increasingly popular Medicare Advantage plans, which are run by private insurance companies with large federal subsidies of roughly $10,000 a year per member, are attracting one million new members a year by emphasizing two selling points: all-in-one benefits, and low (and even zero) premiums.

Advantage plans certainly look good. Under their federal contracts, the two thousand private plans must provide all Medicare services and protections. With the help of the fat federal subsidies of around $400 to $700 per member per month, they nearly always offer extras, such as gym membership or a twenty-four-hour nurse line.

Plus, you can get all that for under $40 a month, though you must continue to pay your Medicare Part B medical premiums. And, on average, adding drug coverage only costs another $15 a month or so. At that price, not surprisingly, 86 percent of members buy plans with drug benefits.

Experts also note that 78 percent of Medicare enrollees live in an area that offers zero-premium plans, including drug coverage.

Still, as attractive as that all sounds, based on complaints and lawsuits, a significant number of members apparently don't realize that Advantage plans have two distinct downsides: (1) limited provider networks, and (2) the legal protection to promise more than they end up delivering.

One of the key differences between Advantage and original is that original Medicare members can go to any doctor, specialist, or hospital anywhere in the country that accepts Medicare payments and not get hit with extra charges for going out of network or not getting prior approval. Although you hear a lot about doctors dropping out of Medicare, the fact is that roughly 90 percent of the nation's 800,000 doctors and nearly all of the 5,700 hospitals participate.

By contrast, Medicare Advantage plans generally restrict members to narrow provider networks, usually concentrated in one geographic area. You might have the doctors and hospitals you need down the road from your home in Virginia. But if you get sick and hospitalized while visiting your in-laws in West Virginia—and people do get sick at the in-laws—you would have to pay out of your own pocket, unless you could convince your Advantage plan that you received medically necessary emergency care.

"We fight with Advantage plans over emergency care constantly," said Judith Stein, executive director of the Center for Medicare Advocacy (CMA), a nonprofit law organization that advocates on behalf of seniors and the disabled. "We just sued a plan that denied a woman on vacation in Florida who got a brain tumor and fell and broke her hip. It cost a hundred thousand dollars to stabilize her. But the plan officials said her care wasn't an emergency or even urgent. They said she had to pay the full hundred thousand dollars out of pocket. We won. We got all but ten thousand dollars covered."

In addition, Medicare Advantage plans reserve the right to promise you more when you are shopping for your annual health plan than they actually deliver during the year. Plans routinely shed doctors and hospitals at any time they choose.

They also regularly alter their approved drug lists, usually by charging more for drugs and moving drugs into higher-cost tiers. And they can even cancel an entire plan with only a sixty-day notice.

"Advantage members are locked in for a year," said the CMA's managing attorney, David Lipschutz. "Why aren't the Advantage plans locked in, too?"

By law, the plans must maintain "adequate" provider networks. Yet following an initial CMS review, plans are merely required to self-attest that their networks are adequate. Furthermore, a Democratic-backed bill requiring Advantage plans to give several months' notice before altering benefits and shedding doctors only for cause, went nowhere in the Republican-controlled congress in 2015. However, under HHS "continuity of care" rules, plans that drop doctors without cause must cover their patients for up to 90 days. That continued coverage can be critical for patients getting chemotherapy, for example.

Don't think you'll never get stung. Losing access to your trusted physicians in the middle of a plan year remains a risk you run. As I've noted, United HealthCare, the nation's largest health insurer, cut its national provider network by 10 percent by ditching thirty-five thousand doctors.

In the process, it dropped Yale University Medical Group, and its 1,200 providers, from all of its networks in Connecticut. That drastic move touched off an uproar in the state. Critics were especially upset because UH had included the Yale Medical Group in the AARP-branded plans it filed with the state and subsequently sold to customers. Then with the customers locked in for the year, the company dumped hundreds of respected physicians and specialists around the state.

"It's like buying a car and getting a bicycle," said Judith Stein.

My Advice. Whether you're new to Medicare or renewing, shop thoroughly at Medicare Plan Finder during open enrollment from October 15 to December 7. Once you punch in your identity and any prescriptions, you'll see an array of plans for original Medicare as well as Advantage plans that you can compare and contrast. Costs might vary widely, but so might the lists of approved drugs and, of course, the provider networks.

Also, if you are renewing any Medicare plan, including Advantage or Part D, your plan must send you a *Plan Annual Notice of Change*. The booklet, which usually arrives in September, should include any changes in coverage, costs, or service area that will be effective in January.

Never renew any health plan without checking that document carefully. For example, Part D plans provide their entire list of approved drugs for the coming year. Do you still see your prescriptions? It's also wise to double-check directly with your doctors and hospitals to be sure they intend to participate in your plan for the coming year.

Surprise 8: The Doctor Will See You—Someday

If your medical problem doesn't sound urgent, too often doctors make Medicaid and Medicare patients wait months to see them.

That's especially true of some specialists and surgeons with offices at hospitals that accept the very low government payments. Hospital specialists must see Medicare patients and accept, say, as little as $40 per visit rather than their normal $400. It's not uncommon, for example, for Medicare beneficiaries to have to wait for four months to see specialists in New York City.

My Advice. If you have the time, identify the top specialist who accepts Medicare and then badger his staff for an appointment.

As a last resort, if you think you are being discriminated against because you are on Medicare, complain directly to the Centers for Medicare and Medicaid Services. Get started by calling 1-800-Medicare, and explain your problem, perhaps by stating how many times you've called for an appointment and quoting from any letters or emails you've exchanged with the elusive physician and his usually polite but unusually ineffective staff.

Surprise 9: Medicare Offers Less Nursing but More Home Care Than You Think

People often get confused about Medicare's rules for skilled nursing rehabilitation care and home health care. Many beneficiaries think Medicare offers virtually unlimited skilled nursing but is less than generous about home health care. Just the opposite might be true for you, depending on your circumstances. (For one family's story, see "Mom's Death on Medicare" on page 100.)

Medicare covers skilled nursing care under its Part A hospitalization coverage. Generally, as I've said, you must be admitted in a hospital for at least three midnights before you become eligible to be transferred to a skilled nursing facility.

Original Medicare pays your skilled nursing costs for the first 20 days of each stay. However, if you are still in the facility on day 101 in 2016, you must pay a daily copay of $161 for days 21 to 120. And after that, you are responsible for all the skilled nursing costs. I repeat, *all* the costs.

In addition, during your skilled nursing stay, you might be responsible for your doctor's services or treatments that are not part of your skilled rehab care per se, such as medicine for an unrelated condition.

Patients who are in skilled nursing facilities when Medicare benefits run out are often desperate to avoid being transferred to a nursing home—or literally wheeled to it down a corridor in some skilled nursing facilities. Instead, many patients want to be sent to a hospital for several days, in an effort to start the skilled nursing cycle over again. But once you've used one 100-day cycle, starting the nursing cycle gets awfully tricky and may require you to go 60 consecutive days without care before reapplying.

If you have Medicare Advantage or a Medigap supplemental plan—designed to cover gaps in Medicare benefits—you might have additional nursing coverage.

Most Medigap plans, which require that you have Medicare Parts A and B, cover the $161-a-day copay for days 1 to 100. Some Medicare Advantage plans offer similar coverage, but only at facilities in their provider networks. So check to be sure you stay in network.

Medicare's home health care rules can seem more humane by comparison, starting with the fact that Medicare pays for home care for as long as you need it. And you can get great care. In a large number of cases, you can qualify for home services such as physical therapy, social services, medical supplies, delivered meals, personal care, and intermittent skilled nursing.

A home health care agency provides the services once your doctor authorizes the care. Medicare picks up the costs of approved home health services, with two considerable exceptions. You will be billed for 20 percent of the cost of durable medical equipment such as a walker or hospital bed. Also, the agency's home care helper usually works an eight-hour shift, leaving you to arrange for whatever additional help you need.

CMS has added star ratings to its "Home Health Compare" lists to help you find a solid agency nearby (www.medicare.gov /homehealthcompare). By 2016, more than half of the eleven thousand agencies on the website page had ratings covering patient care, communication, and an overall score of up to five stars (with three stars as the national average).

Surprise 10: You Can Get Charged Extra or Even Rejected for a Preexisting Condition

Medicare supplement insurers offering so-called Medigap plans must accept you during your initial enrollment period or usually if you lose your coverage at work through no fault of your own. But outside of that, if you want to switch from one supplement plan to another—or from a Medicare Advantage plan—supplement insurers can require you to submit a detailed health questionnaire. Depending on your health issues, they then decide how much to charge you or whether to reject you outright.

Generally, the supplemental insurers will either accept you or not. But some companies, including AARP, Cigna, and Mutual of Omaha, enroll certain people with health issues at around double the usual premium—say, $350 a month rather than $175.

People get rejected for a long list of "knockout" issues, such as heart problems, stroke, rheumatoid arthritis, lupus, amyotrophic lateral sclerosis, and Parkinson's disease. In addition, patients are knocked out for taking insulin for diabetes and for receiving cancer treatment in the previous three years, including taking a costly specialty drug.

My Advice. If you have health issues and are undecided about which plan to choose outside of your initial election period, check carefully with the Medigap insurers on your list to see if any are likely to accept you at a reasonable cost. Or focus instead on Medicare Advantage plans. By law, since the federal government handsomely subsidizes the private insurers offering Advantage plans, they cannot reject you for health reasons or charge you extra. There is one exception: Advantage plans do not accept people with end-stage renal disease, or ESRD. Original Medicare covers them.

Also, if you live in Massachusetts, Minnesota, or Wisconsin, you're in luck. Those states prohibit supplemental insurers from asking you questions about your health, aside from ESRD.

Greg Gudis, owner of BGA Insurance Group in Conshohocken, Pennsylvania, spoke for respected Medicare insurance brokers across the country when he told me, "I exist because the government has made Medicare so difficult to understand. It shouldn't be so impossible for people to figure out. But it is."

MOM'S DEATH ON MEDICARE

Death is mysterious. And so are the Medicare regulations surrounding skilled nursing and hospices, as you can see in this account by writer Kathryn Boughton about the last days of her mother, Frances B. Wohlfert of North Canaan, Connecticut.

Mom fell in late August walking down the hall in our house, severely breaking her upper arm on the left side. She was taken to nearby Sharon Hospital, where a surgeon set the bone. Because she was ninety-three, the surgeon thought keeping her arm stable during the long recuperation would require skilled nursing.

But before Medicare covers the cost of skilled nursing at a licensed rehabilitation facility, it requires that the patient must be admitted to a hospital for at least three days (periods of observation do not count), with transportation on the fourth day. My mother qualified and was admitted to the rehab wing of Geer Skilled Nursing and Rehabilitation Center in nearby Canaan. We were happy about that. Medicare would pay for her room, meals, personal supplies, equipment, and all nursing and rehabilitation services for up to three months. However, we soon learned that there were restrictions and limitations.

My mother was depressed, weak, and tired. She was also in pain, though she stubbornly refused to admit that. Because she would not ask for painkillers, the nurses provided them preemptively, though she didn't metabolize them well, and they sometimes made her seem demented.

She was lucid enough, however, to immediately express her dislike of physical therapy. Fortunately, she was just cooperative enough in her first days at Geer to avoid getting kicked out of the rehab wing as her arm slowly began to heal. Despite her being ninety-three, weak, and in pain, we were told that if she had refused to participate for three days in a row, she would have no longer qualified for Medicare coverage as a rehab patient. And since she was able to take food and medicine orally and did not have a wound that required dressing, she would not have qualified for the skilled nursing benefit any other way.

Medicare would have stopped covering her expenses, and she would have become a private patient at Geer, getting billed $500 a day until the last of her life's savings melted away. We estimated that would take just three months. Then, with her savings gone, she would have been covered again as a Medicaid patient.

In her second week of rehab, my mother suffered a small stroke and was sent back to Sharon Hospital. Medicare's skilled nursing payments to Geer stopped when she was wheeled out the door. We had two options: We could pay $500 a day out of pocket to reserve her room at Geer, or we could roll the dice and hope a bed would be available there when the hospital released her.

Faced with the possibility of having to travel far to see her if she were transferred elsewhere, we opted to reserve her bed. It was important to me to be able to stop by several times a day to see how she was doing.

Mom got back to Geer after only two days. But she "failed to thrive," as people there put it. She was despondent, largely silent, refused the institutional food, and hated the thickened beverages she was served to help her swallow. She seemed a little worse to me every day. She was dying, and all she wanted was to be at home.

In many ways, our decision to bring her home was made easy. She completely refused to participate in physical therapy. Beyond that, I couldn't stand seeing her in misery one day longer.

But when she came home, there were more surprises. I am a writer, not a nurse. While at Geer, I saw how often two people were needed to care for her. Even though she had lost 40 pounds in two months, she still weighed 140 pounds and was so weak it took two people to move her safely while protecting her broken arm. She also needed the support of two people to stand, walk, use the commode, and get into bed.

Fortunately, once she was home, Medicare hospice benefits kicked in. Under hospice, her nursing services, medical equipment, including a hospital bed, commode, wheelchair, oxygen, and the like were all paid for. We also got her pain relief medicines, medical supplies, and bed pads at no cost. A social worker also was assigned to help her and our family. And the rest of the hospice team helped us greatly, too.

But there were limits. Hospice covers home health aids for only one shift a day, nowhere near the round-the-clock care my mom needed. We saw no choice. We paid the extra home health workers' costs out of Mom's dwindling funds: about $250 a day for aids to cover an eight-hour shift each, with me serving as the backup.

The care my mother received in her final days was superb, compassionate, and kind. But it is a bad feeling to have one eye on the calendar as you sit by your mother's deathbed. As she lingered, I kept a nervous eye on her account, wanting her to live forever but not to outlive our ability to provide all the care she needed.

Since my mother had only about $20,000 left, I opened the first bill for her personal attendants with some trepidation—more than $1,500 for her first four days at home. She lingered another ten days, with the bill mounting to more than $6,000.

When death finally released her on November 10, 2015, we were blessed. It was the death she and our family wanted for her: at peace, at home, carefully attended, and still solvent—though barely.

CHAPTER 8

Confounding Billing Codes and Other Bizarre Obstacles

Why Understanding Medical Codes Is Key to Figuring Out Costs

Welcome to the back room of the American health care industry, where the insiders speak in code. As I've touched on earlier, if you don't know the code for the medical procedure or service the doctor wants you to have, it's often difficult to get anyone to tell you in advance whether you will be covered and how much you'll end up paying.

No one you're counting on—your doctor, hospital, health insurer, Medicare—will necessarily help you, as a retired schoolteacher I'm calling Diane to protect her privacy learned sadly.

For more than two months in 2013, the soft-spoken grandmother in her late sixties with a family history of breast cancer tried to get answers to two basic questions: Would Medicare cover her cancer screening MRI this year? And if not, what might the screening cost her? Unfortunately, Medicare refused to answer her questions, because she didn't have the code Medicare beneficiaries need to get such basic information from the government. Diane didn't have the medical code for her procedure.

After years of hearing the health care industry say that better informed consumers hold the key to controlling costs, the media have begun reporting how difficult it is to get doctors and hospitals to reveal their often sharply different prices before you are treated and billed. Now you can add Medicare to that closemouthed list.

When it comes to billing, Medicare and the private health care industry speak in code. By 2016, hospitals had begun billing with ICD-10 codes, which identify 92,000 different medical procedures and services with a unique five-unit set of numbers or letters, plus a concise description. Outside of hospitals, doctors bill patients under the 9,700 Current Procedural Terminology (CPT) codes developed and licensed by the American Medical Association (AMA) for the past fifty years. And to make matters more confusing for patients, Medicare has its own set of codes.

Over the past four decades, the precise sets of procedure codes, especially the CPT codes that tripped up Diane, have become the nation's common shorthand for medical services—and for billing each service.

To make matters worse for consumers, doctors are not ethically bound by the AMA to tell you the codes and costs up front, before you are treated and billed. And Medicare representatives are trained to not tell you the codes, even for a critical procedure, as Diane learned.

Diane has reason to fear cancer. Her mother had a double mastectomy in her forties. Her daughter had the same surgery in her thirties. So far Diane has been diagnosed with troubling dense-tissue breasts and has had two biopsies—both thankfully benign. Given her history, her doctor, Kristen Zarfos, director of St. Francis Hospital and Medical Center's Comprehensive Breast Health Center in Hartford, Connecticut, put her on a cancer screening schedule years ago alternating a mammogram and a breast MRI every six months.

In 2013, Diane's first year on Medicare, the government

covered both procedures. But in late April 2014, Diane said Dr. Zarfos's assistant called with bad news. St. Francis's billing department said that Medicare had changed its breast cancer policy and would not pay for this year's MRI. Diane could have the MRI, the assistant added, but she'd have to pay $1,500 out of her own pocket. Under Medicare back in 2013, St. Francis had billed $5,548.43 for Diane's MRI. But Medicare paid the hospital only $289.54, and Diane didn't pay a penny.

With nothing in writing from the hospital explaining the policy change, Diane's bewildered family contacted the Center for Medicare Advocacy in Connecticut. A friend there, who knew I was writing this book, alerted me.

With the family's permission, I did some checking. Oddly, no one I interviewed had heard of a policy change. Not at Medicare Advocacy, the Medicare Rights Center, the American Cancer Society, New York's Ashikari Breast Center—or at St. Francis Hospital's billing department. "I don't know of any Medicare policy changes," a seasoned billing staffer there told me. "I have her file open in front of me. And I don't see any notes in her file relating to a change in policy."

Did that mean there was a hospital mix-up? Would Medicare cover Diane's MRI after all? Or would she have to pay $1,500? I phoned the Medicare helpline on her behalf three times. But I couldn't get answers without the CPT code.

My calls to the invariably polite helpers at 1-800-Medicare went like this:

> Me: Are breast cancer MRIs still likely to be covered by Medicare, and what would an MRI of both breasts generally cost?
>
> Helper: I personally don't know of any breast cancer policy changes, but I can't tell you anything about any procedure without the CPT code.
>
> Me: The doctor did not give the patient the CPT

code. But I've described the procedure. Why
can't you tell me the code? Is it a secret?

Helper: No, the codes are not secret. But I'm not allowed
to tell you a code. You need to get the code from
the doctor.

After a couple of those catch-22 calls, I tried a new tack.
When Diane asked Dr. Zarfos's assistant for the procedure
code, the assistant gave her the doctor's diagnostic codes, which
explained why her doctor wanted Diane to get the MRI: V16.3
(patient has family cancer history), 610.1 (patient has dense-
tissue breasts).

Me: I have the diagnostic codes.

Helper: We do not discuss diagnostic codes. Tell your
doctor to call the Medicare provider helpline.
The people there can tell the doctor whether
Medicare is likely to cover the MRI under that
diagnosis.

Me: Why can't Diane call that number and get the
answer herself?

Helper: I'm sorry, but the provider line is only for health
care providers, like her doctor.

Me: Wait a minute. You're telling me there's a Medicare phone line with the answers, but only doctors can call it. That makes no sense to me. Does
that sound fair to you?

Helper: Is there anything else I can help you with?

I phoned Dr. Zarfos's office and reached the assistant, who,
according to Diane, had recently spent an hour futilely reviewing her medical file to find a way to get the MRI covered.

The assistant told me, "I don't know what you are talking
about. Eight hundred patients come through here. I don't

recall her." She declined to put Dr. Zarfos on the line: "The appropriate people from St. Francis will call you back." No one ever did.

Meanwhile, no CPT code. No answers. No MRI for Diane.

Donald Berwick, who ran the government's Centers for Medicare and Medicaid Services during President Obama's first term, was surprised to hear about the helpline. "Wow, they can't help you without the code?" he said in a phone interview. "I was not aware of that problem. I would have tried to fix it."

Medicare declined to provide an official to be interviewed. In an email, spokesperson Tami Holzman wrote that helpline representatives "cannot and should not" give out any codes, in part to avoid creating "a perception that Medicare is dictating what treatment is appropriate for the physician to provide."

But Bruce Vladeck, a former head of the Health Care Financing Administration, a precursor of the Centers for Medicare and Medicaid Services, was blunt. "If beneficiaries can describe services in plain English and still can't get basic information without a code," he said, "then, of course, the hot line is not doing its job."

Obviously, in emergencies, few people have the time or inclination to get codes and ask about prices. But the rest of the time, if you choose to consume health care without any idea of your treatment's CPT codes, you might as well eat in restaurants with no prices on their menus. Our doctors, hospitals, and health insurers should make procedure codes and cost estimates easily available to patients. And Medicare should lead.

Some health care experts told me that the government doesn't have the human resources or the billions of dollars that would be needed for software development and retraining to provide pricing without the right code. I don't believe that.

If that excuse was true, how can anyone explain what Jeanne Pinder, a former *New York Times* health reporter turned fledgling entrepreneur, has accomplished? In two years, with just $54,000 in grants and "friends and family money" to start, she created a code search engine at her Clear Health Costs website (www.clearhealthcosts.com). People in a growing number of cities, including New York, Los Angeles, and San Francisco, can type in a procedure, such as mammogram, and a menu window opens listing the variations of the procedure—complete with their five-unit codes. When you click on the one you want, a screen opens showing nearby doctors providing the service and their cash prices for uninsured patients. You can also see Medicare's general payment rate for 8,400 procedures, services, and supplies. Prices, as you might imagine, vary like crazy. The cash price for a 77057 mammogram in New York City ranges from $50 to $607.

If Pinder's seven-person startup can operate a decoder to help consumers budget for care and shop for reasonable prices, why can't Medicare do it for its fifty million beneficiaries, including Diane?

Here's a first step Medicare could take immediately. It should openly provide the ninety-five codes for the twenty-four basic preventive services its helpline implores beneficiaries to get. These services, which include breast cancer and prostate cancer screenings, are usually available to beneficiaries at no extra cost, and undoubtedly help to curb the nation's medical expenses by spotting diseases early.

When a Medicare beneficiary calls the helpline, as I have repeatedly, an automated voice tells you which preventive services you are eligible for and directs you to Medicare.gov for more information about preventive care. That's a terrific service, except that its information is incomplete. The site does not provide any of the preventive codes. So I can walk into a doctor's office for my free annual "wellness visit" (a G0439) and walk out with a $130 to $500 bill for a 99214 "evaluation" that I might have to pay in full.

It's also interesting to note that I did get the codes from the helpline for my preventive services—once. That was when I originally looked into Diane's story for the *New York Times* and identified myself as a *Times* reporter, instead of only little old me, just another Medicare beneficiary.

The helper first said he didn't have the codes, as he is trained to do. But there was a pause as he talked to someone else. Then he said, "I *do* have the preventive codes. You learn something new every day."

I have an idea to help the Health and Human Services Department reach its goal to "harness the power of data and technology to improve the health of the nation." HHS Secretary Sylvia Mathews Burwell should call the General Dynamics subsidiary that runs the helpline under a $200 million contract and request simply that the automated voice system and its three thousand representatives begin directing beneficiaries to HHS's preventive-care information at CMS.gov rather than to the incomplete information at Medicare.gov. The detailed CMS.gov guide has all the codes and descriptions beneficiaries need to get the preventive services from doctors and hospitals that they deserve.

With one official phone call, every one of Medicare's fifty million beneficiaries who need preventive codes would soon get them from a more helpful helpline.

THE LESSONS FROM DIANE'S STORY

How to Get a Good Idea Up Front of What Your Medical Care Might Cost. Like Diane, you need the precise billing code for a procedure or service to get an estimate of what it might cost. You might find the same quality of care at a better price. You can do that despite the hurdles, including if you are in Medicare. But you need to proceed carefully.

At a Hospital. First off, getting your code has become trickier, since US hospitals and other medical facilities began using the ninety-two thousand ICD-10 codes in 2015, while doctors outside of hospitals stuck with the old CPT codes. ICD codes are so precise that they sometimes seem laughable. There are entries for injuries from wandering into an airplane engine. So tread carefully on the tarmac. With all that specificity, where there are, say, four possible CPT codes for a common procedure such as a colonoscopy, there are around forty ICD-10 codes. If you run into trouble getting codes from a hospital doctor, turn to the facility's ombudsman. Part of that person's job is getting straight answers for patients.

With a Doctor. Outside of a hospital, when your doctor suggests an out-of-the-ordinary procedure or costly service, ask her politely but firmly for the CPT codes she has in mind. Though there might be several possible codes, you can bet she's seriously considering only two or three. If your doctor insists that four or more codes might apply, grab a pen and jot them all down. And if your doctor refuses to give you any codes, do what I do: Consider switching to another doctor.

In an Emergency. As I've said, in true emergencies, few people have the time or the inclination to get codes or ask about prices. As my friend Steven Brill, the author of *America's Bitter Pill: Money, Politics, Backroom Deals, and the Fight to Fix Our Broken Healthcare System*, likes to say, "You don't think of the cost when they are wheeling you in on the gurney."

But how often do you take that ride? Some experts estimate that in around 80 percent of cases, you have plenty of time to plan ahead, hunt down your proper codes, and then shop for your best care at a fair price. And that includes people with chronic conditions such as diabetes or coronary concerns.

Getting Codes Online. Finding codes online takes some effort. But it's worth it, because once you have the right codes, you hold the keys to a vault of medical and cost information. You can use the codes to determine whether or not your insurer will definitely cover your specific service. And the codes will lead you to the cost estimates you need to bargain among providers for a better price, either with insurance or for cash without insurance coverage.

Start the easy way, by checking websites that use huge amounts of billing data to estimate typical charges in your area. In addition to Clear Health Costs, which I outlined on page 48, take a look at Healthcare Bluebook (www.healthcarebluebook.com). It tends to report relatively higher amounts that providers accept from insurance plans, and the prices are arranged conveniently by zip code. Also punch up Fair Health (www.fairhealthconsumer.org) for a range of medical and dental costs and reimbursements. The site also allows you to calculate your likely out-of-pocket costs in your zip code. But Fair Health has a drawback: it limits you to fifteen searches a week.

Each of those three sites is easy to use. You can search by billing code or just type a description of the service you want, such as "office visit." The prices that pop up will vary, but they'll at least give you an idea of how much providers charge insurance carriers or Medicare. Your insurance company also might steer you to other comparison sites.

Medicare offers a similar price guide at cms.gov/apps /physician-fee-schedule/overview.aspx. But I've found it extremely complicated to use. On the other hand, if you are web savvy—and patient—you can find the lower rates that providers are accepting from Medicare. Then you could ask your doctor or provider to accept those low amounts from you.

If you need to dig deeper for CPT codes, go to the source: The American Medical Association, which owns the rights to that code set. You can see all 9,700 codes on its website, at www.ama-assn.org. Select "CPT Code/Relative Value Search" under the "AMA Store" dropdown. After you fill out some basic personal information, you'll get a link to procedures organized by CPT code or by description. Since this is a doctor's resource, you might need some medical lingo; searching "hip replacement," for example, yields nothing, while the medical term "total hip arthroplasty" returns seven applicable codes. If this sounds like work to you, you're correct. However, not only can you get your codes and accurate descriptions, but also you'll see the Medicare approved payment amounts that can help you bargain.

In addition, if you need a hospital's ICD-10 code or a Medicare HCPCS code (short for Healthcare Common Procedure Coding System), go to Find-A-Code website (www.findacode.com). Search by the name of the procedure you're considering, and be as specific as possible to get a manageable list. The full set of ICD-10 codes is also available at ICD10Data.com.

Finding the Right Provider. Once you have your codes and pricing insights, call as many doctors or providers in your health plan's network as you like. However, before committing to a provider, double-check with your insurer that the doctor or provider you prefer actually participates in your health plan. Health plans routinely add and shed providers; sometimes doctors don't realize they've been dropped. And doctors decide to join or leave Medicare constantly, too.

Finally, calculate whether you'd save money paying cash, rather than what you'd pay under, say, your health plan's deductible or high coinsurance rate. Cash might be king.

One More Note. If you're trying to find the best value in hospital care, perhaps for treating heart disease, go to Medicare's "Hospital Compare" page (www.medicare.gov/hospital compare), which allows you to search for hospitals in your area and judge the "value" they provide based on their charges and the rather crude measure of—ugh!—their death rates.

Don't Get Pressured into a Questionable Procedure. Diane said hospital staffers asked her to pay $1,500 for an MRI out of her own pocket because, they claimed, Medicare had changed its policy and would no longer pay for her procedure. Diane added that the hospital did not give her any documents supporting the claim. And she decided not to spend $1,500 for an MRI that, at worst, she could have gotten elsewhere for half that price.

Medicare's rules in cases like this are clear: if you have original Medicare, the provider must warn you that Medicare might not pay for the service or item being offered.

The staff should have given Diane an Advance Beneficiary Notice (ABN) saying that the hospital expected that Medicare would not cover the MRI, and therefore she might end up having to pay for it. In addition, the ABN would have had to explain why Medicare might not pay, such as "Medicare pays for this test only once every three years." If Diane had signed such an ABN, she would have put herself on the hook for the charges.

However, by law, if a provider does not give a beneficiary an ABN, the beneficiary cannot be charged for the service or item.

In addition, original Medicare beneficiaries might not have to pay for the care if the ABN is given to them during an emergency or right before receiving a service, such as when they are, like Diane, about to walk into the room for an MRI.

A word of warning: Providers are not required to give an ABN to Medicare Advantage plan members nor to original Medicare beneficiaries for services or items that Medicare never covers, such as hearing aids.

Bottom line: Every time I write about this tricky business of using CPT codes to find out what a medical service might cost, I think of my interview with the outspoken Bruce Vladeck, the former head of the HFCA. He argued strongly that it is "a fool's errand" to ask people to master a complex coding system where there can be fifteen specific codes for one procedure. I disagreed.

But then he asked me this question: "What kind of a society forces people to learn complex codes to get medical services?"

Unfortunately, it's this society.

CHAPTER 9

———•———

Pink Confusion

When Should Women
Get Screened for Breast Cancer?

During a checkup when Hannah Savoy of rural Michigan was only twenty-one, her doctor found a lump in her breast. It turned out to be benign, as was a second lump that her doctors detected three years later. Understandably, Hannah worries a lot about breast cancer. "It's kind of terrifying," she said on TV. "I do my monthly check of my breasts, and if I find other lumps or if a lump has grown, that's when I'll know that it could be something."

Or the lumps could continue to be nothing. It could be that Hannah is one of millions of women who are being overtreated for a disease they will never get.

Driven by studies that concluded that breast cancer screenings are leading to potentially dangerous false alarms and overtreatment rather than prolonging lives, the American Cancer Society (ACS) said in 2015 that women of average risk should have mammograms later and less frequently than the group had advised in the past. That recommendation upset many women, including Hannah: "I think that's just insane."

Call it pink confusion. There are now three distinct sets of breast screening guidelines from more than three respected health organizations, leaving many patients and their doctors wondering exactly what they should be doing to guard against the nation's deadliest cancer, after lung cancer. The ACS, the United States Preventive Services Task Force, and the National Comprehensive Cancer Network (NCCN)—three groups who create influential screening recommendations—agree that annual screening mammography beginning at age forty saves the most lives. Yet their recommendations differ based largely on the dangers associated with overtreatment. The hard-nosed analysis leaves many experts concluding that the health risks for most outweigh the lifesaving benefits for a relative few.

Around 230,000 women will get breast cancer in 2016, and 40,000 with the disease will die. Picture that. Six stadiums full of women will get breast cancer. And all the women in another stadium who already have the disease will be gone by New Year's Eve.

But studies show that if you have an average risk of breast cancer and merely get regular breast screenings, you can reduce your odds of dying from the disease by 30 percent, compared with women who are diagnosed after finding a lump. On average, routine mammograms cost $250, but virtually all health plans pick up the entire expense as a preventive service. So if all 40,000 in that last stadium had gotten screened early, at whatever the cost, up to 12,000 of them might still be there in the upper decks to cheer in the New Year.

The debate—and much of the public confusion—revolves around when women should begin screening for a disease that primarily strikes older women. Around 180,000 of the 230,000 who get breast cancer each year are over age fifty. In fact, the median age of new breast cancer patients has hovered around sixty-one for years. However, very significantly, 40 percent of the lives saved by screening are among women of average risk under the age of fifty, who tend to develop more aggressive forms of the disease.

After its analysis, the ACS concluded that women with no symptoms or family history of the disease could wait until age forty-five to begin annual screening and then switch to screening every other year at fifty-four. Previously, the ACS had recommended annual screening beginning at forty. The ACS added, however, that women between forty and forty-four should still have the option of getting annual mammograms that would continue to be completely covered by their insurers.

In addition, the ACS also no longer recommends clinical breast exams, where a doctor or nurse conducts a hands-on examination looking for lumps or other abnormalities. The ACS concluded that those exams do not prolong lives and actually might do harm by triggering unnecessary further testing for all sorts of false alarms, commonly called false positives. That, too, is a radical change for the ACS. It had long recommended that women—like young Hannah Savoy of Michigan—undergo clinical exams each year beginning at age nineteen.

As controversial as the ACS's new guidelines are, studies show that the routine annual screening finds far too many false positives that lead to needless anxiety for patients; unnecessary testing, such as $1,000 to $5,000 biopsies; and sometimes even surgery. To save one life with mammograms, you have to screen two thousand women, deal with two hundred false positives, and endure ten unnecessary surgeries. What's more, one study reported that 61 percent of women who got mammograms each year between ages forty and fifty got diagnosed with at least one nerve-wracking false positive.

The statistics around the hands-on clinical exams are even worse. According to one study, the exams found 0.4 extra cancers per 1,000—but more than 20 false positives. That's a negative 50-to-1 ratio.

"Any abnormal finding sends a woman into a tailspin," said Lillie Shockney, a breast cancer nurse at Johns Hopkins Hospital in Baltimore. "It's awful." And Dr. Pond Kelemen of the Ashikari Breast Center in Dobbs Ferry, New York, added, "Sometimes women have more stress worrying about all the uncertainties of false positives than they do with a diagnosis of breast cancer. We can treat cancers. But lowering ongoing anxieties can be difficult."

In addition, though one woman in eight gets breast cancer at some point in her life, the odds of an average woman receiving a diagnosis in any five-year period are low, especially if you are young. For example, the risk of developing breast cancer between forty and forty-five is 0.6 percent—or slightly more than one in two hundred. Nonetheless, if you are that one, your early detection gives you a 30 percent better chance of surviving—and you are very grateful for the screening.

In 2016, the independent US Preventive Services Task Force, which helps set the nation's preventive health policies, went a step beyond the ACS. It issued formal guidelines stating that women with average risk can wait safely until age fifty to begin getting mammograms. The task force found that among 10,000 women screened regularly over ten years, only four lives are saved from forty to forty-nine; eight lives from fifty to fifty-nine; twenty-one lives from sixty to sixty-nine; and thirteen lives from seventy to seventy-four. Along the way, for every 10,000 women tested regularly between forty and forty-nine, more than 10 percent of them—some 1,120—figure to have a false positive, inviting anxiety and wasteful extra treatment.

The task force said that its guidelines, based solely on scientific evidence, offer the best balance between the benefits of detecting cancer and the risks of overtreatment. It was quick, however, to add that women should choose for themselves.

The task force's new guidelines could affect millions. By law, the task force's "final" recommendations override the ACA's, which require insurers to pick up the costs of breast screenings as a preventive service. Therefore, experts fear that, if the task force's advice is left unchecked, a growing number of insurers—especially self-insured employers and smaller insurance companies—could choose to stop covering mammograms for women under fifty.

Spurred by health care advocates, the US Congress quickly

passed a bill requiring private insurers to completely cover screening mammograms for women forty and over every year or two without copays, coinsurance, or deductibles through 2017. But many advocates had hoped the bill would mandate cost-free screenings indefinitely. The Susan G. Komen foundation stated that any rollback in coverage would especially threaten African American women, who are more prone than whites to aggressive breast cancer.

Meanwhile, at the opposite end of the scale, the National Comprehensive Cancer Network (NCCN) continues to recommend annual mammograms beginning at age forty for average-risk women. And the American Congress of Obstetricians and Gynecologists recommends mammograms every year or two from forty to forty-nine and then every year after that. In addition, it endorses annual clinical breast exams beginning at nineteen.

Vanderbilt-Ingram Cancer Center's Dr. John G. Huff, who helps develop the NCCN's screening guidelines, said, "While it may be appropriate to give women choices about whether to be screened or not, it will be unfortunate if women who choose screening are denied [the service] because of the loss of coverage."

It's worth noting that around 30 percent of women of all ages who could get breast screening at no cost are not getting the preventive service. Whatever the reason—fear of doctors or of getting a bill or what they might learn—not getting screened becomes literally a crying shame for some of them.

So what should you do? Here's what a number of respected breast cancer specialists recommend for a series of situations you might face.

Can Women with Average Risk Safely Wait Until Forty-Five or Fifty to Begin Breast Screening? The US Task Force aside, many doctors are divided on how long a woman should wait, since a little over one in ten new breast cancer patients are under forty-five.

Dr. Kristi Funk of the Pink Lotus Breast Center of Beverly Hills, California—the surgeon who performed actress-activist Angelina Jolie's preventive double mastectomy in 2013—called the ACS recommendations "harsh and unpalatable." She dismissed the ACS's idea of waiting until forty-five as "dangerous," let alone the task force's guideline of delaying until fifty.

"Around ninety-five percent of all breast cancers occur in women after forty," she said. "So let's start screening normal risk women at forty, and let them decide with their doctors what kind of regimen is best based on their initial screenings."

Dr. Funk added, "I feel the majority of women would gladly have a few extra views each year, or a biopsy for peace of mind, rather than skip imaging until a lump protrudes through the skin, which is where these recommendations seem to be headed." (See page 132 for the Pink Lotus Foundation, which provides complete breast treatment for eligible women at no charge.)

Dr. Kelemen, too, prefers that women begin at forty, but he added that he believes women with no troubling family history or symptoms can safely wait until they are forty-five.

"Where I push back," Dr. Kelemen continued, "is with women under forty who ask for mammograms. I put my foot down and tell them they can wait until forty." Having said that, Dr. Kelemen added with a laugh that he makes sure that his wife who is just over forty gets her annual mammogram—and he reviews the results personally. "I have a rule about not treating family members because you can't be objective," he told me. "But I make an exception for my wife."

Dr. Huff, the chief of imaging at Vanderbilt-Ingram in Nashville, stressed, "The earlier a breast cancer is found, the less aggressive the management of that breast cancer may be. This is why it is critical to maintain reimbursement for screening mammography for women who choose to have it."

Can Women of Average Risk Safely Skip an Annual Exam at Around Age Fifty-Five? The odds say you can. After women go through menopause, breast cancer is less likely to be aggressive. But doctors add that there are no guarantees.

While the ACS and the USPSTF recommend screening every two years for women over fifty-five, the NCCN continues to recommend annual screening. Dr. Huff said that while cancers might be less aggressive in older women, it is still true that the earlier you find a cancer, aggressive or not, the less extensive the therapy for that cancer will be. He said, "We should be concerned not only with survival but also with the woman's quality of life."

Should Women Stop Getting Clinical Breast Exams?
Although breast specialists concede that the benefits of the physical exams are difficult to measure, many argue passionately for them. For example, Dr. Funk called the intimate examination of a woman's breasts "the truest moment of connection between the doctor and patient." She said, "The doctor has to stop looking down into his computer typing in information and billing codes and instead focus his full attention on the patient as a human being who needs his care."

Dr. Kelemen echoed that point, saying the "comforting" exams deepen the doctor-patient bond. He also noted that on a practical level, he "catches things" with clinical exams: "In the past year, in addition to the breast cancers I've detected, I have found two melanomas and two lymphomas that the patients had no idea they had."

How Much Should Women Worry About False Positives?
False positives are false alarms. Usually the mammogram detects something that looks abnormal but, after closer examination, there appears to be nothing to worry about. Experts, including Dr. Funk, agree that even the latest 3-D imaging systems turn up too many false alarms.

According to some estimates cited by people worried about overtreatment, around 10 percent to 15 percent of women with false positives undergo biopsies, in which a sample of breast tissue is removed, sometimes with a needle, and then studied by a pathologist for abnormalities. But Dr. Huff doesn't buy those high figures: "The impact of false-positive screening findings, while not insignificant, has been greatly exaggerated."

According to Dr. Huff's estimates, for every thousand mammograms, fifty to a hundred (5 percent to 10 percent) women are called back for more testing, but usually only for a couple of additional mammographic pictures. Of these women, only about twenty (2 percent of the original thousand) get a biopsy. He added that almost all breast biopsies are now performed as needle biopsies in an outpatient setting with local anesthetic, rather than as an invasive and more costly surgical biopsy in an operating room.

And of these twenty biopsies, five to seven women actually have breast cancer.

Dr. Huff emphasized that those five to seven women have a 30 percent lower risk of dying from the disease compared with women whose cancer was found as a lump. "The majority of women that I've talked with," said Dr. Huff, "would trade the anxiety of a callback and possible needle biopsy in favor of a better prognosis if they are diagnosed with breast cancer."

Furthermore, some experts stress that women should not ignore false positives, especially if they have a series of them. A Danish study of more than fifty-eight thousand women over the age of fifty, for example, found that those who had false-positive mammograms ended up running a 67 percent higher risk of developing breast cancer later in life, compared with women who had negative mammograms. Experts say that women with thick-tissue breasts or a family history of breast cancer tend to have false positives and tend to run higher risks.

Dr. Funk said flatly that she considers false positives a potential signal of an eventual cancer. "A false positive can indicate that the breast is busy making something," she said. "And if it's making something, it could eventually make a cancer."

My Advice. Don't ignore a false positive. After a first false alarm, discuss with your doctor whether you should be screened more closely. And if you have a series of false alarms, it's probably time to insist on frequent monitoring by a breast cancer specialist. You and your doctor should agree on a plan to manage your warnings, based on all available medical information and your tolerance for risk.

When Should Women Undergo Genetic Testing to See Whether They Run a High Risk of Getting Breast or Ovarian Cancer? A big factor that women and their doctors must consider is that genetic counseling and testing is expensive. Even though insurers nearly always pick up the $3,000 to $5,000 cost of a genetic blood test for women at high risk, it's not practical to imagine screening every woman to find the two million who actually carry gene mutations—called BRCA—or other mutation that signals an elevated cancer risk.

Dr. Huff stressed that women who worry they are at risk should undergo a risk assessment before asking for genetic testing. Your local ACS chapter can arrange an assessment with a staff member who will ask you a series of lifestyle and personal history questions to get a sense of your cancer vulnerability.

Beyond that somewhat informal assessment, doctors tend to zero in on genetic testing for women who have these factors:

- going back two generations, two of the woman's relatives on the mother's or father's side had breast cancer;
- a relative had breast cancer before age fifty;
- a relative developed cancer in both breasts at any age;
- a relative had ovarian cancer at any age; or
- the woman is an Ashkenazi Jew, an ethnic group that tends to carry the BRCA mutations.

Normally, BRCA genes help repair your DNA and stabilize your genes. However, if BRCA genes mutate, they don't function properly, and your cells become far more likely to create a cancer.

As we've noted, one out of eight women get breast cancer at some point in their lives. That's bad enough. But a staggering 55 percent to 65 percent of women with BRCA1 mutations develop breast cancer by age seventy, and so do 45 percent of those with abnormal BRCA2. Worse yet, the Mayo Clinic reports that while BRCA mutations account for 5 percent of all breast cancers, they are responsible for 15 percent of highly dreaded ovarian cancer cases.

Angelina Jolie—who carries the BRCA1 mutation and whose mother died of breast cancer at fifty-six—faced an 87 percent chance of getting breast cancer when she decided in 2013 to have a preventive double mastectomy. The actress and United Nations refugee envoy announced her decision in a widely read editorial in the *New York Times*. At that time, she added that she was planning to have more surgery, because she still faced a 50 percent chance of getting ovarian cancer. Two years later, when tests revealed a disturbing level of inflammation in her system, she had her ovaries and fallopian tubes removed. And again she announced the surgery in the *New York Times*.

"I am grounded in the choices I am making for myself and my family," Jolie wrote. "I know my children will never have to say, 'Mom died of ovarian cancer.'"

In her many public statements, Jolie has stressed that women with the BRCA mutations should not rush to get drastic treatment, including the preventive surgery she had. Rather, she has urged women to explore their options with their doctors, including getting genetic counseling before even agreeing to the testing. "Knowledge is power," she said.

"That's what I say to my patients every day: Knowledge is power," said Susan Boolbol, chief of breast surgery at Beth Israel Medical Center in New York. "Know your personal history, know what you can of your family history, and discuss your options with your doctor."

Women appear to be listening. There seems to be little evidence that the "Angelina Jolie Effect" has driven women to demand cancer treatment that they don't actually need. At the same time, at least one study shows that the publicity surrounding Jolie's breast surgery helped to double the number of high-risk women who decided to see their doctors for counseling about what to do next.

If you are a high-risk patient with symptoms or a troubling family history, it's good to remember that under the Affordable Care Act, all insurers should cover the entire costs of genetic counseling and mutation testing. Still, you would be wise to contact your insurer and confirm that the company will pick up the expensive testing costs before you move forward with it. Also, if you are uninsured or meet specific lower-income or medical criteria, your doctor might be able to steer you to a genetic testing company that will do the work at little or no charge.

What Should Women Do if They Are Diagnosed with Tiny Growths in Their Milk Ducts? First off, women who are told they have growths in their milk ducts—about sixty thousand a year—should not panic. A number of experts say many of those women are being overdiagnosed and overtreated. The mammogram might simply be revealing a tiny growth called ductal carcinoma in situ (DCIS) that might never evolve into invasive cancer. Therefore, based on the microscopic appearance of the growths, some experts say it's safe to simply monitor benign growths, perhaps with more frequent mammograms.

Dr. Funk, however, strongly disagrees. "My office overtreats DCIS because two-thirds of those growths will invade at some point," she said. "If you are under sixty-five, we excise the growth and radiate. Usually the growths are larger than they first seem; sometimes three times as large."

She added that, despite her advice, some of her patients only want to be monitored. "So I'm watching them," she said. "That's okay with me, as long as we keep a close eye on them."

Experts say that more than 90 percent of women with DCIS survive if they are treated early. It's worth noting that not only does watching and waiting bring risk, it generally obligates the woman to get her breasts checked by a specialist every six months until she's into her seventies.

What Should Women Do if They Have Cancer in One Breast and the Other Is Healthy? Doctors say that the great majority of cancers in the other breast are discovered during the initial diagnosis of the affected breast. Assuming you don't develop other risk factors, if one breast is healthy, the odds of getting cancer in that breast over your lifetime might be less than one in ten, thanks to modern screening.

Yet a lot of women don't like those odds. As breast reconstruction options have improved, including the technique to preserve the nipples, women increasingly are choosing to have both breasts removed in an operation called contralateral prophylactic mastectomy (CPM). However, that surgery is not a standard recommendation unless the woman runs an elevated cancer risk because of factors such as family history, dense-tissue breasts, multiple benign biopsies, or BRCA mutations. Therefore, some insurance plans refuse to cover the entire operation, which can run from $30,000 to $100,000 when it's complete with reconstruction by a plastic surgeon.

In 2014 the *Boston Globe* reported on ten women who were about to have both breasts removed, some the very next morning, who were suddenly told that Blue Cross Blue Shield of Massachusetts would not pay for removing the healthy breast. Blue Cross, the state's largest health insurer, had covered that operation for years.

Ariel Holmes, a thirty-six-year-old fast-food restaurant manager, decided very reluctantly not to have her healthy right breast removed the next day. She didn't want to wait another minute to get her cancerous left breast removed, and also feared that if she went ahead with both breasts and lost her appeals to Blue Cross, she'd get stuck with bills she couldn't pay.

Her decision forced her plastic surgeon to fit her with a balloon-like tissue expander as a temporary solution while she appealed, rather than the permanent reconstruction of both breasts the doctor had planned.

Dr. Phuli Cohan, a women's health specialist diagnosed with invasive ductal breast cancer at fifty-eight, was also turned down by Blue Cross at the last minute. "It was an awful thing to do to a woman the night before surgery," said Dr. Cohan. "It's inhumane and reckless."

Dr. Cohan's surgeon urged her to proceed with the double mastectomy and promised he would help fight the insurance company. She went ahead with the full operation.

The surgeon also told her there were a number of other women who had gotten similar last-minute calls from Blue Cross. "Then he asked me if I wanted to talk to a *Boston Globe* reporter," said Dr. Cohan. She indeed did.

Two days before the *Boston Globe* reported on the last-minute denials, a Blue Cross official called Dr. Cohan to say the company would pay for her total breast removal and reconstruction after all.

"They were all sweet and nice then," she recalled. But she said she had no doubt that the media attention had caused the reversal, though the company insisted the denials were a mix-up.

Holmes, the fast-food manager, got the apologetic call too, and she planned to get her clean breast removed soon to hopefully keep cancer away for good.

"I feel happy now," she said. "More positive."

But Dr. Cohan was still angry with Blue Cross. "What they did is a form of medical bullying."

She urged women who are turned down by their insurer to

fight back. "You *really* have to fight," she said. "If you are determined, you can win on most appeals with insurance companies. That's been my experience."

Despite the many possible hurdles, a great number of women with one cancerous breast are deciding to have both removed. A study in the *Journal of the American Medical Association* (*JAMA*) suggests that 69 percent of women getting CPMs have no family risk factor of cancer or major genetic problem with the clean breast.

Dr. Michele Gadd, a breast surgeon at Massachusetts General Hospital, calls choosing a CPM a "quality of life" decision. "It's how you feel about your body image, it's avoiding going through thirty years of mammograms, MRIs, and other scares," she said. "When you add up the cost from that standpoint, having a prophylactic mastectomy might be cheaper than lifelong surveillance."

LESSONS FROM ONE WOMAN'S TOUGH DECISION

"My doctor said she didn't like what she saw," said Maggie Murphy, "and neither did I." So began Maggie's intense struggle with the threat of breast cancer—an experience that offers lessons to many women.

Maggie, the former editor in chief of *Parade*, and her primary ob-gyn had been monitoring a lump in her right breast for years when they saw the tiny change early in 2015. Her doctor took out her ballpoint pen and drew a little blue dot the size of the tiny mass she saw. She said, "This may be nothing, but let's get it checked out."

Unfortunately, the needle biopsy was hard to read. Maggie said, "One doctor told me, 'Your breasts are a hot mess. I can't figure out what's going on in there.'"

But Maggie's ob-gyn was emphatic about recommending a

double mastectomy. She said that Maggie, who was fifty-two, had lobular carcinoma in situ (LCIS) in her left breast with maybe a bit of DCIS as well—clear signs of an elevated risk of invasive cancer. Generally, women with LCIS in one breast run up to a 30 percent risk—about double the basic risk of all women—of developing cancer in either breast in twenty years. Given her personal and family history, Maggie's risk of invasive breast cancer was probably about 60 percent, but her doctor thought she could reduce it to 1 percent for life with a double mastectomy.

Maggie recalled, "At one point, my doctor said that if we did not operate, 'Sooner or later, your breasts are going to kill you.'"

Maggie's feisty doctor, who asked that her name not appear in this book, described herself as "radical" about surgery. She lost her mother to the disease and is a breast cancer survivor herself. She imagines that her twenty-seven-year-old daughter will one day choose a double mastectomy as well.

But she told Maggie, "Since I am radical about this, I am going to send you to other specialists who may advise you differently."

As she predicted, when Maggie's genetic test showed she did not have the BRCA mutations, one doctor said she could "watch and wait." However, another called Maggie a "horrible candidate" for waiting.

"No one wants radical surgery," Maggie said, but four factors tugged her toward an operation.

First, though neither her mother, her mother's six sisters, nor thirty cousins had developed breast cancer, Maggie looked into her father's relatives, since either parent can hand down the disease. Bingo: she discovered that her father's sister back in Ireland had suffered from breast cancer.

Further darkening her family history—and far more immediate—Maggie's slightly older sister was suddenly diagnosed with breast cancer. "That rocked me," Maggie said.

And on top of that, her health insurance was running out.

After the Condé Nast publishing company sold *Parade* in 2014, she chose to hang on to the company's generous health plan through COBRA for as long as she could—which was until April 2016. She did not know what sort of insurance she might have after that from perhaps a new employer, or, frankly, whether she would have any coverage at all.

Finally, she couldn't bear the thought of watching and waiting for the full-blown breast cancer she seemed destined to get. "Watching and waiting is a serious job, and I'd end up needing surgery anyway," Maggie said. "Once my doctors concluded that I was a candidate for a double mastectomy, I said, 'Let's do it.'"

Maggie chose "the flap procedure," where the breasts are peeled back, scooped out, and filled with fat from the patient's stomach. The nipples are preserved as well.

"You get new breasts and a tummy tuck," Maggie joked. But no one was laughing about the procedure itself, which involved twelve hours of surgery by a cancer surgeon followed by a reconstructive plastic surgeon; up to twelve weeks for recovery; and an inevitable stack of medical bills.

Maggie was luckier than many others. Her insurance company covered roughly 80 percent of the costs for the cancerous breast, but a lesser figure for the clean one. Maggie finds that "nutty," to use her word. "You would think I would get credit for saving everyone a second trip to the hospital." Maggie believes an operation on her other breast was inevitable down the road. As approved, the operation leaves her facing bills of around $20,000 to $30,000.

"I saved my pennies over the years, so, fortunately, I have the financial ability to do this," Maggie said.

More importantly, she feels that she has put the emotional preoccupation with breast cancer behind her so that she can live her life without that fear.

"Some people will see this as overtreatment," she said. "I see it as a lifesaving decision. After the surgery, my doctor hugged me and said, 'You are going to be fine.' I believe that. I am going to be fine."

FIVE VALUABLE LESSONS

- **Don't Ignore Indicators of Breast Cancer, Such as Thick-Tissue Breasts or Benign Lumps.** Establish an initial baseline with your doctor and monitor your condition closely so that you can catch the disease as early as possible. Maggie established her baseline eighteen years before her operation, when she was thirty-four.
- **Get a Second or Even Third Opinion.** To her credit, Maggie's ob-gyn not only referred her to specialists but to doctors at different hospitals whom she thought would offer different points of view. "Each institution has its own bent," said the doctor. What's more, she got on the phone and made the appointments for Maggie. Few doctors do that much to expose their patients to other points of view. Odds are, you'll have to take control. Always ask your physician and your health plan for the names of physicians who will give you fresh, objective opinions.
- **Double-check Your Family History.** As Maggie learned, her father's sister had the disease, a significant discovery.
- **Hang on to Generous Company Health Insurance.** Those policies are slowly disappearing. If you have one like Maggie did, at a reasonable cost even under COBRA, keep it for as long as you can.
- **Save Your Pennies.** When you get bad medical news, having substantial savings will give you more ability to make the decisions that are right for you. Or as Maggie put it, you get a better chance "to drive your own bus."

FULL BREAST CANCER TREATMENT
FOR THE HOPEFUL, FREE OF CHARGE

Every week, one or two women with breast cancer and limited financial resources were being fully treated by top physicians in the Los Angeles area in 2016 through a foundation promising "Hope for Those Who Lost All Hope." The treatment was being arranged through the non-profit Pink Lotus Foundation run by Andy Funk, who, at thirty-nine, was the country's fifth-ranked Iron Man and the entrepreneurial husband of Angelina Jolie's breast surgeon, Dr. Kristi Funk (whom you met on page 120).

Other nonprofits, such as the Susan G. Komen foundation, provide preventive services to the poor and uninsured free of charge. But Andy Funk told me that his foundation is the first to offer full treatment, including complex surgeries, at no cost to eligible women who have no health insurance or very limited coverage.

"We're keeping our eligibility standards loose for now," he explained. "We want to help patients who can't get care they really need any other way."

Worthy cases identified by the foundation's volunteer screeners were being referred to his wife's Pink Lotus Breast Center, where a team there lined up an area doctor or surgeon who was willing to provide care at a discount or free of charge. No one at the foundation was being paid, including Funk.

No matter how complex the case, even if it involves extensive plastic surgery, patients pay nothing at all.

"We will also fly in patients from the East Coast," Funk added. "The airlines say any publicity about helping a breast cancer patient is payment enough."

In the near future, the foundation hopes to screen thousands of cases a week and refer the most needy to about fifteen area doctors, roughly triple the number of doctors who are participating currently.

Here's my contribution to the Funks' notable effort: If you know someone who might be eligible for breast cancer treatment at no charge, urge her to apply to the Pink Lotus Foundation website, www.pinklotusfoundation.org.

CHAPTER 10

·

Don't Let Dental Insurance Bite You

How to Be Your Own Best Advocate in the Dentist's Chair

As the joke goes, your teeth are fine, but the gums have got to go.

When you shop for dental insurance, you are essentially looking for protection against something as serious as that: major periodontal work, a root canal emergency, a crown, or dentures. Without decent dental insurance, any of those problems can cost you several hundred dollars, if not more.

However, dental insurance is expensive, and even the top policies from big-name companies come with relatively limited benefits and potentially costly loopholes. If you don't study the fine print and understand the gaps in your coverage, you're risking a surprise dentist bill that will wipe that bright new smile off your face.

Insurance expert Wendell Potter said dental care has become so expensive that many of us can't afford to go the dentist. "More than one hundred thirty million of us lack dental benefits—far more than the number of people without medical coverage," he added. And even people with dental benefits usually get billed for 50 percent of the cost of expensive procedures such as root canals and crowns.

My experience is fairly typical. For years, I was covered under a Metropolitan Life Insurance Company group plan from my old employer, Time Inc. It was relatively inexpensive, but skimpy. I paid around $45 a month—$540 a year—largely for limited protection against major problems. Like nearly all dental plans, mine covered preventive care of two routine teeth cleanings and standard X-rays each year. But it paid only 75 percent of the preventive bills. I also had to pay an annual $75 deductible just to say hello to a dentist. And, worse, the plan capped my annual benefits at $1,500 a year. Once MetLife paid out $1,500, I was responsible for every additional dime.

All in all, I was paying around $700 for preventive care and some protection against emergencies.

Over the years, with few exceptions, I needed little more than the preventive cleanings and X-rays. If I had been uninsured, most years I could have paid my dentist about $500 directly for his services and saved $200. But the exceptions included a crown and an expensive root canal emergency that was handled nicely by a specialist—and covered by my insurance. Factoring in peace of mind, I figure I came out ahead by having dental insurance.

When my old employer stopped providing dental insurance in 2014, I knew I still wanted coverage. I also knew that an individual plan would cost me more than $45 a month, partly because there is little competition in the field. In the New York area, where I live, my choices narrowed down quickly to two companies: Delta Dental and MetLife.

Both offered plans at around $40 a month, but one capped benefits at a very low $750 a year and the other at $1,000. Those annual limits were too low for me.

The best deal I found in 2014 was MetLife Plan B Dental. It cost $68 a month—a fat $816 a year. However, there was no waiting period for benefits. Many plans make members pay premiums for six months before receiving any benefits, including preventive care. That essentially forces members to finance their own care. But since I'd had a cleaning, X-rays, and a thorough examination by my dentist in December under my old policy, I decided to wait five months before signing up. That was a gamble, but, fortunately, I had no emergencies. Waiting five months saved me $340 in premiums.

Beyond not imposing a waiting period for preventive service, the Plan B policy covers 100 percent of preventive services, including two cleanings a year and standard X-rays. Also, I didn't have to find a new dentist; my long-time dentist was in the network.

On the negative side, the policy capped benefits at $1,500 a year. That's better than my old plan's $1,000 cap, but still a lot lower than I'd like. With this dental plan, I'm betting that my teeth are fine, and my gums will not have to go.

Still, I thought that was a safe bet until I saw the bill for my first cleaning in June. My dentist charged $667 for what seemed to me to be a routine cleaning by a dental hygienist, plus his three-minute, glad-to-see-you, glance-in-my-mouth examination. The $667 was for "scaling and root planing"—essentially deep gum cleaning. Since the dentist's aid said nothing about scaling or root planing during her cleaning, I thought that what she was doing was preventive care paid for 100 percent by my premiums.

When I questioned the dentist's billing assistant about the charges and noted that I was paying $68 a month in premiums for preventive services, she said, "Paying only sixty-eight dollars is a pretty good deal. I see people paying more than two hundred a month for dental insurance."

I called MetLife, hoping that the $667 scaling was covered 100 percent as preventive care. Otherwise, I feared that my first visit would consume nearly half of my annual benefits. Bouncing from one MetLife staffer to another on the phone, I learned that my scaling and root planing—dental code D4342—was an added service covered at only 50 percent by my plan. However, under MetLife's contract with the dentist, the insurer allows the dentist to collect only $479 for the work, not $667. And of that $479, the insurer pays roughly half, or $254. That left me responsible for $225.

In addition, MetLife's $254 payment to the dentist will be subtracted from my $1,500 annual benefits, leaving me with $1,246.

Long and short, the MetLife staffers explained that my "100 percent covered" cleaning would take a $254 bite out of my annual benefits and cost me around $225 out of my own pocket.

But they also shared some of my concerns about the treatment I received:

- The dental hygienist did not warn me that she was about to begin a costly service. Roger at MetLife said, "I don't know if the dentist is legally obligated to ask for your consent, but he is certainly ethically obligated to do it."
- The hygienist did not confer with the dentist before doing the scaling and deep root cleaning.
- The hygienist did not take any X-rays to confirm that I needed the work.
- The hygienist did not warn me that the procedure might be painful.
- And certainly no one had pointed out that my plan covers only half the cost of scaling and root planing—and that's only once every two years. "You should have had a say about whether you wanted that work done now, or if you wanted to wait," said Roger.

With my MetLife notes in front of me, I called my dentist. He was with a patient. I told his assistant that I had questions about the bill, which boiled down to this: Why didn't the dentist's aid warn me about the costly scaling?

To his credit, the dentist called back within an hour. Before I had a chance to say much, he said, "I looked at that bill for six hundred sixty dollars and said, 'That's crazy.' You won't be charged anything for the scaling work. There was a mix-up about the coding."

As he explained it, his aides do scaling—one level of gum treatment coded as D1110—routinely as part of a preventive cleaning. It's generally not painful, and patients are not charged extra for it. However, he said that when dentists find gum separations from the teeth—so-called pockets—of 5 millimeters or more, they can perform scaling and root planing under code D4342 and bill for that more serious and potentially painful procedure.

My dentist said he had cleaned my 5-millimeter pockets in the past at no extra charge under D1110. "But now the American Dental Association wants us to bill for five-millimeter or more pockets under 4342," he said, "though the treatment you're receiving from my office hasn't really changed. The code changed.

"Billing codes are a nightmare," he said. "My billing assistant spends half her time with those confusing codes."

The dentist also apologized for his aid not warning me about the deep cleaning. "She should have told you about it up front," he said. "It won't happen again."

The dentist accepted the insurer's $254 as payment in full for my treatment and waived the $225 he could have billed me. I owed nothing out of pocket for the cleaning.

However, the insurer's $254 is still being charged against my annual benefits, and my plan will not cover any more scaling and root planing for me for two years. My dentist said he would continue to do whatever work I need but not bill it under the D4342 code.

I believed him when he said he wouldn't charge me extra for the gum cleaning in the future. But I did some Health Care Detective double-checking with the American Dental Association. Turns out, despite what he told me, the ADA'S D4342 does *not* specify the depth of the pocket being treated and certainly does *not* require dentists to do extra work at 5 millimeters. But the ADA's rules also do not require dentists to warn patients before they provide services that they will bill for later. If informing patients up front about surprise bills is a professional rule, it's an unwritten one in dentistry.

So what have we learned from my little episode? Mainly this: Guard against surprises!

- **When you book your visit,** specify exactly which services you expect, by saying, for example, "I'd like to come in for my six-month cleaning." Then, when you arrive at the dentist's office, tell the receptionist which services you expect to get, so there can be no confusion.
- **Stop the exam** if the dentist or an assistant begins to do anything that you don't understand. For example, the assistant might start to prepare you for X-rays, though you haven't asked for that service.
- **Don't rush into major procedures,** assuming that you are not in great pain and don't need immediate care. Serious gum work or root canals can be expensive; you can save hundreds or more if you can take time to compare prices with other quality providers. Your insurance carrier should point you to other specialists in your network.
- **If you get a surprise bill,** become your own advocate. First, question your dentist's billing office; most honest mistakes vanish with one call. However, if you are getting back talk or double-talk, turn to your carrier for help. The MetLife staffers I talked to raised important questions and established, in their opinion, that I should have been warned about the extra cleaning up front.
- **Once you understand the situation,** call your dentist. Chances are, if there's been an obvious office mix-up, as in my case, the provider will apologize and clean it up. And even if there's been a mutual misunderstanding, the dentist might offer a discount on your next visit or some other break to keep a loyal patient.

- **Finally, be skeptical,** without being paranoid. When I told
  my story to a neighbor, he said, "My girlfriend works for two
  dentists. She tells me that they bill for more than they do all
  the time, and sometimes they bill for things they don't do
  at all."

In my case, my dentist accepted responsibility and wiped out
my costs as best he could. But I had to pursue the issue with his
billing assistant, the ADA, MetLife, and finally the dentist himself. Although he was apologetic and cooperative, he did not call
me to clear up the bill in the first place, even though he told me
that when he looked at that bill, he knew it was "crazy."

CHAPTER 11

The Pluses and Minuses of Health Savings Accounts

What You Save—and Might End Up Paying—with an HSA

After some study, Fred Warmbier decided to offer his workers at Finishing Technology, near Cincinnati, a high-deductible health plan to keep premiums down. But he didn't stop there. He recognized that paying a high deductible could be a hardship for any number of his employees who were unlucky enough to get very sick. So Warmbier decided that his firm would pay the second half of the deductible. "Our feeling is that if someone is going through tough medical times, we should help," Warmbier said. "Covering this expense has only been necessary a few times in recent years, which is proof enough for me that this works for us."

Unfortunately, Warmbier is an exception. Far more top executives, especially those running big companies that self-insure their workers' health plans, are increasingly pushing workers to sign up for Health Savings Accounts (HSAs). Many of them are motivated by one overriding factor: HSAs save employers lots of money by shifting the risk of getting stuck with big medical bills from the company to their workers. To open an HSA, the employee must enroll in a high-deductible health plan.

Somewhere around half the big bosses in America are actively pushing their workers to drop the company's traditional health plan and accept the responsibility of buying as much—or as little—health care coverage as they want and that they figure they can afford.

The corporate-driven campaign for HSAs as a substitute for company-provided health insurance is similar to the corporate push for 401(k) retirement savings plans in the 1990s as a substitute for company-funded pensions. Executives argued then that they could no longer afford to provide guaranteed pensions. Furthermore, they said workers should accept the responsibility of saving and investing for their own retirements. Self-reliance! That's the American way.

Now corporate executives are saying they can no longer afford to provide traditional health insurance, and, furthermore, workers should make their own health care choices by saving and paying for their health needs. To paraphrase: Why should the company provide comprehensive health insurance for all when healthy workers would be perfectly happy paying less for less coverage and assuming more risk of incurring unexpected medical bills?

Books have been written about what a failure 401(k)s—"the bastard stepchild" of guaranteed-benefit pensions—have been for workers. But since the 1990s, that hasn't stopped 382 of the Fortune 500 corporations from offering worker-funded savings plans rather than guaranteed company-provided pensions.

Get ready for a rerun with HSAs. If you work for a large company, you or someone close to you is likely to be pressured to sign up for an HSA soon—if you haven't been already. Studies show that the number of workers at big companies who have signed up for HSAs has tripled in the past eight years. Overall, by 2016, there were 14.5 million HSA accounts, with $28 billion in assets, and another million new workers were expected to enroll by the end of the year.

My Advice. Do not rush to join that parade. By and large, you'll be better off sticking with company insurance if your boss allows you to do that.

HSAs can be the best choice, but only for a select group: the young and fortunate. If you are young, remain healthy, and make a good income during your career, you could accumulate more than enough in your HSA to pay for your family's health care and pass on the rest to your heirs. But relatively few hit the young, healthy, and wealthy trifecta.

Think of an HSA as a portable savings account funded partly by your boss—with significant tax advantages for you—that you can use to pay your medical bills. Your employer is sure to underscore the positives:

- You and your employer can contribute up to $3,350 into an individual account, or $6,750 for a family, before taxes in 2016; employers chip in about $1,000 of the annual contribution, on average.
- If you are fifty-five or older, you or your boss can add an extra $1,000 a year to your account.
- You can invest the balance of many HSAs and watch it grow completely tax deferred for decades, assuming that you don't have to deplete it to cover your medical bills.
- You can withdraw the money tax free to pay for any qualified medical expenses, including your health plan's premiums, deductible, and copays, as well as any doctor or drug costs that your plan doesn't cover.
- Since the total balance in an HSA is your money, you can take every cent with you if you change jobs. By contrast, old HRAs, health reimbursement accounts, are funded 100 percent by your employer. You tap HRAs for medical bills while you work for the company, but you cannot take the balance with you if you leave.
- Once you enroll in Medicare, you can no longer contribute to your HSA. But you can continue to withdraw money to

pay your health care bills. You'll owe taxes on the withdrawals, but no penalties.

- You can pass on whatever you have left in your account tax free to your heirs.

That sounds pretty good. So what could possibly go wrong with an HSA?

First off, there's that high deductible. To open an HSA, which you can do on your own or through your employer, you must enroll in a health insurance plan with at least a $1,300 deductible for an individual or $2,600 for a family. Health plans linked to HSAs typically have low premiums, since you will pay more out of your own pocket before meeting the high deductible. HSAs with $10,000 to $15,000 deductibles are relatively common. The higher the deductible you are willing to face each year, the lower your monthly premiums—and the higher the financial risks you run.

For example, if you have a $10,000 family deductible plan, you're responsible for the first $10,000 in medical bills, before your insurer kicks in a dime. What's more, even after satisfying the deductible, chances are you'll owe 10 percent to 35 percent of any additional bills under the plan's coinsurance provisions.

Let's imagine that instead of staying remarkably healthy and building a big balance, you, your spouse, or your kids get sick and drain your savings as you literally deduct your deductible from your HSA account until there's nothing left.

Experts report that the average annual contribution is $2,100, and the withdrawal is $1,000. That means the average worker would have only around $5,000 saved after five years—just about enough to cover a half hour in the ER.

Ask yourself: How would you pay your next big medical bill because of a high deductible? If you don't have a good answer, an HSA might not be a good bet for you.

Even if you stay largely healthy, you might start worrying about tapping your account and decide not to get medical treatment you really need, thereby risking your health and serious illness. Many HSA proponents actually say that they count on some level of self-rationing to drive down the country's medical costs. The Commonwealth Fund, a private foundation for better health, reported that four in ten people with deductibles that equal 5 percent or more of their incomes said they skipped care from doctors, specialists, and labs when they felt sick. The Commonwealth's vice president for health care coverage and access, Sara Collins, told me, "We're seeing a lot of evidence of skimping on necessary care."

And health care consultant Truven Health Analytics reported that many people with chronic conditions were not even seeing doctors for free preventive services, including mammograms and cancer screenings. One result: According to estimates, one-third of people age fifty to sixty-four are not getting preventive services.

Allow me to underscore the obvious: Putting off health care you need is never a good idea and could be a tragic mistake.

And, of course, since many accounts allow you to invest your HSA money in mutual funds, as with a 401(k) retirement account, you run the risk that the stock market could be in free fall when you need your money, say, for an operation. Do you remember what happened to workers' 401(k) savings during the Great Recession of 2008 and 2009? Some people lost half their savings. Imagine being rushed to the emergency room on the day the market crashes. That thought alone might give you palpitations.

Plus, if you ever withdraw the money for a nonmedical expense because of a simple mistake or a family crisis, you will owe taxes plus a 20 percent penalty on every dollar you take.

By the way, it would also be smart to hang on to every medical receipt in case the IRS audits you, and you need to prove that your withdrawals were proper.

As I see it, HSAs might be worth considering, but only under these conditions:

- if you are young, healthy, and exceptionally good at a well-paying job in a growing field;
- if your employer contributes the national average of $1,000 a year for individuals and $1,680 for families; roughly half of the companies offering HSAs do not contribute funds;
- if you are certain you'll have the resources to cover your worst-case deductibles; and
- if you are a prudent investor—with a good tax-filing system.

CHAPTER 12

The Smart Way to Book a Doctor Visit

And Get a Discount, Too

I have one doctor—a specialist on Fifth Avenue across from New York's magnificent Metropolitan Museum of Art—who tells me how much he is thinking of billing me at the end of each visit, and then asks if I can afford it. He does that with other patients as well. "Some of my older patients can't afford me any longer," he told me. "I treat them for free. They've been my patients forever. What else can I do? I can't drop them now."

And I have another doctor, a brilliant internist, who has said to me, "I have never allowed money to stand between me and my patients."

Not everyone is lucky enough to have dedicated doctors like that who believe that the Hippocratic Oath should be updated. Yes, do no harm to the patient. But also do no harm to the patient's financial security.

Based on my personal experience and my reporting, I firmly believe that many doctors would work with patients to keep costs under control if the patients would raise the subject of money. More than once, when I pointed out the high cost of prescriptions, my doctors immediately found ways to slash the prices. I had to introduce the subject. But when I did, the doctors responded.

Physicians are well aware of the high cost of medicine. And most of them, in my estimation, feel an increasing responsibility to provide care at affordable prices. They know generally what studies confirm: Around half of all adults in the United States postpone medical care they think they need—or go without it completely—because of the cost. And that includes one in four in that group who have health insurance. As out-of-pocket expenses, driven by insurance copays, coinsurance, and deductibles, keep climbing each year—by double digits in some plans—enrolling in a health plan no longer guarantees that people can find affordable care.

However, there are many commonsense things you can do to work with your health care providers to get quality care at fair prices. Remember, your provider is a professional, but he's also a merchant who sells his services to a variety of buyers and is constantly adjusting his prices to make the sale. For example, the nine in ten providers who want to do business with the vast number of Medicare patients slash their asking prices and accept Medicare's wholesale rates. And those who treat Medicaid patients accept around two-thirds less. Call that super-super wholesale. Health insurance companies try to get providers to accept just 25 percent more than Medicare rates. But in many cases, they need to offer upward of two to three times Medicare fees in order to attract the best medical professionals.

Who pays retail? Providers reserve those huge prices for the poor souls who show up "naked" with no insurance—and no clue that everyone, including them, can try to negotiate with his or her doctor to get the best care at better prices.

Let's start with what you should always do before you book a doctor's visit.

Ask Up Front How Much the Visit Will Cost. People parade into doctors' offices every day without any idea of how much they might be billed. Does that sound familiar?

When it comes to medical care, many people—especially the

Dr. Welby generation over sixty-five—think of themselves as patients in the hands of a doctor, rather than as health care consumers making rational, informed choices. Ask yourself, Why would I consume health care without knowing what it might cost?

Patients who don't ask about costs aren't the only cause of the information gap surrounding medical costs. The health care industry does not make it easy to get pricing information. Only a handful of the nation's eight hundred thousand doctors post their prices in their offices or on their websites. Most hospitals don't either. And as I reported in chapter 9, Medicare stupidly refuses to openly tell its fifty million beneficiaries what a medical service or procedure might cost them unless they know the precise billing code.

Furthermore, there is no law or even an American Medical Association bylaw that requires the doctor to tell the patient the billing code for the procedures he's suggesting—the critical piece of information the patient often needs to comparison shop.

Fortunately, however, with some Health Care Detective work, you can usually get all the pricing information you need.

Always Try to Stay in Network. If you have a health plan, start with your insurer. First, ask if the doctor is in your plan's provider network. If she's not, you could find yourself being billed anywhere from double to twenty times as much as an in-network provider would charge you.

Then explain the service you want in plain English to someone in your insurance company's billing office. With that information, a billing expert should give you a very good sense of the doctor's charges, including what, if anything, you'll owe out of pocket.

Now take one more step. Check all the information with the doctor's billing office. The doctor might have a contract to provide services to, say, most United HealthCare customers in your state. But he might have dropped out of your specific United plan. Ask very carefully whether the doctor is still in-network and has a "current contract" with your insurer that specifies how much the doctor will get paid for each service in your specific health plan.

Guard Against Balance Billing. Your defense against a surprise "balance bill"—which I'll describe in a minute—is to be absolutely certain that the doctor is a participating member of your health plan's provider network.

Here's what happened to one of consumer advocate Katalin Goencz's clients at esteemed NewYork-Presbyterian Hospital. On a Sunday night, a young Broadway performer fell on her face, literally. She tripped onstage, causing a nasty gash. Her mother rushed her to NewYork-Presbyterian's emergency room, where doctors called in a skilled plastic surgeon.

Before the surgeon began her work, which included six stitches to close the one-inch cut, the girl's mother asked the surgeon if she "took" her EmblemHealth insurance. The surgeon assured her that she did.

But later the surgeon sent her a surprise bill for $1,850. That's when the mother learned that the surgeon was *not* in Emblem-Health's network. She "took" EmblemHealth's payment for her services, put it in her pocket, and billed the mother for the balance of her bill. In all, the surgeon charged $2,600, including an extra $800 for showing up on a Sunday night, and also took EmblemHealth's network provider fee of $746. That left a balance of $1,850, which the surgeon billed to the mother.

The mother has refused to pay what she considers a deceitful bill. The insurer has refused to pay the surgeon any more. And the surgeon has insisted on collecting her full balance. Two years later in 2016, the case was still unresolved.

Bottom line: Never simply ask whether the doctor "takes" your insurance. Like this surgeon, the doctor might happily "take" your insurer's network payment as a down payment on his full out-of-network charge and then bill you for his balance.

Also, if you get hit with a surprise bill, check on whether your state has a law that might help you. Some states do. For example, early in 2015 (but too late for this mother), New York State passed a law protecting ER patients. Essentially, patients do not have to pay out-of-network provider charges for emergency services that are more than the patient's in-network copayment, coinsurance, or deductible. The doctor and insurance companies are left to haggle over the balance in state arbitration.

Ask Whether the Doctor Works for a Hospital. After you are sure the doctor is in your network, always ask if she has gone to work for a hospital since the last time you talked. In recent years, hospitals have spent millions buying up physician practices. If your doctor is now working for a hospital or has simply signed up as a staff physician, the institution might bill you an extra $400 or so in "facility fees" for the doctor's office—even if the doctor is in his same old office miles from the hospital.

Be Specific About the Services You Want. If you want only cancer screening tests, list each one. "Never ask for a routine checkup," advised patient advocate Sareatha Boothe of Milwaukee's Patient Care. "Almost any service a doctor charges for can be called 'routine.'"

And, as I've stressed, if the doctor refuses to tell you what he charges for this or that—or refuses to give you a billing code—find another doctor who will.

Obviously, in an emergency, you shouldn't try to dictate your care or worry about costs. But if you have time to think about your care, think about your costs.

Ask Your Doctor for a Discount. I've told you that chances are, someone in your doctor's waiting room is paying one-quarter to one-half as much as you are, either because they are covered by a low-paying insurance plan such as Medicare or maybe even rock-bottom Medicaid. Most likely, the doctor signed contracts with the government and agreed to accept far less from the feds than he charges you for the same services.

So it might not be unreasonable to ask for a discount. But before you see him, you need to do some research on prevailing costs. And then you need to be honest with yourself and with your physician.

As I've noted, before you go in for any treatment that's likely to be costly, check the websites of Healthcare Bluebook, Fair Health, and Clear Health Costs to get an idea of how much doctors, imaging centers, and hospitals charge for the service or procedure you are considering. If the prevailing rates you find in your area are low, with insurance or not, show your medical provider your research and ask him to meet a reasonable price or beat it. Or, if your research turns up prevailing prices that you truly can't afford, explain your situation in person or in writing and ask for help.

I recently received a 75 percent discount on a complicated back operation from a renowned and compassionate surgeon by being honest with him. The surgeon, who does not accept any insurance, told me that he would ask his billing office to give me a significant discount. And, he added, if that figure was more than I could afford, I should call him. A few days later, his top billing staffer told me that the doctor normally got $40,000 for my operation, but he would accept $20,000 from me.

I knew $20,000 was a fair charge. I had checked with my insurance company and was told that surgeons customarily bill around $26,000 for the operation. But $20,000 was still too much for me. I called the doctor's personal assistant and told him that. A day later, the assistant called back. He said the doctor would perform the operation for $15,000. From the tone of his voice, that sounded like the doctor's final figure.

My wife and I talked it over. I'd seen several surgeons. A well-known surgeon at a top New York hospital, who accepted

Medicare, wanted to fuse a couple of my discs. With my Medicare coverage, that surgeon's operation would have cost me next to nothing.

But this surgeon had wisely ruled out a fusion because of my blood cancer. My multiple myeloma is slowly eating away at my bones; if my bones ever weaken enough for the fusion to fail, I'd be facing horrendous surgery. So I definitely wanted him to do the operation. On the other hand, $15,000 is a significant amount of money.

Carole and I discussed the situation thoroughly and came to a decision. I called the doctor's personal assistant, explained my finances in detail, and told him that all I could afford was $10,000. A couple of hours later, he called back. The doctor had accepted $10,000.

Why did he give me a 75 percent discount? For three reasons: I asked for the discount; he believed that my final offer was all that my wife and I could afford; and he is a compassionate man.

The operation, by the way, was extremely successful, and I'll never forget that when I woke up on a summer Saturday morning in one of New York City's finest hospitals, the first face I saw hovering above me was the surgeon's, smiling down at me.

I joked, "You should be in the Hamptons."

He said, "No, I should be here, looking after you."

Offer to Pay Cash. Increasingly, providers are accepting less in cash from patients on the spot than they could eventually collect from insurance companies. By taking cash, they avoid annoying insurance company paperwork and payment hassles. And by paying cash, patients save money, especially if they have health plans with sizable deductibles or high coinsurance.

Patient advocate Patient Care reported in 2015, for example, that a Wisconsin radiology clinic was accepting $600 cash for a knee MRI—roughly one-third of what it would bill a patient using insurance.

"My favorite was the $5,400 MRI at a medical center in California," said Clear Health Cost's Jeanne Pinder. "The patient paid about $2,500. But he could have paid $725 cash down the street."

By law, people with health insurance are not obligated to use it; they can pay cash legally.

There is one other cash strategy to consider. A skilled internist that my wife and I have seen regularly for years no longer accepts any health insurance, including Medicare. However, with a handshake, he has agreed to treat us both for the entire year for a fixed amount that we pay each January. He gets what he imagines will be his year's worth of fees up front. And Carole and I have the peace of mind of knowing that this gifted diagnostician will treat us at no extra cost if we get sick and require all sorts of extra care.

Of course, the arrangement with our doctor—sometimes called a concierge doctor—is based on mutual respect. My wife and I do not pester him with frivolous calls. On the other hand, it's comforting to have his private contact numbers.

GET YOUR PREVENTIVE SERVICES AT NO ADDITIONAL COST

Preventive services, including cancer screenings and vaccinations, not only save lives but also usually are available to people with insurance at no additional cost. Your premiums in effect pay for those services. Yet according to the US Centers for Disease Control and Prevention (CDC), around 30 percent of people under sixty-five and about *half* of those over sixty-five do not receive all of the preventive services they are eligible to get.

Part of the problem is that most people don't realize how

many preventive services they qualify for. Chances are, that includes you. Try this: check out the Preventive Services Chart at the Cms.gov website. It includes the descriptions and cost information anyone with decent health coverage can use to get more than twenty common preventive services, usually at no extra cost.

Then when you book your next doctor visit, refer to the list and ask about any of the services you want, including a mammogram, a colonoscopy, and your annual flu shot. Many of the preventive services, if not all, will be free.

———•———

CHAPTER 13

Don't Cough in the Doctor's Office Unless You Really Mean It!

Tips to Avoid Sneaky Fees

Here's a cautionary tale that presents four lessons you should consider before your next trip to your doctor.

As Anne Landman's $180 annual physical was about to end, the doctor asked, "Is there anything else you want to talk about?" The Colorado author mentioned a lump in her throat she'd had before in allergy season. The doctor looked, said nothing was wrong—and then billed her an extra $100.

"*One hundred dollars* for one minute peering down my throat," Anne told me. "I thought it was part of the exam."

A conscientious doctor, like Anne's, might take a moment for all the right reasons to respond to a patient's complaint simply to rule out something serious. Still, the doctor's fee-for-service meter might start clicking for that extra look, however fleeting. Worse, I'm sorry to say that there are doctors who ask leading questions to manufacture excuses to poke here or peer there to run up their fees.

Anne's $100 surprise highlights several lessons about what you should do—and not do—when you're with your doctor.

Lesson One: In Our for-Profit, Fee-for-Service Health Care System, Don't Assume Anything

That means when you're with your doctor, don't cough unless you mean it!

Let's assume you made it clear to your doctor that you were coming in only for preventive screenings paid for fully by your insurance premiums. You and your physician should be starting in sync. Still, if your doctor doesn't like the sound of a random cough, a funky heartbeat, or your rattling breathing, she might begin examining you. And at that point—as Anne learned—her fee meter probably starts running, whether the doctor mentions that fact to you or not.

Many doctors stop the exam for a moment and warn patients that they might charge extra for pursuing the symptom they've just picked up. Which means that many others don't. Therefore, whatever the doctor says or doesn't say when you two begin discussing a symptom, you should ask if she intends to begin a "problem-focused evaluation." If she says yes, ask this series of specific questions:

- Why does she want to evaluate you?
- How much might she bill you for the extra care?
- Does the examination need to be done immediately? Even if the exam sounds necessary—say, a chest X-ray or complicated blood work—you might want to shop around for a qualified provider with lower fees.

Medicare patients have a bit of protection. Under the law, doctors must inform them up front about any service that they believe the government will not cover. And they must give patients an accurate estimate of how much they're likely to owe. But unfortunately, there are no requirements like that for patients with private insurance or, heaven forbid, for the about-to-become poor souls who show up with no insurance.

To avoid confusion and potential conflicts about surprise costs, some doctors like to create a clear break between preventive visits and diagnostic exams. When they pick up a symptom during a preventive session, they stop the visit and schedule an exam. But most doctors do not do that. Beyond the obvious financial angle, a great many physicians fear that the patients will not return for the follow-up exam and ultimately won't get the care they need.

Whatever your doctor's normal procedure is, you can sidestep the confusion in advance. If you prefer, when you book your original preventive session, you can request that the doctor book a separate diagnostic session if she comes across anything worth pursuing. But then make sure you do follow up with that doctor or another one to get your symptom diagnosed and fully resolved.

Lesson Two: Raise Legitimate Concerns with the Doctor but Don't Ask for More Services Than You Really Need

Anne's doctor certainly charged a lot for her one-minute throat exam, but it could have been worse. Another doctor might have ordered all sorts of unnecessary and costly tests.

In our fee-for-service system, it's only logical to expect that some doctors and providers will try to pad their bills by pushing tests and procedures on you. Experts estimate the government could wring around 10 percent out of the nation's health care costs by squeezing providers who pad their bills.

Patients should not be held responsible for greedy providers. Still, having said that, there are several things that consumers can do to curb unnecessary services, beginning with this: Do not demand more care than you really need.

Dr. Sharon Orrange, a primary care physician on salary at the University of Southern California's Keck Hospital, said she constantly sees patients who want to indulge themselves with extra care.

"Patients come in with knee pain," she said, "and they start insisting on a knee MRI. Or some twenty-five-year-old with no symptoms says, 'Check my thyroid.' I say, 'Why? You don't need that test.' Many times, it's definitely healthy patients indulging themselves."

To compound the problem, she said hospital satisfaction surveys show that the more laboratory tests, procedures, and prescriptions that the doctor provides, the higher patients rate the doctor.

"Often when I check patients and say, 'You're fine. Go on home.' They say, 'Aren't you going to do some lab tests?' They love blood tests," Dr. Orrange said, "especially when they don't need them."

Fortunately, Dr. Orrange said that USC's hospital administrators encourage their doctors to push back against unnecessary care. But obviously the country's rising health care costs indicate that other hospitals have different policies.

Here are two rules to follow:

- never indulge yourself with unnecessary care; and
- always consider the downside of any test or procedure, because *there are always risks*, as you are about to see.

No Laughing Matter: The Joan Rivers Story

Although this is an extreme example of the risks of any procedure, no matter how safe it might seem, it's worth considering that in 2014 comedian Joan Rivers walked into a respected for-profit New York City clinic for a "routine" examination of her vocal cords that involved general anesthesia—which is a medically induced coma—and never regained consciousness.

Rivers, who was a vigorous eighty-one, had been complaining to friends about her lingering sore throat and raspy voice. Finally, she decided to have a specialist check out her voice box, vocal cords, and upper digestive system. At the clinic, the comedian was given propofol, the powerful general anesthetic that contributed to Michael Jackson's death in 2009. The clinic's medical director then inserted a tiny camera down her throat to explore her digestive system and vocal cords for damage caused possibly by acid reflux, a common digestive problem among bulimics.

During the exam, the medical team appears to have committed a series of egregious errors. For one, the clinic's director allowed Rivers' ear, nose, and throat specialist, who had accompanied the comedian, to examine her vocal cords as well, even though the celebrity's doctor was not licensed to practice at the clinic and, according to state law, should not have been in the operating room.

In addition, the medical director took a cell phone photo of the specialist working on Rivers. He thought the photos would amuse her when she woke up.

At one point, the anesthesiologist maintains that she warned that Rivers' severely swollen vocal cords could seize shut, only to be dismissed by the director as "paranoid" and who added she's "such a curious cat." Rivers' vocal cords soon seized up, shutting off her airway and starving her brain of oxygen. That emergency is often managed with the drug succinylcholine, and, though the clinic maintained the lifesaving equipment of a hospital emergency room, it did not have that drug.

According to the anesthesiologist, Rivers' specialist might have been able to punch a hole in her throat and insert a breathing tube, but the specialist had already left the clinic. Rivers went into cardiac arrest and a coma. She died seven days later at Mount Sinai Hospital without gaining consciousness, when her only child, Melissa, made the wrenching decision to take her mother off life support.

The clinic's medical director, who had allowed the comedian's doctor to examine her, was fired.

Melissa Rivers filed a multimillion-dollar medical malpractice and wrongful-death suit against the clinic, which was settled for a "substantial" amount of money. Rivers' lawyers stressed, however, that Melissa sued primarily to discover exactly what went wrong with her mother's "routine" procedure and to advance laws forcing for-profit clinics to match the same safety standards as hospitals. Rivers' lawyer said, "Profit cannot be placed above patient safety."

As I said, the Rivers case is an extreme example of the risks of a routine procedure. You don't need to worry about your doctor snapping photos before you slip toward a coma during your next procedure.

Still, I'm trying to make this important point: No medical procedure is completely safe. Stuff happens. For example, the New York State Health Department surveyed how frequently patients enter doctors' offices for what they regard as routine procedures and end up in ambulances speeding with sirens screaming to the emergency room. From 2010 to 2013, nearly 2,000 of those patients were taken from doctors' offices to hospitals, and 257 died soon after. No one doubts that in many of those cases, if not most, the doctors discovered that the patients actually needed hospital attention and called the ambulance. But in at least a few of those cases, the patients needed an ambulance because something went terribly wrong during the procedure itself.

You can get the medical care you need and protect yourself by always insisting on what doctors call "evidence-based medicine." Every time your doctor suggests a test or procedure—or before you request one—ask the doctor these five questions:

1. **What medical evidence do you have** that I should get this test or treatment? Your symptoms or lab results should ring a clear signal about the treatment you should receive. Ask your doctor to explain that to you in plain English.
2. **Will it duplicate other tests** or procedures that I've already had? I once had three electrocardiograms, to monitor my heart's electrical activity, in three different offices

within twenty-four hours, because each doctor wanted his own reading. I doubt they were all necessary.

3. **What benefits should I expect?** Will they be lasting? Or only temporary? Force your doctor to be as specific as possible. You deserve to know what to expect. For example, your doctor might say something like: "After four months of physical therapy, you will regain ninety to ninety-five percent of your range of motion in your injured shoulder."

4. **Exactly what risks will I face?** Before I had my first back surgery, I asked the acclaimed surgeon Patrick O'Leary to tell me the worst thing that could happen with the operation. He said, "You could die on the operating table. But that's not going to happen. I've never lost a patient. And you're not going to be the first." Dr. O'Leary was right.

5. **Is the test or procedure truly necessary** and worth the risks? That back surgery was absolutely necessary. By the time Dr. O'Leary operated on me, I couldn't walk half a block before doubling up with pain. The rewards of the operation far outweighed the risks. I woke up pain-free and remained that way for several years.

THE MOST COMMON MEDICAL CARE YOU PROBABLY DON'T NEED

There is an epidemic of unnecessary testing in this country for several reasons. Too many patients demand tests. And too many doctors order them to protect against the overstated boogey man of malpractice suits—and, frankly, to make an extra buck. Procedures such as cardio stress tests can save lives. But tests can also endanger patients. For example, one out of ten people will get a CT scan (computerized tomography) in 2016, and thereby expose themselves to up to a thousand times more cancer-causing radiation than a conventional X-ray.

Moreover, a team of medical researchers at New York's Icahn School of Medicine at Mount Sinai has concluded that many common primary care services are of little benefit to patients. Here are seven of the top services that the doctors, led by Minal Kale, say are overperformed and overprescribed—and waste billions of dollars.

1. **Routine Blood Work.** The Mount Sinai research study, based on 2009 statistics, shows that more than half (56 percent) of the complete blood counts that are ordered to measure levels of red and white blood cells and platelets are not necessary and waste more than $32 million a year. Blood work often costs you around $35 with insurance coverage or around $300 or more without it.

2. **Antibiotics for Children** with Sore Throats. More than 40 percent (40.9 percent) of those prescriptions don't actually help the kids—and waste $116 million. Beyond that, overuse of antibiotics leads to resistance to the medicine when it might actually be needed. The prescriptions run from roughly $4 with insurance to around $50 without it.

3. **Brand-name Statins** to Reduce Cholesterol. More than one-third (34.6 percent) of those prescriptions do nothing more than waste over $5 billion. In addition, not everyone can tolerate statins' side effects. Diet and exercise can lower your blood cholesterol and save you the cost of the medicine—about $3 a month with insurance or up to around $600 without coverage.

4. **Annual EKGs** to Check Your Heart. Nearly one in five instances (19.1 percent) of this common procedure during checkups are worthless and waste more than $16 million. You often pay around $50 with insurance or up to thousands of dollars without it.

5. **Urinalysis.** Again, nearly one in five of these lab studies waste $3.5 million. You might pay nothing for urinalysis if your insurer covers it as preventive care. Without insurance, a test costs around $60.

6. **Imaging for Back Pain.** Most back pain subsides within a month. Consequently, one in six (16.7 percent) X-rays, CT scans, and MRIs don't really help relieve the pain—and they waste $175 million. With insurance, you often pay about $150 for a back X-ray, $300 for a CT scan, and $350 for an MRI. Without insurance, you pay much more: up to $1,000 for an X-ray, $1,500 for a CT, and upward of $6,000 for an MRI.

7. **Over-the-counter Cough Medicine** for Children. More than 10 percent (11.8 percent) of the time, cough medicine doesn't help kids—and wastes more than $10 million. Popular cough medicines cost around $6.

In addition, the not-for-profit American Board of Internal Medicine (ABIM) Foundation's Choosing Wisely research has singled out a couple of other common procedures that it thinks are often not needed:

- **Bone-density Scans.** Foundation researchers say the test makes sense for women over sixty-five and men over seventy, but not for healthy younger people. The cost averages $132.
- **Cervical Cancer Screening.** Since cervical cancer can take ten to twenty years to develop, ABIM thinks women of average risk from twenty-one to thirty can safely wait three years between Pap smears; thirty to sixty-five, every five years; and over sixty-five, no screening at all. Pap smears cost about $200, plus extra lab work that can run $1,000 or more.

Lesson Three: Make Shared Decisions with a Doctor You Trust

Anne Landman and her doctor obviously didn't make a shared decision. When Anne complained about her throat, her doctor should have said something like this:

"I'm not sure that's a major problem. It'll take me only a minute to rule out any worries. However, since I will be going beyond preventive care and actually diagnosing a symptom, there will be a charge. To be safe, I suggest it's best for me to take a look. Is that okay with you?"

Dr. Reid Blackwelder, a past president of the American Academy of Family Physicians, told me, "Patients have the right to make choices about their medical care. And they ought to be informed choices." He added that when he lectures his medical students at Tennessee's Quillen College of Medicine, he emphasizes that they should establish the highest possible level of communication with their patients at three important stages before proceeding:

When Doctors Flag a Symptom. The doctor should emphasize that he is there to advise you, not to dictate to you. "If the doctor wants to take a closer look at your heart or lungs or whatever," Dr. Blackwelder said, "he should explain why that's necessary." He adds that he stresses to his students that they should always speak in plain English rather than in confusing medical terms.

And patients should speak up. If you don't understand what your doctor is trying to get across, say so. Don't feel embarrassed. There is never any shame in saying: "You lost me there. Please explain exactly what you're saying in terms that I can understand."

When Patients Demand Unnecessary Services. The physician should explain politely why he thinks the service is "not medically indicated." That means he should tell you why the service you're requesting will not improve your health and also describe the risks involved. Plus, he should warn you that your insurer would almost certainly refuse to cover any service that he flags as not medically indicated.

Dr. Blackwelder added that, unfortunately, many doctors hesitate to push back against insistent patients because of potential lawsuits. "With our liability laws," he said, "doctors get sued for not doing enough, but rarely for doing too much." Still, physicians should make every effort to talk the patient out of an unnecessary service—and, if they must, they should refuse to provide it.

"Since every procedure carries a risk," he said, "doctors need to explain those risks, including the costs involved, and hold firm against unnecessary demands."

When Patients Say They Can't Afford Needed Care. The physician should spell out his deep concern about the patient's health—as well as the financial burden the patient might face if he ignores care he really needs. Dr. Blackwelder said, "I say something like, 'I respect what you're saying. But think about the costs you'll face if you have a stroke, including the cost of being out of work trying to recover.'"

Dr. Blackwelder added that his doctor group grants 30 percent to 50 percent discounts to the uninsured depending on their income.

Bottom line: In the end, you and your doctor should have a close enough relationship so that you always make collaborative and constructive decisions. So find a doctor you can talk to like an equal, if not a friend for life.

THE DOCTOR WANTS YOUR BLOOD

Before anyone takes your blood (the pinch alone can cost you $35 to $50), be sure your doctor explains why he wants it analyzed. Kyle Thompson-Westra of Chicago told the *New York Times* that he went to a doctor in his insurance network for what he thought was a completely covered preventive care exam and walked out with a surprise $300 bill for blood work. Apparently, the doctor thought several tests should be part of a physical for the twenty-eight-year-old, including one for his thyroid function.

If you ask your doctor up front to explain what he expects to learn from the blood analysis, you might spare yourself costly experiences like that.

Also, ask if the analysis will be done at a lab in your insurance network and how much the work might cost you. If the doctor or his staff don't give you satisfactory answers, stop the exam before anyone draws your blood and ask your doctor for a blood work prescription. With the prescription in hand, you can get the test done at a reliable lower-cost laboratory or clinic, and then review the analysis with your doctor.

In Idaho, the Department of Health's laboratory provides complete lipid panel blood work to all comers around the state once a month for $20 to $25. By contrast, standard out-of-network blood work can cost anywhere from around $200 to upward of $10,000 for a hospital's lipid panel to measure the fats (lipids) in your bloodstream—and presumably to test how much money you have in the bank.

By the way, the same advice applies to urinalysis. One medical professional told me that health plans sometimes cover only four of the twelve factors being measured through urinalysis. She added, "I don't pee unless it's free."

Lesson Four: Skip Your Annual Checkup

Increasingly, medical experts are pushing an idea that would have saved Anne Landman not only the $100 for the peek down her throat but also the $180 for the checkup itself. Experts are saying you can safely skip your annual checkup, at least until you approach your senior years, as I mentioned in chapter 2, "Get the Health Care You Deserve."

Dr. Ezekiel J. Emanuel, an oncologist, is one of them. In the blunt Emanuel family style—one brother (Rahm) the embattled mayor of Chicago in 2016, the other (Ari) a top entertainment agent—he calls annual exams that aren't prompted by a specific symptom or complaint a waste of time and money. As harsh as his assessment is, he has research to support it.

At the top of the pile is a 2013 study by the Cochrane Collaboration. That group of international medical researchers analyzed long-term studies of 182,880 people and concluded that having annual checkups did not improve health or reduce the risk of death, including the risk of dying from heart disease or cancer. Those who had checkups also did not have fewer hospital admissions, less disability, or fewer sick days—and not even fewer worries about their health.

What's more, the study concluded that the patients who saw their doctors for checkups were more likely to end up undergoing unnecessary and sometimes painful treatment for hidden conditions that would not have caused the patients to experience symptoms, let alone die.

As the researchers put it, "The benefits [of routine checkups] may be smaller than expected and the harms greater."

The Cochrane Collaboration is far from the only respected medical advisory group to raise doubts about automatic annual checkups. The lofty United States Preventive Services Task Force—which endorses fifty-two specific preventive services—does not recommend annual checkups. And Canadian health experts have been advising against them since the 1970s.

Still, forty-five million Americans are likely to have routine physicals this year, partly because being told to *not* see your doctor on a regular basis sounds counterintuitive. It seems logical that visiting a primary care doctor regularly builds a bond between patient and physician. Plus, we've all heard stories about how a doctor's visit not only caught an illness early but also saved a person's life. A few months ago, a friend told me a remarkable story about how his new cardiologist simply took his pulse, picked up an abnormal beat, and rushed him to the hospital for life-saving open-heart surgery.

But decades of research show that memorable anecdotes like those are actually anomalies. Screening thousands of healthy people without symptoms to find the one or two who will benefit from an early diagnosis is inefficient, ineffective, and awfully expensive—even without an extra $100 to look down your throat.

My Advice

- **If you are relatively young** and healthy, don't let the calendar dictate your health care. Find a physician you trust and discuss the care you actually need. Assuming that you don't have a troubling family history or any other serious issue, you and your doctor should make an intelligent joint decision about how often you need a physical exam. In addition, do commonsense things to stay healthy, including exercising vigorously enough to raise your heart rate for twenty minutes three times a week. And listen to your body: it will tell you if you need to see your doctor far more reliably than the calendar.

- **If you are fifty or older,** begin scheduling regular checkups. If nothing else, regular checkups allow you to establish a critical bond with your doctor—and that should lead to shared decisions about how frequently she should be seeing you as you age. For example, given my complicated condition, my internist wants to examine me at least once every six months. But the Harvard-trained internist who is looking after my healthy thirty-five-year-old daughter wants to examine her only once every twenty-four months.

- **If you are on Medicare,** schedule an annual wellness visit with your primary care doctor. The wellness visit is not a checkup. It is a preventive service covered at no extra cost by Medicare and many other insurance providers. The doctor or his nurse will take your blood pressure and body mass index (BMI), check your medications, and, most importantly, discuss with you a plan for your health care for the coming year. If you mention a specific symptom or complaint, you and your doctor can discuss the next steps needed to best diagnose your condition and schedule treatment. On the other hand, if you have no issues, you can go home with the peace of mind that you and your doctor are satisfied with your well-being for now.

- **If you develop a persistent symptom,** no matter your age, do not hesitate to seek care. My case is a good example. I was jogging every day and otherwise feeling fine when I first experienced a shortness of breath walking downhill. That made no sense to me. I could have written off the shortness of breath as a mildly annoying consequence of my demanding job. Instead, I didn't hesitate to see our family doctor. After a series of tests, doctors found my blood cancer, multiple myeloma, at the very early smoldering stage before it began damaging my bones and vital organs. By the way, that shortness of breath might have been related to the myeloma or just coincidental. I strongly believe it was related, because I've experienced a shortness of breath when my cancer markers are rising. I also know that I did the right thing by getting that first odd sign of illness checked out by a skilled family physician.

If you need another warning, consider the sudden death of comedian Gary Shandling in 2016. He alarmed a doctor friend so much when he called complaining of aches and shortness of breath that the doctor went to his home. After examining the sixty-six-year-old comic, the doctor told him to go to the hospital if he still had the symptoms the next morning. Shandling reportedly said he'd go, but not until after some morning business. The doctor called the next morning and told Shandling to go to the ER immediately. Shandling phoned 911, but collapsed in the midst of the call and was soon pronounced dead at the hospital of an apparent massive heart attack. Sadly, a limo and driver were outside his home waiting to take him to the ER when he collapsed.

Even if you don't have a limo and driver to take you to the hospital, don't ignore persistent symptoms or a doctor's firm advice.

- **If money is an issue,** as it is for more than 25 percent of patients who don't see doctors when they actually think they should, at least discuss your medical issues with your pharmacist or with the staff at an inexpensive walk-in clinic, where the average bill is about $75. If a pharmacist or a nurse tells you to see a doctor—or if your condition worsens—please go to a physician immediately.
- **One last point:** do get your annual flu shot, which should be available as a preventive service at no extra charge through your health plan at work, Obamacare, or Medicare. Usually around half the people who get the shot do not get the illness. But even in flu seasons like 2014–15, when the vaccine prevented the illness in only one person out of five, I think you still should get the shot. Even a 20 percent chance of avoiding the flu is better than nothing. Plus, those who get vaccinated and still get sick tend to suffer milder bouts of the flu. They have a day or two less of the agony and better odds of avoiding a trip to the emergency room. And that's not nothing.

—————•—————

CHAPTER 14

Stop Paying Twice as Much for Your Drugs

Why Prescription Drugs Are So Pricey

Susan Timoney, a sixty-two-year-old nurse from New Port Richey, Florida, was paying $20 a month for her blood pressure medicine until her doctor mentioned a better idea. He said she could pick up the medicine for free at her local Publix grocery store. And she did. "When you can get your medications for free," said Timoney, "it's great."

It sure is. As I've noted, not long ago my doctor handed me $1,080 worth of nonaddictive, brand-name pain pills—also for free—because I asked for them.

Even if you're not as fortunate as Timoney or me and can't get any of your drugs for free, chances are there are a number of smart moves you can make to save money on the prescriptions you need.

At the very least, you need to know how to protect yourself against the ever-increasing costs of drugs in this country. Drug prices, including generics, have been rising two to four times higher than workers' wages for years. And, if anything, that trend is getting worse.

The prices of everything from lowly generics to high-flying

biotech drugs are approaching unimaginable and unsustainable heights. It's not uncommon for new specialty prescriptions for cancer and other dreaded diseases to cost $1,000 to $1,500 a month. Employers and insurers, who once absorbed drug increases quietly, are now announcing that they can't afford to continue doing that. Instead, they are shifting runaway prescription increases onto workers and retirees in the forms of higher copays and deductibles—if not entirely new and narrower health plans. Consequently, to cite the findings of one report, worker health plan deductibles have risen six times faster than worker wages since 2010. *Six times!*

Public anger also is increasing as families and neighbors see their out-of-pocket drug costs double or triple overnight. They sense what national studies confirm: One-third of the people taking several prescriptions are cutting their food budgets to pay for their drugs.

The public's anger is approaching a tipping point. Something has to change. And fast.

WHY DO AMERICANS PAY MORE FOR DRUGS?

Studies show that Americans pay up to 100 percent more per capita for pharmaceuticals than citizens in the thirty-three other developed countries in the Organization for Economic Cooperation and Development (OECD). Drilling deeper, people here are shelling out more money for drugs than people in France and Canada, even though, on average, Americans take fewer prescription medicines than they do.

Specific examples are even more startling. My *Reader's Digest* colleagues in Germany, which has had national health insurance since 1883, generally paid a $5 to $10 copay for their prescriptions. Not a pfennig more. In Great Britain, to cite another example, a steroid inhaler called Pulmicort that retails for around $175 here is provided free to asthma patients.

Other developed countries, in sharp contrast to our system, effectively set a national wholesale price for each drug sold through their government-run single-payer systems. Drugmakers, for example, must apply for permission to raise prices, citing evidence such as rising inflation to justify the increases. In Japan, by law, drug prices must *decrease* every two years. And so it goes around the globe.

What's more, drug prices here appear primed to continue rising, though they are not in the rest of the world. The nonprofit, nonpartisan Health Care Cost Institute reported, for example, that generic prices rose 5 percent in 2012—more than twice the rate of inflation. That was bad enough. But the institute said brand-name drugs soared 25 percent.

Since then, big pharmaceutical companies such as Pfizer and Merck & Co. raised their prices an average of 13 percent in 2014 and another 8 percent or so in 2015—all as part of what's become a relentless industrywide march of price hikes year after year.

In all, in just seven years, from 2008 through 2014, the prices of nongeneric drugs increased by about 125 percent.

And the band plays on. The federal government estimates that Americans spent an eye-popping 12 percent more on drugs in 2015 than they did only a year before.

Our Free-Market System Gives Drugmakers a Green Light to Keep Raising Prices. Rather than having a government brake pedal to slow down price increases, we rely on free-market competition among pharmaceutical companies, including the makers of cheaper generic drugs, to keep drug prices at reasonable levels.

Obviously, our system favors the drugmakers. Instead of having to negotiate with an entity as public and powerful as, say, the Department of Health and Human Resources, the manufacturers conduct discrete and largely secret bargaining sessions with an endless parade of buyers, including the nation's roughly

5,000 hospitals, 125 major chain pharmacies, and 50 leading national health insurers. Deals are also brokered by powerful middlemen, called group purchasing organizations and medical benefit managers, who leverage the massive number of workers they represent to sometimes get around 30 percent discounts on very high-priced drugs.

Still, the piecemeal bargaining gives the drugmakers, especially the global powerhouses loosely called Big Pharma, such as Novartis and Pfizer, the upper hand in setting prices.

Dr. Marcia Angell, the former editor of the *New England Journal of Medicine*, summed up our system: "Unlike every other advanced country, the United States permits drug companies to charge patients whatever they choose."

More of the Rising Costs Are Being Dumped on Consumers. Employers and insurers are shifting rising drug costs onto their workers and plan members. Historically, health care spending in this country has rested on the assumption that health insurance, provided largely by employers as a benefit, will cover a significant part of the overall costs. But that assumption no longer holds. A growing number of employer-backed health plans are increasing deductibles to $2,000 or more—as well as adding special deductibles for drugs alone. Insurers are also discouraging patients from choosing the most costly drugs by requiring them to pay higher copayments or coinsurance, after the members have paid their deductibles in full.

Simply put, health plans are reducing their prescription coverage, especially for the most expensive specialty drugs, while forcing members to pay more. The Kaiser Family Foundation reports that one in four people say that someone in their family didn't fill a prescription in the past year because of the cost.

And what's worse, the sickest patients who need the most expensive drugs for cancer and other dreaded diseases are being forced to pay the most: often as much as 75 percent in so-called coinsurance for top-tier drugs costing $1,000 and more a month.

Drugmakers Keep Setting Astronomical Prices for Their Miracle Medicines. In recent years, a number of manufacturers have created lifesaving blockbusters for cancer, multiple sclerosis, autoimmune disorders, and the chronic liver disease hepatitis C. The drugs are saving lives, but at a high cost. Many of these miracle drugs are so unique and effective that they have become monopolies the day they hit the market. Faced with little or no competition, too many of the manufacturers have decided to charge as much as the market can bear. That means that one of the miracles surrounding these drugs is that anyone can afford them—especially an average person too sick to keep working.

A major case in point is Gilead Sciences's hepatitis C cures, Sovaldi and Harvoni. Back in 2012, when it became time to set a price for Sovaldi, Gilead executives weighed a series of factors. To name a few, the intertwined factors included the $11 billion cost of acquiring the company that had created the drug, plus the expense of guiding the drug through clinical trials before winning approval from the US Food and Drug Administration (FDA) in 2013. In addition, the executives had to consider the drug's projected marketing expenses. Even the price of the chemical ingredients. And, of course, there was the intrinsic value of the drug itself, which in twelve weeks of treatment can eliminate a disease that affects three million people in this country.

Ultimately, the executives weighed all those factors, and surely scores of others, and came up with a price: exactly $1,000 per pill. Not $1,014. Or $996. But precisely one grand.

"They rounded the price. They do that," one of my doctors remarked sarcastically.

The $1,000-a-day price seemed especially arbitrary because the scientist who created the drug said that the cost of manufacturing a full supply of Sovaldi was $1,400—nowhere near the $84,000 the company was charging in 2016. When the scientist—who collected $400 million when the drug was sold to Gilead—was asked on national television why the drug is priced so much higher than its manufacturing cost, he said: "That's a good question."

Gilead has argued that the drug is priced correctly at $1,000 a day, because an $84,000 supply actually cures hepatitis C in more than 90 percent of the cases.

Yet, here's the topper: Gilead has quietly entered into deals to have its $1,000-a-day wonder drug made and sold in India and Egypt for $10 a pill. And I'm betting the company is making a profit at that price, too.

Late in 2015, US Senate investigators slammed Gilead for pricing Sovaldi so high. And the Obama administration pointed to the $11 billion of new spending for hepatitis C treatments, in general, as one of the significant reasons that retail prescription spending rose 12.2 percent in 2014. "This rapid increase, which was the highest rate since 2002, was in part due to the introduction of new drug treatments for hepatitis C, as well as of those used to treat cancer and multiple sclerosis," the administration said.

What's more, the hepatitis C drugs alone helped drive up the costs of Medicaid prescriptions by nearly 25 percent, since many low-income people with the disease get their care through that joint federal-state program.

In the end, American taxpayers are getting stuck with these bills, as I explain fully in chapter 16, "The Wonder Drug Racket."

Pharmaceutical Companies Are Ratcheting Up the Prices of Obscure Drugs to Unimaginable Heights. There are more examples of this blatant grab for profits by drugmakers than you dare to count—and more victims of it than the pharma executives would dare to meet.

Consider twenty-nine-year-old Jordan Haynes of Pemberville, Ohio. He takes Xyrem twice a day to control his narcolepsy. "Without that drug, I'd be a different person," said Haynes, who works in the post office while studying to get into medical school. "I'd be about eighty pounds heavier and constantly fighting to stay awake and concentrate."

Back in February 2011, the drugmaker, Jazz Pharmaceuticals, was charging Haynes's health plan $3,511 a month for his medicine. That already sounds high. But since then, he estimates that Jazz has raised Xyrem's price around 15 percent four times a year, like clockwork, to reach today's peak of $12,000 a month.

"If I lost my insurance, I don't know where I'd turn," said Haynes. "The company [Jazz] said they'd lower the price for me personally through an assistance program. But they won't say by how much. And they're sure not telling me why they keep raising the price of Xyrem on me."

One of the godfathers of aggressive pricing is J. Michael Pearson, a former management consultant who became a billionaire for a time running Toronto-based Valeant Pharmaceuticals International. Pearson followed this simple management philosophy: He nearly never saw a drug price he didn't want to increase.

Pearson helped to refine the modern pharmaceutical company strategy of acquiring drugs from other companies and boosting their prices, while also slashing investment in research and development. That's a neat formula to boost revenues and spike profits. When he took over Valeant in 2008 at a relatively youthful forty-six, most major pharmaceutical companies invested around 20 percent of revenue in R&D programs headed by highly paid scientists who kept trying to develop breakthrough drugs. Costly and heartbreaking failure was common. But the companies kept investing, because one big win by one big scientist could bring in $1 billion a year and wipe away a lot of tears.

Pearson flipped that business model on its head. In 2007, the year before he took over, Valeant spent 14 percent of its revenue developing drugs. In 2015 it spent 3 percent, according to Wall Street research. Under Pearson, the company has closed around a hundred deals to amass an inventory of drugs and has boosted many prices out of sight, sometimes on the very day an acquisition closed.

From early 2013 to late 2015, Valeant hiked the price of ninety tablets of its Glumetza for diabetes from $896 to $10,020; a hundred capsules of Syprine for nasty Wilson disease from $1,395 to $21,267; and a hundred capsules of Cuprimine, also for Wilson disease, from $888 to an incredible $26,189.

There's more. From 2014 to late 2015, the company rocketed the price of a hundred capsules of Demser for adrenal gland tumors from $9,979 to $32,794, and—get this—twenty-five ampoules of Isuprel for irregular heart rates from $4,489 to a heart-stopping list price of $36,811 a month, or $441,732 a year. Even a multimillionaire's heart would flutter paying that much.

Pearson defended his strategy of shrinking research and ballooning prices by saying he had a duty to make as much money as possible for his shareholders. Among the widows and orphans depending on Pearson for shelter and food were more than thirty hedge funds in 2015, led by the $6 billion Sequoia Fund, which owned around 10 percent of the company, and the $14 billion Pershing Square Capital Management, which controlled about 8 percent.

Bruce Booth, a prominent life sciences venture capitalist, spoke for many when he said that ratcheting up prices of old drugs with no R&D risk-taking "hurts the industry and innovators."

And legendary—and notoriously tight-lipped—investor Charlie Munger, who saw the effects of Valeant's pricing as chairman of Los Angeles's Good Samaritan Hospital, said publicly that Valeant was engaged in "price gouging," was "deeply immoral," and was "a sewer." Then he apologized to sewers.

Fueled by complaints from doctors and patients in 2015, the media zeroed in on Valeant's decision to hike the prices of two of its heart medicines, Nitropress and the Isuprel that I mentioned, by 212 percent and 550 percent respectively—all on the day it acquired their rights from another manufacturer. Other stories showed that the company had raised total drug prices an average of 48 percent a year since 2007—and by 93 percent in 2014 alone.

Leading senators from both parties moved to investigate Valeant, and federal prosecutors in Pennsylvania, New York, and Massachusetts launched probes. The Pennsylvania investigators and the Justice Department's civil division began looking into whether Valeant was overcharging Medicaid. The New York and Massachusetts federal investigators were studying the company's pricing decisions, distribution—and, perhaps most importantly for consumers, its patient assistance program. (See "Do Drug Company Patient-Aid Programs Help the Needy or the Greedy?" on page 192.)

The public's anger about Valeant increased when a Wall Street research firm claimed that the company was creating fake revenue by recording "phantom sales" through its patient assistance program at the mail-order specialty pharmacy Philidor RX Services. The research firm concluded that Valeant appeared to be cooking its books.

The stock price of the onetime Wall Street darling dropped 19 percent that day alone—and more than 69 percent in one quarter, reducing the value of CEO Pearson's ten million shares from $2.6 billion to, dare I say, a mere $722 million. And the beating continued. Early in 2016, the stock lost half its remaining value in one day. Though he still owned a chunk of Valeant, J. Michael Pearson was a billionaire no more.

Meanwhile, Valeant denied any wrongdoing and quickly cut ties with the specialty pharmacy, adding that it was "disturbed by the reports of improper behavior at Philidor."

Hedge fund manager William Ackman of Pershing Square cut through the company's PR announcements: "If it turns out Pearson has been found to have committed a crime, he'll be out."

It didn't come to that. With the stock plunging, Pearson announced his resignation early in 2016.

But take note: Ackman is on record as saying that ultimately Valeant will endure as a profit-making company. "Life will go on for Valeant," he said. "We don't think the business model is broken."

With Public Anger Building over Rising Drug Prices, Along Came "The Most Hated Man in America."

What pharmaceutical executive would put cancer patients, HIV survivors, and sick babies at risk of brain damage, blindness, or death by hiking the price of his lifesaving medicine overnight by 5,000 percent—from an affordable $13.50 a tablet to $750 a day? Say hello to Martin Shkreli, the thirty-two-year-old son of Albanian immigrants who found work here as janitors. Young Shkreli began as a hedge fund manager and then went into pharmaceuticals with the Valeant strategy: Acquire drugs from other companies and shoot their prices to the dark side of the moon.

But the smart young man with a missing moral compass went too far too fast with his 5,000 percent price hike for his Daraprim, a sixty-two-year-old generic that controls devastating parasitic infections. His brazen move ignited a furious public outcry for him to lower the price of Daraprim, which, by the way, sells for a dime in India.

But more importantly to you and me, his heartlessness exposed how many modern pharmaceutical companies set their prices well beyond what consumers can afford without significant help from their insurers or the government—or from sympathetic neighbors who pass the hat for the uninsured.

When news of Shkreli's 5,000 percent hike went viral online, the young, self-assured drug executive stared into the national TV cameras and spoke the truth about how drug companies price their products. They ask for what the market can bear.

"I will teach the public how our health care business really works," he said. "It's a free market. And it's up to each company to decide what's proper . . . I don't think that ought to be a crime."

Indeed, setting high prices and raising them relentlessly are not crimes; they are the industry norm. Thanks to Shkreli's morally repugnant decision to grab every dollar the market could bear, the public got a center-aisle view at how "free-market" pharmaceutical price gouging works. And now a lot of politicians say they want to outlaw the worst of the industry's "profiteering," including Hillary Clinton.

As the Internet exploded with anger over the 5,000 percent hike, Clinton said, "Price gouging like this is outrageous."

"Inject him with a migraine," another person tweeted, "increase the price of Tylenol to $850 a pill, and see how he likes it."

And the BBC called Shkreli "The Most Hated Man in America."

Then things got worse for him. Unfortunately for him, he came across on national television as young, twitchy, and arrogant. For instance, he defended the increase as "altruistic." What the public didn't understand, he lectured, was that he was going to use his profits to make a better drug and build his year-old Turing Pharmaceuticals into a bigger biotech company.

In other words, he was gouging the sick today to help them tomorrow.

Medical experts noted quickly that today's Daraprim works fine; doctors weren't clamoring for a better drug. Plus, they added that the former hedge fund manager had no expertise in pharmaceutical research or development.

Shkreli played his "free-market" card. "I'm a capitalist," he said on CBS TV. But he conceded, "I can see how it looks greedy." So could millions of others.

Shkreli also did not help his image as a responsible pharmaceutical executive by tweeting the lyrics from a particularly charming Eminem song: "The media points a finger at me, so I point a finger back at 'em, but not the index or the pinkie."

With fingers flying and the TV camera lights blazing late in 2015, Shkreli announced that he was "open" to adjusting the price of Daraprim to break even or perhaps make what he called "a small profit."

He never did.

Instead, his past as a failed hedge fund manager caught up to him. FBI agents arrested him on charges of a securities fraud trifecta of lies, deceit, and greed. According to the indictment, he allegedly used a drug company he founded before Turing as a personal piggy bank to misappropriate $11 million to pay back his unhappy hedge fund investors. He pleaded not guilty.

What Shkreli Teaches Us. I'm telling you the Shkreli story in detail because there is a critical lesson here. Whatever you think of the "punk capitalist," do not write him off as a bad apple—not even as a worm in the apple—as pharma executives (and some pharma-friendly lawmakers) have tried to do. Instead, think of him as exhibit A in the case against responsible-sounding drug executives who keep raising their prices to whatever the market will bear—while sticking you and me with the bill through higher insurance premiums, rising deductibles, and increased costs for Medicare and Medicaid.

As Shkreli pointed out, he didn't invent this game. He is far from the first drug CEO to jack up prices to unconscionable heights. And the point is that he will be far from the last.

As he's insisted, it doesn't appear that Shkreli did anything illegal by mercilessly raising prices in our broken health care system.

Pharmaceutical industry critics such as Peter Bach, director of Memorial Sloan Kettering Cancer Center's Center for Health Policy and Outcomes, have pointed to Shkreli's price hike as yet another example of how the health care system is rigged against patients.

"He made it clear that the system is so broken even a child could manipulate it," Bach said.

Although few pharma executives in pinstripes dare a 5,000 percent bite overnight, many of them are inflating the nation's health spending far beyond Shkreli's gluttonous dreams. Year after year, they raise prices of their medicines for common ailments such as diabetes and high cholesterol by 10 percent or so—three to four times the annual inflation rate. Those relentless annual increases have a far more profound effect on the public than any rogue's increase of an obscure drug, despite the disproportionate publicity "the bad apple" gets.

According to one study, large pharma companies more than doubled the prices of four of the ten most commonly used drugs from 2011 to 2014. Patients with rheumatoid arthritis (RA) and multiple sclerosis were hit especially hard. AbbVie increased the price of Humira for RA by more than 126 percent, for example, and then launched a massive ad campaign to push the drug.

Overall, from 2011 to 2014, sales of the top ten drugs increased by 44 percent to $54 billion. But total prescription volume was down 22 percent. That suggests that big pharma's relentless price hikes are compelling consumers to go without their medications.

Drug companies claim that they need high drug prices to recoup the costs of developing new drugs, which can hover around $2.6 billion each over ten years, according to the Pharmaceutical Research and Manufacturers of America. They note that despite the R&D investment and countless clinical trials, the FDA approved only forty-one new drugs in 2014. And that was a record year.

What the industry protectors don't volunteer is that nine out of ten pharmaceutical corporations spend more on marketing than R&D, including around $6 billion a year in direct advertising to consumers. Direct advertising like the Humira campaign is outlawed in other countries.

Dr. Vikas Saini, the president of the Lown Institute, said the pharmaceutical industry claims about R&D are overblown.

"Innovation has just become a slogan for a lot of big pharmaceutical firms," he said. FDA records show that only about one-quarter of newly approved drugs in 2014 were the first of their class of drugs, less than half offered any actual improvements, and only a portion of those came from the historic Big Pharma firms.

"It's unfair to make a bad guy out of [Shkreli] and stop there," Dr. Saini added. "The entire health care system is filled with decisions made far from the public interest."

As I've said, there is no law against raising prices. The Food and Drug Administration has no authority over drug prices. And critics say that congressional investigations into Valeant and Shkreli's Turing Pharmaceuticals won't go nearly far enough. They say Congress also should turn its attention to big pharmaceutical players that keep raising prices because they know some employer or insurer or Medicare or Medicaid HMO will pay the prices and then pass on the cost to you and me.

Like the people running Rodelis Therapeutics, who acquired cycloserine for drug-resistant tuberculosis and boosted its price from $500 for thirty pills to $10,800 for a time before selling out. Or the execs at Horizontal Pharma, who increased the price of its Vimovo for arthritis by 597 percent. As well as our friends at Actavis, who jacked up the price of its generic version of the antibiotic doxycycline for Lyme disease from $20 a bottle to $1,829—an unfathomable 8,281 percent increase in one year.

And how about a special shoutout to Warner Chilcott? It agreed to pay $125 million, including $23 million in criminal fines, in 2015 to settle federal charges that the unit ran an elaborate kickback scheme to prod doctors to prescribe at least seven of its drugs, including the osteoporosis treatments Actonel and Atelvia. In a rare move, federal authorities followed up in 2016 and arrested Warner Chilcott's former president, W. Carl Reichel, for allegedly conspiring to pay kickbacks to doctors, and indicted Dr. Rita Luthra of Longmeadow, Massachusetts, for allegedly accepting around $23,000 in bogus payments. Both pleaded not guilty.

Prosecutors said the former Warner Chilcott president

designed a sales strategy to entice doctors to prescribe his company's drugs in return for bogus speaking fees and lavish dinners. The physicians were paid to give speeches they often did not give; instead, they shared expensive dinners with sales representatives, the indictment said.

In addition, in another doctor kickback case in 2016, the Manhattan US attorney asked Novartis to provide documents for 80,000 events in which the government alleges the drug company treated doctors to expensive dinners in return for prescribing its cardiovascular drugs. Last year, Novartis paid $390 million to settle yet another kickback case involving its tactics to increase sales of five of its drugs, including cancer drug Gleevec, which costs less than $200 to make and costs more than $10,000 a month.

Let's face it: The prescription drug game is stacked against you. But you'll see in a minute that once you become a Health Care Detective, there are seventeen smart ways to get the prescriptions you need and often save money, too.

But first, there's one other thing we can all do. Let's apply the antiterrorism motto to pharmaceutical price gouging: "If you see something, say something."

If one of your drugs, even a generic, doubles in price overnight, or you hear about a sick neighbor struggling to pay soaring drug costs, point that out on social media, and tell me about it on Facebook—or better yet, on my website at www.healthcaredetective.us. When you sense a story beginning to build in your area, alert your local newspaper or TV station.

In the end, public outrage helped to expose Valeant's pricing strategy and to nail Martin Shkreli. An aroused public speaking with an amplified voice can accomplish wonders against big pharmaceutical companies that want to protect their public images.

THE PUBLIC WANTS POLITICAL ACTION

No one should be surprised that the Kaiser Family Foundation reported that the public said the top priority for the president and Congress in 2017 and beyond should be making drugs for serious diseases affordable. The number two issue: lowering the cost of all prescription drugs.

Political leaders are listening. The Los Angeles–based AIDS Healthcare Foundation launched a California initiative for 2016 that would mandate that drug manufacturers grant the state's health programs (including its giant Medicaid program Medi-Cal) a 25 percent discount. A similar movement was under way in Ohio. As you should expect, leading Big Pharma companies lined up to fight the California initiative, including such trusted household names as Johnson & Johnson (pledging $5.7 million for opposition ads), Bristol-Myers Squibb ($2.9 million), Purdue Pharma ($1.1 million), Pfizer, and Daiichi-Sankyo.

As you know, health care became a major campaign issue in 2016. Politicians on the left rallied for Medicare for All, and those on the right vowed to kill Obamacare. But neither of those extremes amounts to much more than fund-raising gambits—red meat appeals for supporter greenbacks. Focus instead on Hillary Clinton's top four ideas to curb drug prices, plus Dr. Ben Carson's out-of-the-box musings of souping up HSAs for every family. You will be hearing more about versions of those two sharply different approaches as the left-versus-right health care debate rages on.

Hillary has proposed this series of government reforms:

- **Cap Consumer Costs.** Under this plan, the federal government would prohibit health insurers from collecting more than $250 a month, or $3,000 a year, from its customers for drugs, a move that in theory would spur insurers to refuse to cover expensive drugs unless the manufacturers gave them steep discounts. California's ACA health plans are already capping costs at $250 a month, and those limits will extend to all state health plans in 2017.

- **Allow Medicare to Negotiate Prices.** Federal law specifically prohibits Medicare from negotiating with drug companies for lower prices. Some experts believe that Medicare could use its fifty-million-member clout to save each beneficiary more than $500 a year *if* it also restricted the number of drugs it agreed to cover, as the VA does. Beneficiaries would have fewer drugs to choose among, but at lower prices. Supporters see it as an acceptable trade-off to help the millions of older and disabled people struggling to afford their medications. But such a major change figures to be debated long and loud.

- **Give the Federal Government the Power to Block Profiteering.** Many on the left want the federal government to have the authority to prohibit exorbitant insurance company rate hikes and any "excessive profiteering" by drug manufacturers.

- **Let Consumers Buy Drugs from Abroad.** As you might know, it is illegal to import prescription drugs, including imports from reputable mail-order pharmacies. This cautious proposal would allow Americans only to import medications that drugmakers have exported to Canada to guard against bogus products. Still, Canadian drugs are roughly 30 percent cheaper than they are here.

During the 2016 Republican presidential primary, Dr. Ben Carson, a retired neurosurgeon, championed nothing short of replacing Obamacare, as well as Medicare and Medicaid, with— drum roll, please—me and you.

Under his plan, the federal government would deposit a lump sum in each American's souped-up Health Savings Account each year, perhaps on your birthday. The sums would vary from, say, a basic $2,000 for individuals to $5,000 for Medicaid members and $12,500 for Medicare beneficiaries—regardless of the person's medical condition or needs. The rest would be up to you. You could put as much money into your account as you like tax free—or as little.

But what would happen if—despite your best efforts—you got sick and came up short paying your medical bills? Where would you turn? The retired brain surgeon had an answer: "Each family should become its own insurance company." You shouldn't look to the government for help, as the public does now. You should turn to your own family: simply borrow from a relative.

In other words, don't call Uncle Sam. Call your uncle Vinnie.

You may not hear much about Dr. Carson in the future, but ideas built on self-reliance are popular on the right; conservatives believe self-reliance would lead to reasonable self-rationing of unnecessary care. So you'll hear more about ideas such as transforming Medicare into a voucher program and turning Medicaid into a block grant program run by states to cap payouts to the poor.

When you hear these ideas, you might ask yourself this: What is attractive about a national policy of self-reliance that would cause tens of millions of citizens to pay more and, in many cases, go without the care they need? Wouldn't that be a heartless and irresponsible way for the government to treat its citizens?

New York governor Nelson Rockefeller, a Republican, crystallized the point decades ago: "If you don't have good education and good health, then I feel society has let you down."

Despite the public's hope that lawmakers will improve health care, don't even bet on major changes in the ACA. The truth is that powerful health care players like Obamacare more or less the way it is. By guaranteeing millions of new health care customers generous federal subsidies each year, health care players will continue to do well under this system. Before the early 2016 stock market slide, stock prices of the five largest for-profit health insurers had tripled, and other health care stocks had quadrupled since the law was passed.

In addition, other providers, including doctors with more patients, drugmakers with more customers, and hospitals with fewer charity cases, are doing fine, too. Or as one physician lamented to me about his daughter who just entered the profession: "The best she'll make is $250,000 a year. How can she get by on that?"

Resist the urge to shed a tear. Doctors make around $200,000; specialists, $400,000; surgeons, $600,000; and the health care rock stars—renowned surgeons, celebrity plastic surgeons, and hospital administrators—bring home $1 million to $4 million.

What's more, what's good for the health care industry is fine with politicians in both parties whom the corporations support with lavish campaign financing. As a result, preserving today's health care system enjoys strong bipartisan support.

Consider this instructive example: In 2012 John McCain (R-AZ) teamed up with Senator Sherrod Brown (D-OH) on legislation to allow Americans to reimport drugs and save money. When it became clear that the bill was about to be defeated, McCain denounced the drugmakers: "[The pharmaceutical industry] will exert its influence again at the expense of low-income Americans who will again have to choose between medication and eating."

It's interesting to note that the nation's pharmaceutical and health device interests shelled out $229 million lobbying Congress in 2014—three times more than the entire defense and aerospace industries spent combined. Or as Vermont senator Bernie Sanders puts it, "The health insurance and drug companies are bribing the US Congress."

Nevertheless, despite whatever happens in Washington,

there are a number of smart moves Health Care Detectives can make to get the prescriptions they need, as I'll show you in the next chapter: "Seventeen Ways to Save Money on Drugs."

MEDICARE FOR ALL, BY THE NUMBERS

For some insight into whether a government-run Medicare for All program would be better for average people than our present system, look at this set of numbers generated by Bernie Sanders's proposal in 2016:

- All 320 million American citizens would be eligible for a single-payer health care system similar to today's Medicare coverage for seniors and the disabled. That means that at any age, you could go to a doctor, specialist, or hospital you like in the expanded Medicare system—which should include just about every provider and facility.
- To cover the estimated $15 trillion cost of universal coverage over ten years, the government would raise taxes around $1 billion a year, or by about one-third—the largest tax increase since World War II.
- The government would impose a 6.2 percent health care payroll tax on employers; steeper income taxes on families making upward of $250,000 and topping out at 52 percent for those making $10 million or more; taxes on estates of over $3.5 million; higher capital gains taxes; and a 2.2 percent health care premium tax on the rest of us.
- But after paying the taxes under Medicare for All, a typical family earning $50,000 would save around $5,000 a year in health care costs, since the new system would

replace private health insurance and provide zero copays and deductibles, as well as dental coverage and long-term nursing—and still cost that family only $466 a year.

- Finally, employers would save $9,400 a year on the typical working family, since the cost of covering the family would plunge to $3,100.

DO DRUG COMPANY PATIENT-AID PROGRAMS HELP THE NEEDY OR THE GREEDY?

At first glance, the pharmaceutical industry's patient assistance programs appear to help everybody. But if you bend over to get a closer look, you'll see that the programs can bite you in the end.

Take Valeant's program, for openers. The company largely steered patients seeking assistance to pay for the company's dermatology drugs to one mail-order specialty pharmacy—which in turn used that customer volume to receive sizable insurance reimbursements from carriers and self-insured companies. That looks like everybody wins!

Valeant collected around 7 percent of its revenue from the specialty pharmacy Philidor RX Services. And by using Philidor, assistance patients didn't have to pay anything like Valeant's list prices, such as more than $1,000 a month for its acne medicine Solodyn and over $500 for a small bottle of its aggressively marketed toenail fungus ointment Jublia. For example, rather than paying the drug's high tier-three copay, many customers paid only $25. Some got their copays waived entirely. Jublia, by the way, has a complete cure rate of less than 20 percent after forty-eight costly weeks of treatment.

But there's a catch in Valeant's program that is largely mirrored by the pharmaceutical industry's patient-aid efforts.

By making it easy for doctors to have the pricey prescriptions filled without a hassle, Valeant got a steady flow of customers, including many who had no idea that they could be buying less costly drugs and get effective generics instead. For example, Valeant's Wellbutrin XL, a thirty-year-old antidepressant, commanded a list price of more than $1,000 for a month's supply in 2015, while generic substitutes were going for as little as $4 a month.

Even when some insurers refuse to pay for costly drugs such as Wellbutrin XL, drug companies can make a lot of money through the assistance programs. If enough insurers pay for the drugs, the manufacturers more than make up for those that don't. Experts estimate that manufacturers can make 4-to-1 to 6-to-1 returns on their investments with copay coupon programs like Valeant's.

Plus, companies with assistance programs—and Big Pharma, in general—get to portray themselves as heroes for giving people a few thousand dollars in benefits while they pocket their negotiated drug prices from insurers. And if the drug helps you, the company figures it probably can hold on to you as a lucrative long-term customer.

This is big business. Two former Philidor employees told the watchdog Southern Investigative Reporting Foundation that at one point the pharmacy was filling more than twenty thousand Valeant prescriptions a week, effectively discouraging those patients from asking independent pharmacies or their insurers about less expensive substitutes. In addition, more than 90 percent of the patients who filled prescriptions with Philidor came back for refills or continued therapy. Philidor's former CEO called that a "tremendous retention rate."

You don't have to be a math genius to know that the Niagara of sales meant that a lot of unnecessary costs were being dumped onto health insurers and their customers. Ultimately, the insurers pass on those costs to you and me in waves of higher premiums.

WHAT SHOULD YOU DO?

Your misgivings about the industry's ethics aside, if you need assistance buying a promising drug—and there isn't a lower-priced generic available—what would you do? Here are eight tips to consider:

1. **Sign Up for the Immediate Savings.** I think most people should sign up for the savings, even if they worry about the long-term effects of assistance programs on overall drug prices and rising premiums. I signed up twice. I got my $571-a-day Revlimid for $25 a month from the Celgene company in 2013. I also tried AbbVie's expensive testosterone booster AndroGel with the company's $10-a-month coupon. I used the coupon for a true trial period. I ultimately decided the extra testosterone wasn't helping me enough to make me a long-term user at, sooner or later, a far higher copay, or, heaven help me, the full retail price of $300 to $400 a month.

2. **Double-check Whether There Is a Generic Available.** The FDA approves roughly thirty new generic drugs each month. So check with your doctor or pharmacist every few months to see if there's a new generic that's cheaper than the drugmaker's brand-name option. A $4 version of whatever you're taking might pop up.

3. **It's Easy to Find Drug Assistance Programs.** Most drugmakers, including heavyweights AbbVie and Bristol-Myers Squibb, offer extensive assistance programs. You can research company programs through the pharmaceutical industry's Partnership for Prescription Assistance (PPA) website (www.pparx.org). Enter the drugs you take, fill out a short profile, and up pops a list of programs.

Since there are more programs than the website shows, also check the website of the nonprofit Patient Access Network Foundation (www.panfoundation.org), which allows you to apply online. Better yet, ask your health care provider or hospital to apply for you to avoid the tedious chore of doing it yourself.

4. **Private Foundations Can Help, Too.** Sometimes the company making the drug you need won't have a program that fits you, but don't give up. There might well be private foundations that can help you. Start with the advocacy organization for your disease, such as the American Cancer Society or the Cystic Fibrosis Foundation. Staffers there are plugged into the available resources and want to make them available to as many patients as possible.

A good independent organization that offers help paying for prescriptions and therapies for a variety of diseases is the HealthWell Foundation (www.healthwellfoundation.org).

5. **You Also Can Search the Internet.** If all else fails, you can always go mano a mano with your computer search engines. Simply plug the phrase "[your disease] patient assistance" into an online search, and up should come a list of helpful programs.

6. **Once You Find an Aid Program, It's Often Easy to Qualify.** If you're applying for a very expensive, top-tier wonder drug, chances are you will need to ask your doctor to submit a note saying that the drug is medically necessary; he'll probably have to repeat that each month.

You'll also have to disclose your income. But since the program's income limits commonly reach six figures for families and not much less for couples, many people will likely qualify as I have.

7. **You Might Get Very Attractive Deals on New Drugs.** For example, consider Takeda Pharmaceuticals' offers for Ninlaro, the oral version of its cancer drug Velcade. Takeda won FDA approval for Ninlaro in late 2015, less

than two years before it was slated to lose its Velcade patent protection—and the monopoly that has allowed it to command more than $1,500 a dose.

Takeda representatives quickly began beating the drum for Ninlaro to cancer support groups. At one California meeting in 2016, attended by a friend of mine, the Takeda rep declined to quote a retail price for Ninlaro. All she would say was that it would cost *no more* than Velcade, which of course commands $1,500 a dose. As *Saturday Night Live*'s Church Lady would say: "How convennnn . . . ient!"

But here's the kicker: introducing Ninlaro was so important to Takeda that it offered to give the first monthly course of it to patients free of charge—and invited uninsured patients to apply for a free year's supply.

8. **Don't Get Yourself into a Lose-Lose Proposition.** Of course, free trials don't last forever. They are meant to turn you into a paying customer. So if a wonder drug like Ninlaro worked for you—but your insurer refused to pay for it at any point—you could be staring at a five-figure monthly bill, and you'd be scrambling to find a different drug plan or an assistance program that would step in and cover your five-figure monthly bill. That's hardly the equivalent of "everybody wins!" It's more like a lose-lose. So check that the drug is on your insurer's approved list, or that it is likely to be, if it's new to the market. Then proceed with your eyes open and your wallet squeezed as tightly shut as possible.

—— • ——

CHAPTER 15

Seventeen Ways to Save Money on Drugs

Easy Ways to Work with Your Doctor, Your Insurer, Your Pharmacy, and Others to Get the Best Prices

With the costs of drugs stacked against you, as you can plainly see from chapter 14, you need some good news, and we're going to get it from the little blue pill Viagra. That billion-dollar drug provides a classic example of how a consumer can save money by being a Health Care Detective and asking a few questions.

Let's assume that you (or your partner) want to try Viagra. Since the meanies at many health plans at work and virtually all Part D providers don't consider sexual pleasure a medical necessity, you will probably end up paying cash for the pill. Sensing occasional high demand among customers—reflected by Viagra's "huddle-with-me" ads that run in football season— some pharmacies want hundreds of dollars for one pill. Obviously, abstain; you have better options.

If you are fortunate, your plan at work might allow you to get six pills a month for a $30 copay. That equates to the price of a latte, or $5 each. With your doctor's okay, you could also invest in a quality $20 pill splitter and cut the most powerful dosage,

100 milligrams (mg), into two 50 mg pills, a common dosage that would effectively cost you $2.50.

If you're not covered, however, figure on a steep $50 a pill. A search at the comparison-shopping website GoodRx (www .goodrx.com) in 2016 turned up its lowest prices, ranging from $44 to $52, at major chains in one California town—and, yes, that's for one pill. Prices at competitor Milligram (www .milligram.biz) were nearly identical at $46 to $54.

Viagra manufacturer Pfizer felt your pain, up to a point. Its website was offering a half-price coupon on your first three prescriptions. The catch? You had to buy at least six pills per prescription. You laid out $300 for eighteen tablets and "saved" $150. Yet you would be down to a relative bargain of $17 a pill.

There's one more trick: Although Pfizer won't license a true Viagra generic copy until its patent expires in 2017, there is an inexpensive version widely available today. The brand is Revatio, though it's better known by its generic name, sildenafil. Chances are your pharmacist has it tucked away behind his $50 Viagras. Sildenafil comes only in 20 mg tablets, so you'd need two or three to measure against Viagra's 50 mg pill. But in 2016, you could buy 90 of the 20 mg tablets through Blink Health for $62.50.

Instead of shelling out $50 for each Viagra pill, you'd be paying 69 cents for a sildenafil.

Remember, however, that this is a free market. Pharmacies can charge whatever they want. Steve Patton of the price-tracker website PrescriptionBlueBook.com spotted an alternative version of Viagra selling for $204 in one chain store in 2015 and $1,633 in another—which he called "the highest markup I've seen in my forty years as a pharmacist."

So those are your Viagra options: $1,600 or 69 cents—or just about any price in between. Happy shopping. Here are sixteen more ways to reduce your prescription costs, based mainly on 2016 prices, organized by where you can pursue savings and beginning face-to-face with your doctor in her office.

ASK YOUR DOCTOR

Why Are You Prescribing This Specific Medicine? Your doctor should be able to fully describe the benefits you'll get and *when* you should expect to experience them. For example, women with common urinary tract infections should feel better after a few days on the antibiotic nitrofurantoin. If not, at the least, they should stop wasting money and consult with their doctors about what to do next.

The stakes get higher with chronic conditions. When my doctors said I should switch from Revlimid, which was no longer controlling my blood cancer after five years, to the new and more powerful Pomalyst, they said they would be able to measure whether my blood tumors decreased within the first month of treatment. I'm happy to say that's exactly what happened; otherwise my doctors and I would have been scrambling for options as my tumors continued to multiply.

No matter how serious your condition is, pin down your doctor to a target date of when you should be getting better. If you don't get the benefits by then, don't wait. Get back to your doctor and ask if you're wasting money—and risking your health—on the wrong medicine.

Why Are You Suggesting This Specific Dosage? Generally, you want to take the least amount of medicine that works. There's an obvious financial angle as well. Sometimes, slightly different dosages of the same medicine can cost hundreds of dollars more, as it did with metformin, a drug to control blood sugar. GoodRx, which tracks the prices of more than six thousand FDA-approved drugs at seventy thousand pharmacies, reported in 2015 that a Kmart wanted $800 cash for a different dosage of the drug available at Walmart for $4. Presumably with some help from their doctors, nearly all of the people paying $800 could find a safe way to control their diabetes with the

$4 version—to say nothing about what savings like that would do to improve their blood pressure.

Also, be especially attentive if you are seeing a so-called dispensing physician; that is, a doctor who gives you the drug directly and either bills you or your insurer rather than writing a prescription that is filled by a pharmacist. Studies in 2015 in several states, including California, Ohio, and Illinois, indicate that some dispensing doctors were charging much higher prices for unusual dosages of common drugs such as generic Vicodin, a combination of the pain medication acetaminophen and hydrocodone, as well as the opioid painkiller tramadol and the muscle relaxant cyclobenzaprine.

Is There a Lower-cost Generic Available? On average, brand-name drugs cost four times as much as generics. And sometimes, switching to a generic can save you much more. You could have bought a generic called pravastatin for high cholesterol for $4 in 2016, compared to upward of $230 for brand-name Crestor. Although pravastatin acts like Crestor, it is not an exact FDA-approved copy. However, Crestor was one of a number of high-priced drugs that was expected to get FDA-approved copies in 2016. The savings figure to be huge. Generics with the same active ingredient, quality, safety, and strength as its branded original were expected for the following: Humira for rheumatoid arthritis at $3,800 for a standard dose; Benicar and Zetia for cholesterol at $230 to $270; and three drugs for HIV—Norvir at $265, Kaletra at more than $900, and Epzicom at more than $1,200.

Here's a tip: If your popular brand-name does not yet have a generic option or an FDA-approved copy, keep asking your doctor and pharmacist about alternatives. There's a good chance a low-cost option will pop up sooner or later.

Is There an Over-the-Counter Alternative? For example, you can buy allergy nasal sprays Flonase or Nasacort Allergy

24HR for about $20 over the counter, compared with around $150 to $300 for similar prescription drugs such as Veramyst, Rhinocort Aqua, and Nasonex. Over-the-counter drugs rarely cost more than $20. Just check the active ingredients carefully with your pharmacist before you buy. Pharmacists tend to know more about specific over-the-counter alternatives than many doctors do.

Conversely, Is There a Prescription That's Cheaper Than the Over-the-Counter Product? Generic Prilosec (called omeprazole), for reducing stomach acid, is an example of a prescription drug costing less than an over-the-counter option. Prescription omeprazole has been available in 10 mg, 20 mg, and 40 mg capsules. Both the 20 mg and 40 mg prescription capsules can easily be found at under $10 for thirty capsules— about 33 cents each. Better yet, the 20 mg strength has been on several pharmacy generic lists for $4 for thirty capsules—or 13 cents each. By contrast, the over-the-counter product, which comes only in 20 mg, tends to cost around $20 or more for forty-two capsules—or 47 cents and up.

Do You Have Free Samples? That's the five-word question I asked one of my doctors, and he handed me the $1,080 worth of the new nonaddictive painkiller that I mentioned earlier. When I told the doctor that my pharmacy wanted a whopping $20 a pill, he gave me a stack of sample packets that the drugmaker's salesmen had left at his office. Then, without my saying anything beyond thanking him, he checked his supply with his nurse and gave me a second stack. Drug companies hand out around $18 billion worth of samples a year, and many doctors fill their cabinets with the free stuff. The samples could be yours, if you ask.

Do You Have a Manufacturer's Discount Card for the Drug? The same drugmaker salesmen who leave samples might also give your doctor so-called savings cards for their company's most expensive medicines. For example, a savings card could allow you to try a costly drug, such as AbbVie's testosterone booster AndroGel, for as little as $10 a month, as I did. If your doctor doesn't have a savings card for the brand name he's suggesting, check the manufacturer's website. Ohio pharmacist Roni Bennett said that in her experience, manufacturers offer volume-building savings cards for nine out of ten of their brand-name drugs.

Is It Okay to Split the Pill, or Take It Every Other Day, to Cut My Costs in Half? Never do this without checking with your doctor. I said, *never.* And never ever consider it for time-release capsules; it's feasible only for certain pills or tablets. Tablets that have FDA approval to be split are scored, including metformin for diabetes and Paxil for depression.

Other examples of popular drugs that are indented to split easily include two antidepressants: alprazolam, the generic for Xanax; and sertraline, the generic for Zoloft. Alprazolam's 0.5 mg and 1 mg tablets cost almost exactly the same—around $12 for sixty tablets. So if you split the 1 mg tablet with your doctor's okay, you can save 50 percent. As for sertraline, it costs even less—around $10 for thirty-day supplies of 25 mg, 50 mg, or 100 mg strengths.

There are also a number of medicines that aren't indented but can be split safely with your doctor's approval, according to GoodRx. They include atorvastatin, the cholesterol-fighting generic for Lipitor; and the Alzheimer's disease drug memantine, the generic for Namenda. Atorvastatin can be found for around $15 for each of its strengths of 10 mg, 20 mg, 40 mg, and 80 mg, while memantine offers even greater savings, since it is more expensive. Sixty tablets of both the 5 mg and 10 mg dosages cost around $50. Hey, who doesn't want to save $25?

Will You Write the Prescription for No More Than Fourteen Days? If your doctor is suggesting a brand-name drug for a chronic condition, don't automatically buy a full month's supply. Instead, ask her about starting with a fourteen-day supply, so that you both can see whether the medicine is helping and not causing nasty side effects before you sign up for more.

ASK YOUR INSURER

Please Identify Three "Preferred" Drugstores Near Me. Since pharmacy owners, like any other merchants, can charge whatever they want for a drug, the exact same medication could go for anywhere from $4 to $400 (or more!) in your neighborhood. No exaggeration.

On average, your insurer's preferred stores should offer you savings of roughly 5 percent to 25 percent on prescriptions. And sometimes more: My month's supply of Lyrica for my neuropathy costs $25 at my plan's preferred Walgreens, but around $45 at nonpreferred CVS.

In addition, some health plans cover drugs with a reasonable copay at preferred pharmacies but do not cover them at all at nonpreferred stores.

Also, take the extra step of checking the prices at each of the preferred stores. One or two might offer better "preferred" discounts than others.

Insurers shuffle stores on and off the preferred lists so routinely that sometimes even they can't keep the information straight. For example, in 2014 Aetna inaccurately listed around five thousand pharmacies serving more than four hundred thousand customers either as being in network when they were not, or as being preferred with the best prices—again, when they were not. It's wise to double-check with a new pharmacy before you fill a prescription.

Finally, always ask your insurer about the preferred stores for the coming year. One year, when CVS was my plan's preferred chain, my insurance carrier steered me to a CVS one block from my New York City home. The next year, the same insurer sent me to a different CVS—five blocks from the original one. That seems crazy. But store managers have a lot of freedom to set drug prices and switch loss leaders.

Is My Drug in Your Formulary? This question can be critical if your doctor wants you to take a costly prescription for a serious illness, especially a top-tier specialty drug. If the drug isn't on your plan's formulary—its approved list—you could be out of luck or out a lot of money.

A little background: Both private insurance plans and Medicare Part D providers compile lists of drugs they will cover. Within this formulary, drugs generally are divided into four tiers, from cheap tier-one generics to tier-four specialty medicines requiring costly coinsurance, with branded options in between. With occasional exceptions, the Department of Health and Human Services demands that insurers offer at least two drugs in each category, such as two anticoagulants, two thyroid agents, and so on. But insurers can add or shed which drugs they'll cover, and they often do that based on cost. In January 2016, for instance, two giant pharmacy benefit managers for large employers ditched more than fifty drugs, including brand-name Viagra and the exorbitant hepatitis C drug Harvoni. Insurers make changes like those because a safer or more effective option is available, or maybe, more likely, a cheaper one.

Obviously, as I've noted, always ask your doctor whether you can take an effective lower-tier medicine.

The real challenge for you and your physician begins when a tier-four drug you need is not on your insurer's list. You do have options. But do not try to tackle this one alone. Ask your prescribing doctor to lead your appeal, which is called "an exception." Insurers frequently cover specific medicines based solely on an informed physician's recommendation. But not always.

If you and your doctors are turned away, you will have to follow a mandated, time-consuming appeal process, which can take your case before an independent arbitrator or perhaps ultimately a judge. Let's hope your insurer listens to your doctors, and you never have to push your appeal beyond that. (For more on appealing a denial, see Emil Pusateri's story in chapter 20.)

Can I Save Money Ordering Through Your Mail Order Program? You may be able to get three-month supplies of medications for chronic conditions like diabetes and high blood pressure at zero copay, including free shipping. But you must order through your insurer's specific plan. Also, as with any mail orders, you could face delivery snafus, including delays and damages. On top of that, many insurers are offering ninety-day supplies at their network pharmacies at mail-order prices— such as Caremark plans at CVS, Express Scripts, and Optimum at Walgreens.

ASK YOUR PHARMACY MANAGER

Will You Match the Lowest Price I Can Find? Many pharmacies, even in chains, will match a lower price you can find at other stores. Philippe Boistard of Battleboro, North Carolina, paid $139.99 and $9.99 for two prescriptions at his pharmacy. That was until he discovered that his local Walmart would sell him the same drugs for $30 and $4, respectively. His first store manager agreed immediately to match the Walmart prices. "There were two sets of prices," said Boistard. "The price they charge you, and the price they are willing to match. But if you don't ask, you don't get the good price. It's ridiculous."

Doug Hirsch, the founder of the GoodRx price-tracking company, agrees. "Pharmacists have chased me out to the parking lot trying to close a sale on a prescription I could get cheaper at another store," he said. "Pharmacies bargain on prices all the time."

However, there are limits. Do not expect the pharmacy to match prices you find online or from an overseas supplier. Generally, the store manager will match prices you can document from a nearby brick-and-mortar competitor.

Please Check My Prescription's Cash Price Against What I'll Owe Under My Insurance Plan. From time to time, you also might be able to save by paying cash, especially if you have a plan with a high deductible or a limited list of approved drugs.

The GoodRx website (and its free mobile app) can often find attractive cash prices near you—plus manufacturers' discount coupons that can save you up to an additional 80 percent. The website is easy to use. Just type in the name of your medicine and select the correct dosage. Up comes a list of nearby stores selling your medicine, beginning with the lowest cash price— with or without a discount coupon.

All in all, I've found that GoodRx usually offers the best prices. In addition, check out the Milligram website as well. It sometimes offers lower prices from independent pharmacies not covered by GoodRx.

Also, take a look at WeRx's website (www.werx.org), especially if you live in an ex-urban area. It features a map of your zip code showing the exact locations of nearby stores and their competing prices. Like Milligram, WeRx covers independent pharmacies that you might not see at GoodRx.

Finally, for convenience, consider the much-publicized Blink Health. You order your drug online (www.blinkhealth.com) and pick it up at a drugstore near you. One caution: Although the website claimed it offered "the lowest prices on over 15,000 medications" in 2016, GoodRx had lower prices on half the drugs I spot-checked. So think before you blink.

GoodRx's editor in chief, Elizabeth Davis, singled out three drugs available through her website at especially favorable cash prices in 2015:

- Follistim AQ is a common fertility medication that isn't covered by many plans. Typically, its cash price is not all that far off from the website's discount price of $600 and up. But GoodRx had added a fertility pharmacy that was offering the drug for $270 at www.goodrx.com/follistim-aq.
- Adderall (generic: amphetamine and dextroamphetamine) often isn't covered or carries a high coinsurance cost. Typically it costs over $100 out of pocket at big chains or up to $170 at some independent stores. But GoodRx showed the drug used to manage attention deficit hyperactivity disorder (ADHD) available at Walgreens and Costco for only $45.
- Retin-A (generic: tretinoin) is often covered for treating acne. But it's rarely covered at all if it is prescribed for other uses, such as improving wrinkles and skin tone. The off-label brand-name cash price is usually around $200 at Target and about $215 at the Safeway chain and at Rite Aid. But GoodRx had it available for just $40 at the Kroger chains: Kroger, Ralphs, and Fred Meyer stores.

Can You Steer Me to Assistance Programs from the Drug Manufacturer, Nonprofit Groups, or the Government? Since you will be discussing personal details, it's best to arrange a private meeting with your pharmacist. Show up with your drug list and be prepared to discuss your finances. A well-informed pharmacist or pharmacy manager should be able to refer you to local assistance programs.

In addition, as I've mentioned, I know from personal experience that a well-informed pharmacy staff can sometimes help households making $85,000 or more get assistance that covers the entire cost of an expensive drug, including cancer medicines listed at upward of $800 a day.

ASK YOUR CHAIN STORE DRUGGIST

Is My Drug on Your Deep-Discount Generics List? That's how Susan Timoney got her blood pressure medication for nothing. The Publix chain offers a handful of common generics for free to attract customers to its grocery stores. In addition, giants such as Walmart, CVS, and Costco, which tend to offer the best prices overall, also sell a select set of generics for roughly $4 to $10 each.

Those $4 deep-discount programs can be a great deal, but there are serious caveats. First, relatively few generics are covered. And if you're not careful, you can get clipped for extra hundreds of dollars.

"Those four-dollar programs include less than two percent of all prescription drugs available," said Steve Patton, founder of the PrescriptionBlueBook.com website, which tracks the wholesale prices of around five thousand FDA-approved drugs. "And you can get gouged more than three hundred dollars on just one prescription that isn't in the program."

The big-box chains claim that their discount programs cover hundreds of drugs and save consumers a great deal of money. But a close reading of the chains' lists of approved generics shows that they are pumping up their numbers by counting various dosages and versions—such as gels or tablets—of only around one hundred of the country's nine hundred distinct generics.

For example, if you take meloxicam for arthritis or atenolol for high blood pressure at a few common dosages, you're in luck. In 2015 you could buy a thirty-day supply of either medicine for $4, or a ninety-day supply for $10, at Walmart and Target. CVS also was offering ninety-day supplies of either drug for $11.99, after you paid a nominal annual fee to join its Health Savings Pass program.

Those prices are relative bargains compared with what you would pay at many independent pharmacies, which generally try to make at least a $10 profit on every prescription.

But it's a completely different story if your precise generic—including its dosage and form—isn't on the discount list. Then the programs are like magic: they make the money in your wallet disappear.

After you spot your drug on the approved list, check the fine print for the precise dosage and exact version of the medicine that is covered, such as a gel or extended release. If your prescription is for a slightly different dosage or type, the store might ask you for $300 extra.

For example, a New Jersey chain store I checked personally was selling the ninety-day supply of the 20 mg antidepressant paroxetine on its approved list for only $10. However, if your doctor had prescribed the 25 mg extended-release version, the store wanted $321.84. Why $311 extra for the 25 mg version? The pharmacist gave me a succinct answer: "The twenty-five-milligram pill isn't on our discount list."

Still, deep-discount programs can save you money. Just be careful:

- Check two or three of the chain store discount lists; the pharmacy staff should hand you a printed copy if you request it. If you spot any $4 generics of medicines you take, ask your doctor whether they would be as effective as your prescriptions.
- Don't fill a new generic prescription until you pin down the dosage and what type of medicine it is to be sure the specific drug is on at least one approved list.
- And if you take a deeply discounted medicine from time to time, don't refill it automatically; review the approved list first to be sure your precise dosage and form is still covered—and you're not about to be billed an extra $300.

One Last Tip: Take Your Medicine. Roughly half of all drug-related admissions to hospitals and nursing homes are triggered by people not taking their pills as instructed. Sadly, as we've discussed, around one person out of five cuts back because of costs. But in many cases, people simply lose track of when they are supposed to be taking what. Especially if you pop several pills a day—my one-day record was eighteen. If so, invest $10 or so in a pill organizer. Then put the organizer next to your toothbrush, so you see it a couple of times every day.

In addition, I've begun wearing a watch with an alarm. It reminds me to take my Lyrica twice a day—when I remember to set the alarm (and sometimes, even worse, when I remember *why* I set it).

Our oldest daughter asked me recently when I thought I was at the top of my powers. I said, "I can't remember."

CHAPTER 16

The Wonder Drug Racket

Secrets to Getting a Costly Specialty Drug at a Price That Won't Bust You

If you develop a serious illness, like I did with my blood cancer multiple myeloma, your doctor is likely to prescribe what's called a specialty drug. Today there are five hundred to seven hundred specialty drugs, and more coming to market seemingly every month. Some of them—the true wonder drugs—are turning deadly diseases, like mine, into chronic conditions. And the scientific discoveries behind those breakthrough medicines are leading to cures for specific cancers, though the defeat of the 3,000 named types of cancer still remains a decade or more away.

But along the way, the prices that the wonder-drug manufacturers are demanding are inflating our national health costs, driving up insurance premiums, and pushing tens of thousands of sick people into insolvency. And there's no end in sight for this price spiral. Sixteen percent of what Medicare Part D members spent on all drugs in 2014 went for specialty drugs, up from 11 percent in 2013.

Effective wonder drugs expand their manufacturers' customer pools by extending the lives of millions of people. Diseases that once killed become profit centers. According to estimates, with sales increasing around 20 percent a year, specialty drugs will account for almost half of all pharmaceutical manufacturer revenues by 2017.

In a twist of that knife to patients, the drugmakers are charging about double here than they do in Canada and elsewhere. As I explained in chapter 15, other countries with single-payer government health programs negotiate for deep discounts. But our government, by law, prohibits even Medicare from negotiating for discounts, thanks to bought-and-paid-for lawmakers in both parties.

Exceptional specialty drugs become monopolies. Patents protect the drugs from competitors, thereby allowing the creators to pretty much charge as much as they want. That helps explain why my monopolistic wonder drug Revlimid, a thalidomide derivative with an estimated 14 cents' worth of ingredients, was retailing for $540.61 a pill in 2016, according to price tracker Milligram—and commanding around a steep $380 from insurers. That's how much collectively people with blood cancers like mine, and their insurers, appear willing to pay for it until the happy day when the drug's patent runs out and low-cost generic options hit the market.

As pricey as it is, Revlimid is far from the most expensive wonder drug out there. The last chemotherapeutic agent that *When Harry Met Sally* screenwriter Nora Ephron was taking in 2012 to combat acute myeloid leukemia was said to be priced at $30,000 a month—more than seven times what an average worker earns a year.

And then there's the drug that experts call "the world's most expensive": Alexion Pharmaceuticals' Soliris. It fights two rare immune system disorders that destroy red blood cells—at an insane price of $669,000 per patient per year in 2015.

Whatever the price, once you are told that there is a drug that could keep you alive for years, if not "cure" you, who wouldn't struggle to find a way to pay for it through your insurance, or government assistance, or a private grant, or neighborhood casserole dinner fund-raisers?

Assuming that my cancer meds keep my myeloma in check for a decade, I will cost my insurers around $1 million—at today's prices, without factoring in inflation. And my family's out-of-pocket costs could approach $100,000. Under Medicare Part D's so-called catastrophic care, I could end up being on the hook for the rest of my life for 5 percent of the drug's cost, or roughly $550 a month at 2016 prices.

For many people on specialty cancer drugs, especially those like me in Medicare, the big question they face is: Will I die before I go bankrupt? Half of Medicare households bring in less than $24,150 a year and spend around 14 percent of their money on health care alone, compared with about 5 percent for all other households. No wonder that each year millions of Medicare beneficiaries run through their savings paying medical and drug bills that the government doesn't cover and end up broke and on Medicaid. Sad and true.

The shameful fact is that this country is forcing millions of its sickest and oldest people to face the nightmare of choosing between eating dinner or taking life-prolonging drugs. And pinstriped dudes running Big Pharma companies are largely to blame. Their companies have become too big to care about their customers. Big Pharma's marketing plan is simple: Our customers will pay through the nose for our products, or die trying.

The drugmakers, of course, argue that their specialty-drug prices are reasonable. They say that patients are paying for the companies' billions of dollars of research and development. But as I've documented, studies show that the R&D expenses of major drug companies average only around 15 percent to 20 percent of gross revenues—and amount to a baby bite out of their net profits. Furthermore, with few exceptions, they spend up to twice as much on S&M (fifty shades of the truth through Sales and Marketing), rather than on R&D.

Shocked by the ever-rising prices, a few teams of hospital oncologists have refused to sell cancer drugs in their hospital pharmacies unless manufacturers cut their prices by around

25 percent to 30 percent. Even after these discounts, the drugs still easily run around $9,000 a month, or $108,000 a year—or double an average family's annual income.

WHAT SHOULD YOU DO?

If your doctor ever says you need a specialty drug, despite everything I've just told you, do not panic. There are several smart moves a Health Care Detective can make to get the medicine you want at a price you can afford.

First, Check with Your Insurer. If you are covered at work, say, by a company with more than 500 employees, you might be in luck. Some corporations still pick up all of a worker's drug costs over $1,000 or $2,000 a year, though that sort of cost-cap benefit is disappearing. As I detailed in chapter 1, my old employer paid drug expenses beyond $1,000 for all of its workers for years. But then with only a few weeks of notice, the company eliminated the benefit entirely in 2013.

Also, if you have an Obamacare health plan, your combined medical and drug costs are capped at around $6,400 for an individual and $12,800 for a family in 2016. And those caps will climb to $7,150 and $14,300 in 2017. That's a lot of money out of your pocket, but hopefully not a ruinous amount.

Second, Calculate Carefully How Much the Drug Will Cost You. Aside from corporate coverage, Obamacare, and Medicare, many health plans require members to pay coinsurance of anywhere from 20 percent to 75 percent of the cost of their highest-tier specialty drugs. Jot down your estimates, take a deep breath, and keep reading.

Third, See if the Drug's Manufacturer Will Help You. If you are facing daunting costs, there's a good chance the drugmaker will assist you, even if your family brings in $100,000. In my view, since wonder-drug manufacturers are so vulnerable to charges of profiteering off society's sickest people, they have created teams of empathic specialty-drug staffers to arrange grants and other forms of support for families in need.

When I was struggling to learn how much my Revlimid would cost me a few years ago, the staffers at the drug's manufacturer, Celgene, were the most courteous, compassionate, and helpful I contacted. On several occasions, workers there called me unsolicited to check on my progress and to reassure me that they would work with me to find an affordable solution.

My old employer's health plan ended up capping my Revlimid at $60 a month in 2013, or a manageable $2 a pill. Then Celgene stepped in and cut my cost to $25 a month for the last few months of that year. I'm confident that Celgene would have continued subsidizing my costs. But unfortunately, beginning in 2014, my former employer again reduced benefits for its retirees, thereby forcing me to enroll in Medicare's Part D drug program. The federal government's antikickback laws prohibit drug manufacturers from subsidizing Medicare Part D members to buy their products, so Celgene could no longer offer me the $25-a-month copay.

To make matter worse, under Part D's flawed catastrophic care provision, there is no dollar limit on what anyone might have to pay for exorbitant drugs. Instead of paying the Celgene-subsidized $25 a month for my Revlimid, I faced having to pay around $800 a month under Medicare. But fortunately, I got a grant from a nonprofit group.

The lesson. If you can't imagine how to pay for an exorbitant specialty drug, don't curse the manufacturer. Instead, call the company and ask for help. Or, okay, curse the manufacturer for its outrageous drug prices. And then call for help.

Fourth, Apply for Assistance. There are several hundred foundations, organizations, and nonprofit charities offering financial aid and other assistance, including help covering the entire cost of prescriptions. Many are disease specific, such as the Leukemia & Lymphoma Society for blood cancer patients and the Cystic Fibrosis Foundation for that lung disease. Others are private, independent charitable organizations, such as Good Days, formerly the Chronic Disease Fund (www.gooddaysfromcdf.org), and the HealthWell Foundation (www.healthwellfoundation.org). Both have helped hundreds of thousands of patients.

In addition, as noted in chapter 14, the pharmaceutical industry seems to recognize the mess that many of its firms have created with their often outlandish pricing and therefore offers substantial copay assistance through its Partnership for Prescription Assistance. You can search programs by drug name at www.pparx.org. And nearly all drugmakers maintain their own assistance programs—even the notorious Martin Shkreli's Turing Pharmaceuticals.

Also, RxAssist (www.rxassist.org) and NeedyMeds (www.needymeds.org) have comprehensive directories of assistance programs that are searchable by diagnosis, state, and other relevant terms.

Experts also recommend the Patient Access Network (PAN) at www.panfoundation.org. The website offers a comprehensive list of copay support programs, arranged by diagnosis. You can apply online or through many doctors' offices and specialty pharmacists. Or call PAN directly at 1-866-316-7263 and explain your situation. Awards, which vary by the illness, can reach six figures a year.

Most hospitals and many physician practices have staffers available to assist you. And, as I've mentioned, your local pharmacists can help you apply as well.

Nearly all assistance programs have income limits, but the caps can be surprisingly generous. Typically, you can get help even if you're earning up to 400 percent or 500 percent of the federal poverty level, or as much as $79,650 for a couple or

$121,250 for a family of four in 2015. But by and large, state programs, especially red states, have much lower income limits.

Other qualifying factors vary. For example, some programs require that patients have health insurance; others help only those without insurance.

I certainly can't guarantee anything. But people in tears facing huge costs have gotten grants overnight that covered the entire cost of their tier-four drugs. One patient told me, "I answered a few simple questions, and the next day I had a ten-thousand-dollar grant."

Fifth, If All Else Fails, Consider Enrolling in Obamacare. Even if you can't get premium subsidies because you earn too much or because you have coverage available to you at work, all Affordable Care Act health plans offer the remarkable cap on costs I mentioned a moment ago. Obamacare caps your combined medical and drug costs at around $12,800 for a family. Therefore, Obamacare might be your least expensive option even without subsidies. And remember, you cannot be turned away because of your health.

CHAPTER 17

What to Do When the Doctor Suggests a Costly Procedure

Don't Get Blindsided by a Budget-Bashing Bill

My doctor said I should get an expensive procedure from a specialist who isn't in my health plan's provider network. That would cost me at least $10,000 to $20,000. What should I do?

As health correspondent for *Parade*, I got questions like that regularly from our worried readers. But in virtually every case, aside from emergencies, people have many more options than they realize. If your doctor suggests a costly procedure or service, here are five steps to get the care you need with a minimum of financial risk.

Step One: Get a Second Opinion

Do not feel embarrassed about telling your doctor that you want another opinion. If he's suggesting a costly procedure, he feels that you're facing a serious concern, so neither of you want to make a mistake.

In my opinion, your doctor should volunteer to help you identify that second doctor—and a third one if you need a tiebreaker—just as Maggie Murphy's doctor did when Maggie was considering whether to have a double mastectomy. (For Maggie's story, see chapter 9, "Pink Confusion: When Should Women Get Screened for Breast Cancer?")

If your doctor isn't helpful, take that as a sign that you may not have the level of primary care physician you need. You want a quarterback, like I have. He should know you well enough to call the next play. But he also should give you time in the huddle with him to discuss his call and decide whether you want to run that route or not.

If you find yourself more or less on your own, call your insurer for the names of board-certified specialists in your plan's network and then get back to your original doctor to discuss the one or two who stand out. Board certification is the medical profession's equivalent of the Good Housekeeping Seal of Approval, as I'll explain more fully in a minute.

You can check a doctor's credentials on the website of the American Board of Medical Specialties (www.certificationmatters .com) or call the ABMS at 1-866-ASK-ABMS (275-2267).

Diligent Health Care Detectives might have to make a dozen calls stretching over several days. But the effort is worth it to get an informed second opinion from a network board-certified specialist that confirms the first suggestion—or perhaps concludes that you don't need the procedure after all.

Don't be surprised if the second doctor says you don't need extra care.

The *Journal of the American Medical Association* reported in 2015, for example, that common breast biopsies to diagnose cancer are nowhere near as conclusive as many patients and experts assumed. Somewhere around 13 percent of healthy patients in the study were misdiagnosed and therefore faced additional and costly treatments they didn't need.

Assuming that study reflects what's happening generally, we're talking about a lot of people getting unnecessary care.

Dr. Joann G. Elmore, a professor at the University of Washington School of Medicine in Seattle and one of the lead researchers, said, "It is often thought that getting the biopsy will give definitive answers, but our study said maybe not."

So what should you do if, for example, your doctor tells you that your biopsy is troubling? First, do not rush to schedule surgery. Even if you might need it, you do not need it tomorrow.

As I described in Maggie's breast cancer story, get a smart second opinion. You might not even need a second biopsy immediately. You might simply ask another cancer specialist to check your doctor's reading of your biopsy slides and give you her independent opinion.

Although I've singled out breast biopsies, this advice applies broadly to any troubling initial recommendation.

Step Two: Confirm What the Procedure Will Cost

Start with your insurance company. You want the "contracted rate" the insurer pays its network providers. Or you ask for the "usual and customary" rate if you are considering someone out of your network. Do not just read your policy closely. Insurance policy language is tricky stuff. Get an insurance staffer on the phone, and write down the date, that person's name, plus exactly what the staffer tells you. If what you're hearing doesn't sound right, speak to a supervisor.

With one of my back operations, two staffers at my health insurer initially told me that the usual and customary fee for my procedure was about $30,000, depending on exactly what the out-of-network surgeon ended up doing—and that my plan would cover more than 80 percent of that. Both staffers figured I would owe around $5,000.

That didn't sound correct. I thought I'd have to pay about

30 percent under my plan's coinsurance rules, or roughly $9,000. Although both assured me I wouldn't owe that much, I insisted on speaking to a supervisor.

Guess what? The supervisor told me that my plan didn't cover the operation I had in mind at all. Forget the coinsurance. I'd have to pay the entire bill. And my policy did not even provide an out-of-pocket maximum.

"You have a really bad plan," she said. I considered that an understatement.

Generally, usual and customary fees are set at what your insurer believes around 80 percent of providers in your area charge for your procedure. If, say, your out-of-network surgeon plans on charging more than that usual and customary fee, figure you'll be billed for every dollar above it, plus a 30 percent coinsurance. So if the usual and customary fee for your operation is $20,000 and your surgeon charges $30,000, you'd owe the extra $10,000, plus $6,000 for your 30 percent coinsurance of the usual and customary $20,000. Your cost: $16,000.

Your financial risk can get even higher out of network. Your plan might not cover that doctor's fees at all, or perhaps only up to double the low rate that Medicare would pay. And even if your policy said it pays, say, 70 percent of out-of-network charges, watch out. That 70 percent is calculated on what your plan pays a network doctor. If the network doctor has agreed to perform the procedure for $2,000 and your out-of-network provider charges $4,000, you'd owe the additional $2,000, plus another $600 for the 30 percent coinsurance on the in-network's contracted rate of $2,000.

After you've nailed down how much your insurer will pay for the procedure you want and you've found a board-certified provider you prefer, always double-check with that provider. Despite all your good detective work, steel yourself for six of the most depressing words in our broken health care system: "We don't take that insurance anymore."

Step Three: Look for a Lower Price, as You Always Should

Searching hard for a better price becomes imperative if you have a high deductible of $5,000 to $10,000, or no insurance at all.

As I've said, the prices of procedures vary so absurdly that patients are saving thousands of dollars by getting complicated care way across town or across the country, even after factoring in airfare and family hotel bills. For example, a government survey reported in 2015 that the same heart failure care ranged from $9,000 to $51,000 in the same city of Jackson, Mississippi. And an identical joint replacement went from $5,000 in Oklahoma to more than $200,000 in California. (For more on medical travel, see chapter 6, "How to Keep the Doctor and Hospital You Like.")

Obviously, don't lock in the first price you see; keep dialing for dollars until you find a quality provider charging around half of the highest rates you see.

Step Four: Offer to Pay Cash

As I've mentioned, assuming that you have a sizable deductible or no insurance, you might be able to negotiate a steep discount by paying cash to providers and hospitals. Let's say a radiologist normally charges $1,000 for an ultrasound scan but usually accepts 60 percent of his asking price from an insurance plan, or $600. He's really not losing a penny if he takes $600 from you, and he might accept $500 on the spot to avoid the usual hassle of waiting months for the insurer to pay him.

In addition, some providers routinely accept 50 percent to 80 percent of their asking prices, and others take as little as 10 percent if they believe that is all that the patient can afford.

However, do not expect providers to volunteer that they discount their prices. You'll have to raise the subject and then negotiate.

Among hospitals, the trend of negotiating for cash stems in

part from new state and federal rules aimed at protecting uninsured patients from price gouging. Under the ACA, for example, not-for-profit hospitals cannot charge needy patients much more than Medicare would have paid them.

A billing professional at a Utah health center spoke for many hospital pros when she told me, "There is a new attitude here. Any amount of money we accept from you is money that didn't walk across the street to our competitors."

Step Five: Proceed with Caution

Let's assume you've done everything right leading up to, say, your back operation. You have worked with your insurer to identify a few qualified network surgeons and focused on the one who impressed you the most when you interviewed him. You also have a clear idea of what he'll charge and what you'll owe him.

That's good. But you're not done yet. You still need to guard against huge financial risks by quizzing the surgeon about other doctors who might be treating you while you are hospitalized, including the anesthesiologist and the assistant surgeon.

The *New York Times* put a spotlight on surgeons who bring in out-of-network assistants who sometimes charge forty times or more than the in-network rate—and often collect every penny.

Peter Drier, a thirty-seven-year-old bank technology manager, checked carefully with his insurer before his neck surgery in 2013. He knew he'd have to pay around $3,400 for his in-network surgeon and the anesthesiologist to cover his deductible. But his insurer had agreed to pick up the rest of their bills. In all, the network surgeon figured to collect about $6,400.

Yet despite Drier's planning, he was blindsided by a bill for $117,000 from an assistant surgeon he didn't recall ever meeting.

It's common for doctors to call in others to assist them with patients. But the widening gulf between in-network and out-of-network fees has turned this common practice into a thorny trap for trusting patients. Hospitalized patients—and not only those sedated on a gurney—usually have no idea whether the unfamiliar doctors checking in on them are in their provider network, or even who asked them to assist. Yet the out-of-network doctors can bill rates that dwarf the network charges. No one should be surprised that sometimes the big-billing assistant shares the big bucks he collects with the network doctor who brought him in. The *Times* called the arrangement "drive-by doctoring."

Some unethical doctors and hospitals are also gouging patients in other ways:

- Doctors perform services a nurse could handle and bill the higher rates.
- Doctors exaggerate how much care they actually provided and bill insurers with medical codes that pay more—a ploy called upcoding.
- Two doctors bill for a procedure that one could do.
- Hospitals call in out-of-network doctors to provide services a network doctor could perform.
- Hospitals make extra money by outsourcing services they once provided at no extra cost.
- An increasing number of in-network hospitals now staff their emergency rooms with out-of-network doctors who bill separately.

So much gaming of the system goes on that Howard A. Corwin, a former clinical professor at Tufts University School of Medicine, concluded, "There is widespread dishonesty that leads to unjustified expenses throughout the medical profession." He added, "Honest doctors are demoralized and suffer from this system."

Unfortunately, hospitals that join insurance networks are rarely required to provide only in-network doctors, laboratory testing, or X-rays. For example, Drier's Lenox Hill Hospital in

New York City sent his blood to an out-of-network laboratory for testing and arranged for a $950 EKG that commonly costs half that amount—or as little as $50 to $100 in area clinics.

Drier, by the way, refused to pay what he considered the assistant surgeon's "illegal and immoral bill." And his insurer paid the entire $117,000.

Here are five things you can do to try to protect yourself from drive-by doctoring.

- **Get It in Writing.** If you are about to be hospitalized for surgery or for an extensive procedure, ask your doctor's billing office for a written estimate of what you might be billed, including the names of the assisting physicians and their likely billing codes. Then check with your insurer to make sure the assistants are in network, or at least that they have agreed to charge reasonable fees.

  Asking for a written estimate is a reasonable request. In return, in our litigious society, you might have to assure the doctor in writing that you understand that you are getting only an estimate of his services and that he has your approval to do whatever might become medically necessary.

  Ask for a clear worst-case cost limit. Stress to your doctor that you have two goals, aside from a successful outcome: First, to reach a shared decision about the care you need, including the help of any assistants; and second, to guard yourself against surprise bills.

- **Complain to Your Insurer.** If the doctor you want refuses to give you a reasonable estimate up front, report that to your insurer. Your insurer should be willing to help you negotiate with the doctor or assist in finding another qualified provider. In the end, the insurer doesn't want to get stuck negotiating a doctor's surprise bills either.

- **Avoid Hospitals That Staff Their Emergency Rooms with Out-of-Network Doctors.** Plan ahead. Assume that when you least expect it, you or your jungle-gym-climbing kid will need to be rushed to the emergency room. When circumstances allow you to choose, you want to go to the nearby emergency room staffed by doctors in your health plan, rather than one operated by out-of-network contractors with out-of-sight fees. A study in Texas showed that half of the hospitals with United HealthCare, Humana, and Blue Cross Blue Shield—the state's three biggest insurers—had no in-network emergency room doctors.

That's bad. And nationally, it's worse. According to some estimates, 65 percent of all hospitals now contract out their emergency rooms.

- **Go to Hospitals Where Every Provider Is in Network.** Robert Devlin of Bronxville, New York, was worried that some providers of his upcoming surgery would not be in his health plan. He checked with his hospital and was relieved to learn that since NewYork-Presbyterian Hospital was in his insurance plan, by hospital policy, everyone who took care of him was also in network. So before you go in, ask if your hospital is as generous to its patients as NewYork-Presbyterian—the nation's largest nonprofit hospital.

- **Know Your Rights.** There ought to be a national law, like there is in Australia, guaranteeing that patients are told what they should expect to be charged before they are hospitalized.

    In addition, more states should follow New York and pioneer laws eliminating surprise bills. Under New York's "Emergency Medical Services and Surprise Bills" law enacted in 2015, if the hospital is in your plan's network, you only have to pay network rates, even when out-of-network providers treat you, including in the ER. Patients are protected from surprises, including in an emergency when they might be incoherent on a gurney.

Also, if you are uninsured, the provider must tell you the estimated amount he intends to bill you and get your okay—

provided you ask him for that information. In addition, he must identify any out-of-network assistants he plans to call in, such as anesthesiologists, pathologists, and assistant surgeons. And the uninsured do not have to pay "excessive" ER bills.

In short, under New York law, you can't be billed at out-of-network rates unless you sign off on them when someone shoves a stack of paperwork in your face. So always study those hospital waivers carefully before you sign.

CHAPTER 18

If You Go to the Hospital, Don't Pay the Bill

Nine Ways to Save Money at the Hospital

A friend of mine had heartburn. Only she didn't realize that. She rushed to the emergency room fearing a heart attack. One thing led to another, and after she was finally diagnosed accurately and released, the hospital handed her a bill for $93,000.

"The bill almost gave me a heart attack," said the woman, who asked not to be identified. "I'm uninsured and middle class. I don't have that kind of money. What can I do?"

By now you may have heard that up to 80 percent of hospital bills contain errors and 50 percent—*one-half*—have significant mistakes. So if you get a $93,000 bill for heartburn, or anything like it, think of that amount as no more than the hospital's opening asking price. Then don't pay anything until you play that popular game Let's Make a Deal.

While you're staring at your otherworldly hospital bill, take some comfort in knowing that you have more options than you might realize, depending on your income and where you live.

First off, you might live in one of the eight states that has capped the amount hospitals can bill the uninsured by 2016.

The best of the laws call for "Medicare equivalency": Hospitals are prohibited from billing uninsured middle-class families more than what they would accept from Medicare.

In California, for example, hospitals generally can't bill you more than Medicare rates if you make less than 350 percent of the federal poverty level—around $40,000 for individuals and $80,000 for families of four. In Illinois, the cutoff is 300 percent to 600 percent. That top figure works out to easily more than $125,000 for a family of four, depending on whether the patient went to a reasonable rural hospital or a pricey big-city facility.

Other generous states include Connecticut, Maryland, and New Jersey. Your state, particularly if it's blue, might have a version of this law or assistance programs protecting families making around 350 percent of the poverty level.

In addition, an IRS provision bars the six out of ten of all hospitals that are nonprofit facilities from billing the uninsured more than they generally bill the insured. And some sympathetic hospitals cover Medicare's $1,288 Part A deductible for people who can't afford to pay it.

If possible, well before you go to the hospital for, say, a scheduled surgery or to deliver a baby, check on what financial assistance is available by meeting with your hospital's ombudsman: Yes, the facility should have a person on staff looking out for the patients' welfare. Do not start with the billing department; staffers there often get paid mainly to collect money.

Explain your financial situation in detail during your face-to-face with the ombudsman. Bring along any pay stubs or tax returns that might help make your case. Even if there is no state aid program available to you, you might be able to work out a deep discount or at least arrange a payment plan that makes sense for you. In fact, you might find that your hospital is surprisingly reasonable. Many hospitals would rather work out an agreement up front rather than chase after people for months or years to get paid.

On the other hand, let's assume you didn't negotiate in advance, and you get a surprise bill—like the $23,000 bombshell another friend of mine got in 2015 from a suburban New York hospital for an ordinary colonoscopy that often costs around $3,000, tops.

If your hospital slaps you in the head like that, especially if you've been hospitalized for a day or more, request a fully itemized bill that reflects each of your charges. Many hospitals lump charges under a single heading with an ambiguous name. This style of "bundled" billing can hide improperly billed items and allow honest mistakes to go unnoticed. Itemized bills rip the cover off complex bills and reveal each item and its cost. You have the right to get a fully itemized bill.

Once you have it, you should spot any obvious nonsense, like the laughable $160 charge for a warm blanket or repeated $12 charges for the hospital's "mucus recovery system"—tissues.

But chances are you'll be staring at page after page of billing codes and cryptic descriptions that you don't fully understand. For instance, patients in an operating room are billed anywhere from $60 to $200 a minute depending on the procedure, so you need to confirm that you're paying for the right procedure. Also, hospitals often mistakenly charge two or three times for the same item. For instance, you might be getting billed in the operating room for a "surgical kit and tray" and then double-billed for a "knife or other instruments." Or you might be billed $149 for the magnetic pad holding the instruments, which is a little like a mechanic charging you for his toolbelt.

With some luck, if the errors you find are honest mistakes, you might get the charges dropped with one call to the billing department. However, if the situation begins to drag on, or there's a lot of money at stake, you probably would be wise to hire an expert to review the bill with you.

Your primary care doctor, or someone in her office, might agree to help. Or you can turn to one of the thousand or so health care advocates, one of the country's fastest-growing cottage industries. In my opinion, the leading firms include the following:

- Patty Stone at Stone Ortenberg Support, in Menlo Park, California, helped pioneer the field back in 1992 (www .stoneortsupport.com or 1-650-323-0216).
- Pat Palmer at Medical Billing Advocates of America, in Salem, Virginia, is another longtime consumer adviser and a mentor to many advocates (www.billadvocates.com or 1-855-203-7058).
- Katalin Goencz at MedbillsAssist in Stamford, Connecticut, provides help with claims, insurance choices, and other medical concerns (www.medbillsassist.com or 1-203-569-7610).
- Jane Cooper at Patient Care, headquartered in Milwaukee, serves corporate and individual clients across the country (www.patientcare4you.com or 1-414-271-1790).

Depending on the complexity of your bill, figure that you would pay roughly $100 an hour or one-third of the discount your advocate gets for you. Whatever the fee, if you are dealing with a stubborn billing team at the hospital, you almost certainly will come out ahead by being represented by a professional.

Advocates say they usually find enough errors and raise enough questions to cut a big bill by anywhere from 10 percent to 50 percent.

Candace Butcher of Medical Billing Advocates, for example, rattled off one case of overcharges and billing errors that would have cost a client tens of thousands. One client went to the ER with a head injury and was sent home with a bill for $45,199— including $13,017 in erroneous charges. Astoundingly, $10,022 was for a trauma team that was never called in.

Or how about this doozy? A birth with complications billed at $332,085 contained $128,328 in overcharges—mostly for *routine* supplies, services, and equipment.

Even when you've negotiated up front, the bill can go wrong, as it did for a mother I'm calling Shyla, from San Francisco. As her delivery date neared, she and her husband double-checked that both her ob-gyn and the hospital, California Pacific Medical Center, were in their Anthem health plan network. But after her difficult delivery, when the last thing she needed was more stress, she started getting surprise bills for $55,000. The reason? The bills stated that California Pacific was actually *out* of network.

More than two months later, after hours spent trying to reach someone helpful at Anthem, and preparing to go to court if necessary, a letter arrived from Anthem, confirming that all the charges would be covered at in-network rates. The $55,000 was just a billing error. Shyla's family owed only about $1,200.

But the experience took a toll on the new mother. "It's been so, so stressful," Shyla said. "We just felt so helpless."

On the other hand, Shyla might have avoided headaches by hiring an advocate. One advocate told me, "Sometimes it's so easy for me to get a fifty percent discount, I almost feel guilty charging the patient a fee."

SHOULD YOU SUE?

Probably not, unless you run into horrendous circumstances and see no other comparable solution. For example, imagine that you got misdiagnosed years earlier and you now face late-stage cancer, along with the bills for your inadequate care. Lawyers say that is exactly what happened to Elissa McMahon at New York's Lenox Hill Hospital.

In 2012, the Boston-area social worker was told she needed surgery to remove a fibroid—an abnormal but commonly benign growth near her uterus. She decided to have the surgery at Lenox Hill. Staffers there reassured her that her tests came back negative for cancer.

But two years later, her back pain was so severe that she went to an emergency room. Scans soon showed that she had a large tumor on her spine and cancerous lesions in her liver. Moreover, a Dana-Farber Cancer Center oncologist in Boston told her that 25 percent of Lenox Hill's initial pathology slides revealed evidence of cancer. The Lenox doctors apparently had missed the disease, and now she faced stage 4 uterine cancer as a forty-four-year-old single mother of a teenage son.

McMahon decided to sue. "I'm dying," she said, "and I have nothing for [my son] Jack."

And here's where the tale gets darker and shows that suing is never an easy road.

McMahon soon learned that the statute of limitations to sue had expired a few months *before* she learned she was sick, let alone before she was initially misdiagnosed. Since New York is one of only six states that lack a so-called date of discovery law, patients must sue no later than two and a half years after the medical mistake *occurs*, rather than the more logical date that a patient *learns* that the mistake was made.

McMahon and her attorneys are pushing for long-shot changes in the state law, called Lavern's Law, named for forty-one-year-old Lavern Wilkinson, who died in 2013 when Kings County Hospital misdiagnosed her lung cancer. By the time that Brooklyn mother sued, like McMahon, the window to sue had slammed shut.

The Lavern bill passed the New York Assembly, supported by democratic Governor Andrew Cuomo in 2015, but died in the Republican-controlled Assembly, where it appeared to be languishing in 2016 as well.

The Lesson. If you have good reasons to believe you have grounds to sue, do not waste time. Even in the best of circumstances, suits tend to drag on as cases become more complex and you face the prospect of your health deteriorating and your resources dwindling. Filing a lawsuit can be like enlisting for war; make sure you're prepared for the battle—or seek a less all-consuming option, like signing up a tough patient advocate to fight for you.

NINE TIPS TO SAVE MONEY IN THE HOSPITAL

On average, expect to be billed around $4,500 a day in 2016. Figure you'll be charged for every minute you're hospitalized, plus for each doctor consultation, facility fee, test, service, Band-Aid, yummy meal, and Kleenex. So, if you land in the hospital, your goal should be to make your stay as efficient as possible—and get out as quickly as your recovery allows. Here are nine sensible tips:

1. **Don't Demand More Care Than You Need.** Which is another way of saying, Don't play doctor and drive up your bill unnecessarily by 20 percent or more. As much as you can, come to joint decisions with your doctors about each test, scan, and procedure. But back off if the doctor insists that something you suggest is not necessary medically.

2. **Bring Your Own Medicines.** You'll get slammed for every pill from the hospital pharmacy. But in my experience, the hospital will usually allow you to bring pills from home that you take regularly to control, say, your cholesterol, blood pressure, back pain, and so on. By the way, you run a better chance of getting an okay if you bring them with you and then ask for permission to take them.

3. **Also, Bring Your Own Medical Equipment.** For example, your cane, walker, wheelchair, or even your CPAP machine. Hospital technicians will check, but if they decide your CPAP is delivering the right continuous positive airway pressure to control your sleep apnea, you'll save money in your sleep, compared to renting the facility's machine.

4. **Don't Chat with the Doctor.** The longer you talk to him, the more he can bill you. Discuss your condition as thor-

oughly as you both want—but not the New York Mets pitching staff.

While I was captive in a hospital bed, a partner covering for one of my specialists tried to engage me in a discussion of his neighborhood's many flying insects in an absurdly obvious attempt to prolong his "consultation" and inflate his fee. I cut him short, partly to save money but mainly because he was so damned boring.

5. **Schedule Your Surgery Early in the Week.** Light weekend staffs can force you and your doctor to wait hours, if not days, for lab results and other important services that might be essential for your recovery.

6. **Ask Your Surgeon If He's Planning to Operate on You and Someone Else at the Same Time.** Some surgeons do that. Doubling up on long, complicated operations might be cost-effective for the surgeon, but it can prolong your time in the operating room—which in effect you are renting by the minute. Obviously, get a straight answer before you schedule the surgery. If he is doubling up, get his assurance in writing that it won't affect your operation.

7. **Make a Record of Your Care as Best You Can.** If you're like me, you won't remember half of what the nurses and doctors tell you while you're hospitalized. You *are* sick, after all.

   Forget about trying to keep a daily journal; that requires far more concentration than you're likely to have. Instead, ask your mate or a close friend to take notes during consultations when they're around.

   Also, if you are alone and have a smartphone, tape record important discussions, especially your discharge instructions. I like the app TapeACall.

8. **Get Copies of All Your Test Results Before You Head Home.** In addition to wanting them for your personal medical records, they'll come in handy to check any surprise charges.

9. **Try to Get Out a Day or Two Early.** Ask what the staff expects you to do before they feel they can safely discharge you, such as getting up and down the hall without a walker or climbing a flight of stairs. Then build up to the tasks.

You can save thousands by getting out ahead of schedule. But don't push it, like I did.

During a hospitalization a couple of years ago, the physical therapist wanted to see me walk the hall with ease two days in a row. The first day, I breezed through. But the second day, I had to force myself to maintain my pace. Of course, with my stubborn overachiever tendencies no doubt inherited from my maternal Neapolitan grandmother, I didn't tell him I was straining.

I got discharged a day early, but I felt lousy and slept most of my first day at home. The next day, I was back in the hospital running a high fever, and I stayed hospitalized for three more days before I recovered completely.

Lesson learned, and now lesson shared: Risking your health is never smart, no matter your genetic bent.

HOW TO GET TO THE HOSPITAL WITH LESS FINANCIAL PAIN

Before she became a savvy consumer advocate, Sareatha Boothe of Milwaukee remembers calling an ambulance for her son, who was suffering a severe asthma attack. He needed oxygen immediately, and he got it. The ambulance ended up driving two blocks to the nearest ER. Boothe's bill: more than $1,500.

"When it's your child in an emergency," she said, "you don't think to get a network ambulance. You just want to get to the ER fast."

No matter how healthy you feel today, you should be prepared to be transported to the hospital you prefer, at a reasonable cost, if you fall down tomorrow. An ambulance ride can cost from $150 in network to upward of $4,000 out of network. And emergency room visits run from $1,200 to $10,000 and up. Obviously, a smart plan to get to the right hospital can save you hundreds, if not thousands of dollars—and preserve your well-being as well.

Look at your refrigerator door. If you don't see the telephone numbers of your health insurer's in-network ambulance service and the highest-rated network hospital posted there, or someplace nearby, you need to get that information from your health insurance today and keep it handy.

Of course, in any true emergency, call 911. The dispatcher will send the closest ambulance, and you'll be rushed to the nearest hospital for the urgent attention you need. Never risk your health just to save money.

But otherwise, assuming you are up to it, you can ask the in-network ambulance team you've called to take you to the network hospital you want. Emergency workers are trained to speed you to the nearest hospital. But generally, they have the authority to take you to another hospital if the longer trip won't endanger you.

If you live in a suburban or rural area, your local ambulance service might be run by volunteers who'll accept whatever your health plan pays, plus perhaps a modest fee of around $25 a ride or a subscription charge of $35 a year. And in some towns, a volunteer service might be free of charge. A volunteer adult and student program in Darien, Connecticut, for example, is said to be one of four services that relies heavily on student volunteers. The free emergency service is funded largely by donations from grateful town residents.

Also, ambulance industry experts say you should avoid private ambulance services that solicit your business. Not only might their emergency service be substandard, they generally will bill you for much more than your insurance pays.

"The cost can be several thousand dollars," said Jane Cooper, the health care advocate, "and the bill can be very unexpected."

Not all ambulance rides go to a hospital. For example, immobile patients need transportation to treatment centers or from one nursing facility to another. In those cases, be sure to ask your insurer what documentation it needs to justify the service. If your plan requires a formal preauthorization, you will have to get a doctor's note explaining the medical necessity for the rides. Depending on where you live and your condition, your health plan might cover an ambulance, a wheelchair van, or perhaps an ordinary taxi.

If you can, pin down costs with your health plan ahead of time, no matter the type of transport you need, to avoid hassles like this one:

One of patient advocate Patty Stone's clients couldn't walk after a serious car accident and needed rides to and from a rehabilitation clinic. She used ten ambulance transits. At first, her insurer, Cigna, refused to pay for any of the rides. Then it paid for some trips fully and others at a discount. But when it came time for the last session, Cigna said *all* the rides should have been preauthorized and demanded that Stone's client pay around $33,000.

Stone pushed back hard, and after eighteen months of wrangling, Cigna paid all but about $1,000.

One Last Note on Medicare. Medicare generally covers ambulance services, including for emergencies, scheduled treatment, and even air evacuation, if the transportation is deemed necessary for the patient's health. The coverage falls under Part B and is subject to deductibles and copays.

As it does for hospitals and physicians, Medicare publishes a schedule of charges. But as you would expect, it is dizzyingly complex. If you need a straight answer, call the Medicare help desk at 1-800-Medicare.

CHAPTER 19

If You Get Bad Medical News
Follow This Positive Action Plan

For Frank Pasquini, a newly retired fund-raiser for nonprofits, the bad news came in threes. He was admitted to a hospital for testing when he returned home to Wilkes-Barre, Pennsylvania, from a well-earned vacation at the New Jersey Shore complaining of sharp abdominal pain. His test results hit him like a series of hammer blows: He was diagnosed with colon cancer, followed quickly with prostate and bone cancers.

"All this was cooking in me for a while," Pasquini said. The diagnoses led to an intensive month of surgeries and treatment, plus continuing care that included chemotherapy. More than a year later, in late 2015, he said he was happy to have survived: "I'm lucky to be vertical."

What's more, his recent scans were good, and his doctors had starting calling him "a walking miracle."

Still, he was frustrated about how his cancer had derailed his life. "The status quo is totally acceptable," he said. "But I can't wait to get back in circulation."

After the initial shock began to wear off, Pasquini had to grapple with the vexing questions that people must face when they get news of serious illness:

- How do I find the care that gives me the best chance to survive?

239

- What will my illness mean to my family?
- Who should I tell—and not tell?
- Will I be able to keep working?
- Can I pay the bills?
- What if I don't recover?

Fortunately, there are many resources to help you meet each of the challenges. But I'm not going to kid you. I know from my experience with my treatable but not (yet) curable blood cancer, multiple myeloma, that you need all the support you can muster from your family, your doctors, your friends, your employer, and myriad health care professionals. Some of these people will be as close to you as caring social workers at your nearby hospital or as distant from you as script-reading bureaucrats at your health insurer and, sadly, occasionally at Medicare as well.

EVERYONE GETS SCARED

Although I'd known for months that I might have multiple myeloma lurking in my bloodstream, when my oncologist phoned me while I was on business in London in 2008 with the confirmation that I did, in fact, have the cancer, the news staggered me. I thought I had gotten my death sentence.

Other people I've talked to who've been diagnosed with serious illnesses have used the same death penalty metaphor. But I'll be damned. None of us can remember the crime we committed.

Carol Vanstory, an oncology social worker at the Geisinger Health System in Danville, Pennsylvania, said that bad medical news can carry the same impact as the sudden death of a beloved relative. "I think at some point," she said, "everybody gets scared."

I was literally shaking for days after I received my diagnosis. I was scheduled to attend an all-day business summit chaired by our new *Reader's Digest* CEO, and I told my doctors that I had no idea how I could get through the meeting. One prescribed Neurontin. That morning, with no time to test its effect on me, I popped one. Maybe two. Suddenly, instead of being scared, I was jovial. I had cancer. And I couldn't stop smiling.

The CEO didn't know me well enough to judge my mood. But after the meeting, one of my close colleagues asked me if I was okay. "You were downright giddy in there," she said, looking at me strangely. "That's not like you."

I never took another happy pill. Instead, I tried to focus on the positive.

New York psychoanalyst Louise Fay observed that, following the initial shock of a dire diagnosis, people tend to revert to who they are at their core. "If you're a fighter," she said, "you vow to beat the cancer. If you tend to deny and delay, you may put off treatment. And if you're a positive person, you try to find a way to stay as positive as possible.

"The disease doesn't define you," she said, "you define it."

Since I had a trusted primary care doctor and oncologist, as well as a close physician friend, I was luckier than most people in those early days. I called them constantly to help me tiptoe away from despair. Even more importantly, I had the love of my close-knit family: my wife and best friend of over fifty years and our two terrific daughters, beloved son-in-law, and our two fantastic grandsons to get me through this initial fears-and-tears period.

Up or down, I have never shed a tear over getting cancer. That is a bad break in a life of phenomenally great breaks, led by falling for my sweetheart Carole Danese at nineteen and marrying her at twenty-two, when I was making $74 a week as a newspaper reporter. Her mother, who had big-city dreams for her intelligent daughter, nearly drowned in her tears in the first pew of St. Joseph Church in Bogota, New Jersey, and I have the wedding pictures to prove it.

I know who I am. I am a proud, hard-charging family man who isn't afraid to laugh at myself. And I've got a life story to prove it.

One Christmas, when I was the editor of Time Inc.'s *Money* magazine, Carole and I were invited to President Clinton's White House holiday party. My amazing assistant beat the other company mucky-mucks to The Hay-Adams' hotel suite with the best direct view of the White House. I got fitted for a tux, and Carole bought a smashing gown. As we were about to head down to our shiny black limo for our six-minute ride to the White House, I couldn't resist bragging:

"When you married me at twenty-two in Bogota, New Jersey, did you ever think in your wildest dreams that someday I would take you to meet the president and first lady of the United States?"

Carole said: "Frank, when I married you, I wasn't thinking."

We laughed all the way to the White House.

Social worker Vanstory said that most people cope reasonably well with serious illness and preserve their senses of humor, provided they stay grounded through their inner strength and solid outside support. The support can come from many sources, starting with the patients' loved ones, but also from others facing similar challenges. Hundreds of organizations, such as Cancer Care and the American Heart Association, offer online groups, workshops, and referrals to help patients meet one another and share experiences.

Vanstory stresses that nearly everyone gets past the initial feelings of despondency and despair. Once your shock begins to fade, find the ways that lift your mood—and then focus on getting your best care.

FINDING YOUR RIGHT CARE

When you get really bad medical news, you sometimes need to ask how much time you have to plan your care. Again, I was more fortunate than some. My doctors in New York told me I had six months or more before I would have to begin some form of chemo. That gave me plenty of time to zero in on Dr. Kenneth Anderson at Boston's Dana-Farber Cancer Institute, one of the world's multiple myeloma experts. However, it wasn't at all clear that he was accepting new patients.

I called Dr. Anderson's office cold and introduced myself to his assistant, Lisa Popitz.

"I'm Frank Lalli. I have multiple myeloma, and I'd like Dr. Anderson to accept me as a patient."

Lisa said, "Are you . . . Frank Lalli?"

I said, "Yes, I'm Frank Lalli."

"Are you *the* Frank Lalli?" she asked.

Not many people have ever asked me that.

I said, "I'm not sure."

"Are you the Frank Lalli who was the editor of *George* magazine?"

I said, "Yes." I edited *George*, the magazine about politics and power founded by John Kennedy Jr., between my years at Time Inc. and *Reader's Digest*.

She said, "*George* was my favorite magazine. I am so pleased to meet you. Now tell me again exactly what you would like me to do for you."

A week later, Carole and I were at Dana-Farber, sitting across from Dr. Anderson, the most charming Irish elf you could ever meet at the end of a rainbow.

"I am your doctor," he said. "You can call me anytime with a question or a concern." Since then, he has gotten back to me almost immediately, including today (as I write this), when he reached me within two hours to tweak my medications.

Don't Delay

With his stomach pain and spreading cancer, Frank Pasquini knew "time was of the essence." He relied on his family doctor to quickly assemble a team, including an oncologist, urologist, and surgeon. "You're putty in their hands," he said. "I was totally reliant on their skill, energy, and knowledge—and they saved my life."

Although our experiences differed, our stories underscore the importance of always having a primary care physician you trust and then becoming a Health Care Detective to find the specialists you need.

"Everyone should have a PCP [primary care physician] who really is your trusted medical adviser," said patient advocate Jane Cooper of Patient Care.

In a crisis, you need a frontline doctor you respect. That's the reason many experts urge patients to keep shopping for a family doctor until you find one you can talk to openly and who listens. Relatives and friends might have suggestions, and so will your health plan. In some cases, your insurer might require you to choose a network PCP. Still, don't rush. Get at least three names, and ask to interview each one. Forgive the melodrama, but act as if your life depends on picking your best medical partner, because someday it might.

Finding the right specialist can be even more challenging, since you need to drill down to identify the most qualified board-certified physician or surgeon—one with documented peer-reviewed experience in the specific procedure or treatment you need. That means a panel of the top physicians in their field have reviewed the doctor's record and certified their excellence.

That sort of expertise can be prohibitively expensive. To avoid nasty surprise bills, start your search within your health plan's provider network. Don't limit yourself to local physicians; check for experienced physicians at large medical centers and teaching hospitals at the forefront of medical research, preferably within driving distance. If a specialist you like is out of network, you might be responsible for double the charges, but getting truly top-notch care can be well worth the expense.

As I touched on above, consider only physicians who are board certified by top experts to treat your specific condition.

"That is absolutely critical," said Dr. John J. Connolly, CEO of Castle Connolly Medical, publisher of the guidebook *America's Top Doctors.*

The certification for, say, cardiology or pain management means that the physician has not only received extra training in his specialty but also has been judged and endorsed by fellow experts. As a result, certification in any field is a world away from a doctor calling himself a specialist, or "self-certifying," as far too many doctors do.

"People don't realize it," said Connolly, "but once a doctor is licensed in any state, he can call himself any kind of specialist he wants."

As I said, you can check credentials at the American Board of Medical Specialties website (www.certificationmatters.org). Try entering the city of the physician's main hospital affiliation; his office address might not help you locate him. You also can call the ABMS at 1-866-ASK-ABMS (275-2267).

Many experts tend to prefer specialists affiliated with major teaching hospitals or academic health centers. In addition to the physician in your field, you potentially would have access to the hospital's other leading specialists if your condition became more complicated and you needed the care of a tight-knit multidisciplinary team.

And, of course, check the physician's disciplinary history. "That can help you avoid the real bad actors," Connolly said.

For example, on the Minnesota Board of Medical Practice website, users can search doctors by name and see a detailed profile that includes disciplinary actions as well as education, training, and experience. In addition, California and some other states include disciplinary actions on a physician's licensing information.

The fastest and easiest way to find this information is through an online search using the term "medical disciplinary action" and the physician's name and state. You also can go to a state's main website and look for the Medical Board or Board of Medicine. Some state websites are easier to navigate than others, so you might have to poke around to pin down the report you want. But it's worth the extra effort to rule out a questionable doctor.

Once you find the physician, experts note that you should not be alarmed if your relationship with your specialist differs from what you have with your family doctor. If you are dealing with a chronic condition such as Crohn's disease or diabetes, you may well want a similar level of intimacy. But good rapport might not be so important if you want the best neurosurgeon to remove a benign brain tumor—hopefully a onetime event.

Experts estimate that 95 percent of people stay with the specialists their primary doctors recommended. But Dr. Patrick Lee of the Lynn Community Health Center in Massachusetts warned that such a level of trust can be a mistake. He said flatly, "Folks sometimes feel stuck after getting a referral." He added that if you have any concerns, always go back to your family doctor, talk through your worries, and, if need be, ask for more names.

As you weigh your choices, Connolly advised, you should keep looking until you book the very best specialist you can. "Nobody wants second best in health care," he said.

WHO SHOULD YOU TELL—AND NOT TELL

Dr. Katie Grimm, a palliative care consultant in Buffalo, New York, said patients should resist the temptation to hide their distress from family members. "Patients work very hard to protect their families from what they know," she said. At the same time, family members hide their emotions in an effort to protect one another. Communication breaks down, and everyone feels worse.

She said it's better for the family to acknowledge the reality of the diagnosis and to face it together. "It's okay to plan for the worst, while always working to recover," she said.

Within our immediate family, we made a decision not to tell anyone about my cancer until I had completed my four-month drug regimen, and I could assure everyone that the worst was behind me for years to come. Why should anyone worry about me more than they needed to? I didn't even tell my brother in Chicago.

When I began making the calls, one family member and friend after another expressed shock at the news. But they said they understood why I had kept my illness secret and supported my decision.

Only one friend disappointed me deeply. She was insulted.

"How could you be a friend of mine for forty years and not tell me about this?" she said loudly and angrily. "I know everything about multiple myeloma. I could have gotten you to the right doctor."

Suddenly my cancer was all about her. She was angry with me because, at my most vulnerable period, I didn't put her at the center of my life next to my immediate family and didn't feed her self-important image of herself.

I hung up on that friendship.

Pasquini, who also has a tight family network, received an outstanding amount of support from friends and former colleagues. Three friends from work organized a "retirement" party through social media that attracted two hundred people and raised enough for the railings, hospital bed, and other items he needed at home while he recovered.

"I'm still semi-homebound," Pasquini said. "Phone calls from friends mean an awful lot to me."

While no one doubts that patients deserve support, experts note that too often the closest family caregivers are left to deal with their fears and frustrations alone. It's often helpful for caregivers to attend support group meetings to learn more about their loved one's illness and possible treatments, and, perhaps as importantly, to exchange ideas with other people facing the same challenges.

People can find support programs as nearby as a local social service agency or through online sites, including the website of the National Alliance for Caregiving (www.caregiving .org).

OBLIGATIONS AT WORK

After my diagnosis, I asked an attorney I respect deeply a straightforward question: Now that I have cancer, what are my obligations to my company, and what are its obligations to me?

He did some research and called the next day. "As long as you can do your job, you have no obligation to tell your employer anything," he said. "But at the moment that you feel you can't do your job, you should inform the company. And from then on, the company has an obligation to support you."

Years later I ran into the *Reader's Digest* CEO. The first thing she blurted out was that she had no idea I was ill during the eighteen months I worked for her.

On a grander scale, legendary musical artist David Bowie told very few people that he was dying of cancer. Even after he died in 2016—two days after releasing his twenty-fifth album, on his sixty-ninth birthday—his advisers declined to confirm the type of cancer (liver) that had taken his life in only eighteen months. Yet he fully informed the key producers of his 2015 Off-Broadway musical, *Lazarus*, which, by the way, reflected his state of mind: the show is named for the biblical character that Jesus raised from the dead.

Back here on earth, around one-third of people with incurable cancers continue to work. Yet newly diagnosed workers in particular often face thorny issues, depending on how supportive their employers are; generally, the bigger the firm, the more likely that it has helpful HR policies. For example, many workers hesitate to ask for time off for treatment for fear they will lose their jobs. Skipping care, of course, is never a good idea.

Patients can end up in the emergency room with a crisis and big medical bills.

Instead, workers should determine their rights and then ask for fair treatment when necessary. At the very least, under the federal Family and Medical Leave Act (FMLA) you are entitled to twelve weeks of unpaid leave within any twelve-month period if you work for a company with fifty or more employees, or for a public or government agency of any size. During your leave, you can keep your health insurance, although other benefits, such as accruing vacation time, are not guaranteed.

When you return, your employer is required to place you in an "equivalent" job at appropriate pay compared with what you had when you left.

Hopefully, your employer has even more generous policies. For example, you might be able to collect pay for your unused vacation or sick days during at least part of your time away.

Some employer-provided benefit plans include the option to buy short- or long-term disability insurance, which is usually inexpensive and typically pays around half of your average weekly earnings while you are unable to work. However, these policies notoriously might not cover preexisting conditions. Check carefully with your HR department before signing up, or you might pay premiums for nothing.

A loss of earnings can be devastating, especially for people earning hourly wages, who might have limited savings. With the exception of filing for Supplemental Security Income (SSI) or Social Security Disability Insurance (SSDI), Vanstory said, "There's nothing more out there that gives income." If you think you might be eligible, you have nothing to lose but time by applying online for SSDI benefits. Go to the Social Security Administration (SSA) website (www.ssa.gov), click the "Benefits" tab and then "Disability." One more click will show the range of documents you'll need to apply. It's an extensive list that includes details about you, your medical condition, and your work history.

If you're not comfortable filing online, make an appointment with your local Social Security office and bring every one of the necessary materials with you. The staffer considering your application might terminate the interview abruptly if you fail to bring one key scrap of paper.

You must go to a Social Security office to apply for SSI, and you must bring the same array of information you need for a disability application. You can make an appointment to apply for either program by calling 1-800-772-1213.

In addition, there are benefits such as food stamps and cash assistance available, but the programs vary dramatically by state and are often severely limited. In South Carolina, for example, the maximum monthly temporary cash assistance benefit for a family of three was $240 in 2015, while it was $636 in Maryland. South Carolina also imposed a sixty-month lifetime limit for receiving the temporary cash, plus a work requirement that can add a mean-spirited burden on people who are ill.

There also might be limits on how long you could receive food stamps, now under SNAP (Supplemental Nutrition Assistance Program), as well as income and asset limits.

Generally, the assistance programs are administered at the county level, so contact your county social services office for details and help in applying for these and other benefits you might be eligible to get.

PAYING THE BILLS

Headlines about medicines that cost $1,000 a pill and $500,000 operations add stress to families facing whatever might follow a serious diagnosis. No one is immune, even the insured. A study by Duke University and the Dana-Farber Cancer Institute found that cancer patients with insurance faced an average of $712 per month in out-of-pocket costs in 2011—a figure that has surely risen sharply since then, along with the surge in high-deductible plans that suck away your money.

The wife of one cancer patient told me, "Caring for my husband is taking all the emotion and energy I have. I can't deal with bills right now. For the last five months, I've been sticking them in a drawer unopened. So far, nobody is calling us to collect."

Although I have no doubt that she is doing her best, ignoring bills is not wise. Honest negotiation trumps angry confrontation. Experts suggest that you explain your circumstances to your creditors and assure them that you will work with them on a fair outcome in a timely way.

You might say, for instance, that you will be turning to your bills next month after your husband returns home from the hospital. If you describe your circumstances thoroughly and honestly, chances are you will reach an understanding that serves you and your creditors.

The vast majority of doctors and hospitals would much rather work out a payment plan with you than turn bills over to a collection agency that keeps around 50 percent of whatever it recovers.

Having said that, do not hesitate to question any billing items that seem inaccurate. As I've mentioned, if the bill is especially high and the errors egregious, you might want to hire a medical advocate to negotiate for you at around $100 an hour. They can be worth every dollar, since they can sometimes get bills cut by one-third or more with phone calls to, say, a local hospital billing official that the advocate deals with regularly.

However, there is no licensing organization for advocates yet, nor a comprehensive directory. One typical directory website is the ADVO Connection Directory (www.advoconnection.com), but, like others, it and others list only their members. Given the lack of regulation, it's important to ask a number of questions before hiring anyone, such as whether the advocate has health care training; how long she has been an advocate; and whether the aid is limited to negotiating bills, or includes services such as finding your best insurance options or dependable low-cost providers.

One pioneer that I've mentioned is Medical Billing Advocates of America in Virginia, founded in 1997 by Pat Palmer after she struggled to understand her family's medical bills. In addition to serving consumers, MBAA trains others to spot billing errors. Some of those graduates now head their own advocacy firms. You can find them at www.billadvocates.com or call 1-855-203-7058.

When medical bills become overwhelming, some families decide to tell their stories in the media and solicit donations. Supporters can organize charity walks or arrange fund-raising nights at restaurants, with a percentage of sales going to the patient, similar to the retirement event Pasquini's friends held for him. Bear in mind that if you solicit funds, you will need to set up special bank accounts to accept the donations. Your bank will have specific rules about the accounts; someone there can guide you.

Another option is crowdfunding. Instead of telling your story to your local newspaper—or in addition to that—you can post a funding request online at websites such as GiveForward (www.giveforward.com) or GoFundMe (www.gofundme.com), complete with a dollar goal and a completion deadline. There are fees involved, but donors often cover them.

GoFundMe claims that it helps raise $1 billion a year and that medical bills are its top fund-raising campaign. The site's success stories range from raising $14,462 for an injured teacher to $134,205 for a young father reeling from a sudden diagnosis of stage 4 cancer.

REDUCING YOUR FUTURE BILLS

Once you gain control of your most pressing bills, you should turn to cutting the expenses on your horizon, including any astronomical drug costs, costly upcoming procedures, and your health insurance.

With drug prices rising year after year, including 10 percent for 2016, millions of people are seeking financial assistance. Fortunately, there are many places to turn for help with prescription copayments, even if your family brings in more than $100,000 a year. As I've mentioned, one good place to start is the pharmaceutical industry's own patient assistance website, at www.pparx.org.

In addition, among the many nonprofit private foundations, the HealthWell Foundation at www.healthwellfoundation.org or 1-800-675-8416 offers an excellent range of programs. (For more on private foundations, see chapter 14, "Stop Paying Twice as Much for Your Drugs.")

If your doctors are recommending a wonder drug at $1,000 a month—or a higher price that even Donald Trump couldn't afford forever—work with your doctor to appeal to the drug manufacturer for "compassionate care." Or call yourself, at least to get started. A vast majority of drugmakers maintain generous assistance programs. As I've mentioned, thanks to the Celgene company, I was once paying only $25 a month for its Revlimid, while it was retailing for more than $500 a day.

Indeed, the pharmaceutical industry's knee-jerk response to criticism of runaway prices is to brag about how it makes drugs available to patients at a fraction of their retail price. Take the industry at its word—you might catch a big break. (Also see chapter 14 for more on the best and worst of the pharmaceutical industry's patient assistance programs.)

In addition, about half the states have modest State Pharmaceutical Assistance Programs, called SPAP. To find out if your state offers SPAP or similar programs, go to your state department of health website or check with your state representative's office. Unfortunately, you may face severe income limits.

You also might be able to save hundreds, if not thousands, by shopping for services, including MRIs, other scans, and blood work. When Gary Thorne, a fifty-five-year-old auto shop owner in Exeter, Pennsylvania, was diagnosed with multiple myeloma, he realized quickly that his insurance plan's hospitalization did not cover tests. His hospital's "list price" for a midspine MRI with contrast that his doctors ordered was $2,700; hospital staffers offered it to him for $2,100 in cash. But that was still too high for Thorne. He went shopping, first at a freestanding imaging center, which asked for $1,500—nearly half the hospital's list price. Not bad. But he moved on to another independent center and got the MRI for $625—just 23 percent of the original MRI list price and a savings of over $2,000.

Thorne got similar results with a bone X-ray. He paid $75, not the hospital's $400 list price. And the major cancer center where he underwent treatment agreed to a "special price" of $25 for blood work that normally would have cost $250 or more.

With everything seemingly negotiable, Thorne concluded, "Getting a big discount just depends on the facility and how willing they are to work with you."

If you are facing a very costly operation, and your plan has denied coverage or you have no insurance at all, you might want to consider having the operation performed overseas to save tens of thousands of dollars. As I've mentioned, you won't be the only one exploring what's called medical travel. About a million Americans seek care out of the country each year, many of them going to Mexico for oral or cosmetic surgery not covered by their insurance plans, and others to Asia for more pricey procedures such as joint replacement or heart surgery.

A small but growing number of self-insured corporations offer medical travel as a benefit covering 100 percent of the employee's costs, including airfare, lodging, and food for the worker and a companion. In addition, some companies throw in a $5,000 incentive bonus. The companies still come out ahead, because operations overseas at globally accredited hospitals cost roughly half or less of US rates. For example, a hip replacement for a Florida woman cost $11,000 in Malaysia in 2015, including two weeks in a first-rate hotel while she received physical therapy. That operation would have cost about $30,000 here.

If you work for a company with around a thousand or more employees ask your HR department about medical travel overseas as well as domestic travel to a leading out-of-state facility, such as the Cleveland Clinic for heart problems or the Mayo Clinic for cancer treatment. (For more on medical travel, see chapter 6, "How to Keep the Doctor and Hospital You Like."

By the way, one significant factor holding back medical travel: Only one-third of American citizens have passports.

With a couple of smart moves, you also might be able to save money on your health insurance or at least break even while upgrading your coverage. And, remember, thanks to the Affordable Care Act, insurance companies can no longer refuse to cover you because of your condition. That can be a godsend to anyone diagnosed with a chronic illness.

If you are still working and have a company-provided health plan, it's very often best to stick with it. I shopped around after I got my bad medical news but wisely decided to stick with my Time Inc. insurance for as long as I could.

If you aren't working and not yet eligible for Medicare, you might find solid coverage at an affordable price with Obamacare. Don't let high premium list prices or high deductibles scare you off. If you are no longer working regularly, chances are your income is low, and that could help you to qualify for the government's generous premium subsidies and maybe cost-sharing assistance as well. According to a survey by the research firm HealthPocket, around 85 percent of all Obamacare members received premium subsidies in 2015 and, on average, paid only $101 a month. The people who didn't get subsidies averaged $364.

Obamacare open enrollment is from November 1 to January 31. However, if you have a "life event," such as getting laid off and losing your insurance, having a baby, or moving to a new coverage area, you get a sixty-day "special enrollment" window to shop and sign up. To check the rules and compare coverage, go to HealthCare.gov. And yes, the ACA computers are fixed and performing nicely. Or simply call 1-800-318-2596 and speak to a human being who, by the way, gets paid to patiently answer all your questions out of his employer's fat $200 million call-center contract with the government.

Once you are eligible for Medicare, either because you turn sixty-five or become disabled, think carefully before choosing between original Medicare and a private Medicare Advantage plan, as I've noted. Since I have a chronic illness that could create complications at any time, I want access to as many doctors, specialists, and hospitals as possible. In addition, I worry about being hospitalized under an Advantage plan and getting stuck with thousands of dollars of surprise bills. Therefore, I chose original Medicare.

With my original Medicare Parts A, B, and a Medigap Part F supplement plan, I can see any participating doctor anywhere in the country without a formal referral or prior authorization. And remember, 90 percent of doctors and nearly every hospital accept Medicare patients.

Original Medicare is not cheap, however, especially for someone like me who was hospitalized in 2014 and again in 2015. Medicare Part A, which covers in-hospital care, has no monthly premium, but it carried a $1,288 deductible in 2016. Part B, which pays for preventive services, physician charges, and other services, will cost most people an affordable $104.90 a month in 2016, usually deducted directly from their Social Security checks. But if you earn a lot, you pay much more. Couples making more than $214,000 pay nearly four times as much: a fat $389.80 a month.

Plus, you'll have to pay an extra $50 a month or so for Medicare's Part D prescription drug coverage. As I've stressed, shop carefully. Part D plans vary greatly in cost and coverage, since each has its own list of approved drugs at various prices. At the very least, make sure your drugs are included and affordable.

And as I have noted, before you sign up, compare your Part D options head-to-head through Medicare Plan Finder at Medicare.gov.

On top of adding Part D, you'd be wise to buy a Medigap plan to cover "what Medicare doesn't cover," as the Medigap ad that seems to run on a loop on cable TV puts it. Although it's widely believed that Medicare covers 80 percent of its beneficiaries' health costs, experts say the program actually pays 70 percent or less.

If you can afford it, Medicare Supplement Part F offers the most comprehensive benefits, including paying the difference between what a provider charges and the amount Medicare will pay; you get virtually no bills. However, monthly premiums can run from around $150 to $300 or more, depending on where you live. There is a low-premium, high-deductible option available, but those plans boil down to a form of self-insurance. You'd have to shell out more than $2,000 to cover the deductible in 2016 before the plan pays a penny of your medical bills.

My zero-deductible Part F Medigap plan from United HealthCare cost me a little over $140 a month in 2016 after my lump-sum contribution of $1,400 a year from my old employer. I think the insurance is well worth the price for my peace of mind. I know my plan will pay for just about everything that original Medicare doesn't cover.

On the other hand, you can join the one-third of all Medicare beneficiaries and enroll in a private Medicare Advantage plan offered by nearly all the big-name insurance companies, including Humana, Aetna, and United HealthCare. For a relatively low premium or no premium at all, in addition to your Part B hospital premium, you get "all in one" convenience. In addition to hospital and doctor benefits, the vast majority of plans cover prescriptions, and some also offer dental and vision benefits.

By law, Medicare Advantage plans also cap your out-of-pocket expenses at $6,700 in 2016.

As noted, the major drawback is that nearly all Advantage plans offer only providers in a narrow geographic area, sometimes as limited as one county. If you go out of the network for care, perhaps to see an acclaimed specialist halfway across the country, you might have to pay the entire bill. Obviously, that prospect presents too much of a risk for me.

Plus, Advantage plans generally charge you around $250 a day for your first four days in a network hospital before picking up the rest of the tab. By contrast, original Medicare doesn't begin charging its $322-a-day copay until day sixty-one; there is no charge for your first sixty days.

I cannot imagine ever enrolling in a Medicare Advantage plan. I have zero interest even with a zero premium.

One More Important Note. Medigap insurers might not pay for treatment of certain conditions during the first six months in your plan. Before you sign up, check to confirm that each of your conditions is covered from day one. A couple of months without coverage could cost you thousands of dollars.

Finally, if your income and assets get very low, look into Medicaid and the Children's Health Insurance Program. Each state sets its own eligibility limits, from having to live on less than 18 percent of the federal poverty level—which was a merciless $4,365 for a family of four in red states Texas and Alabama in 2015—to 201 percent, which is a comparatively more humane $48,500 for a family of four in blue Connecticut and Washington, DC. In many states, the income limit is 138 percent of the FPL, or $33,465 for a family of four.

ADDRESSING MORTALITY

No question, bad medical news forces you to think about the potential end of your life and what you'll leave behind. But frankly, I haven't dwelled on that, beyond updating my will and carrying a card whenever I leave home that shows I have a living will. I've lived with my chronic cancer for eight years as I write this, and I'm counting on at least eight more.

Victor Thuronyi, a Washington, DC, tax lawyer with a treatable cancer, stressed that anyone with a manageable disease does not need to rush to address end-of-life issues. "You pay more attention when you have a diagnosis like that," said Thuronyi, "but you don't need to do much right away."

He and others note that one thing you should do immediately is set up a health care proxy, so that your wishes about your acute care can be carried out if you're ever unable to communicate or make decisions. "You should have a living will, as well as a durable power of attorney," he said. "If you're delirious, and some medical action needs to be taken, those documents can be critical."

Ideally, with the help of an estate lawyer, start by completing the "advance directive," also called the living will. In that document, define exactly what care you will and will not accept if your illness becomes terminal or you have a serious complication or a catastrophic accident.

Estate lawyers commonly charge $1,000 to $2,000 to write a living will. A durable power of attorney can cost another $1,000.

You can create a living will without an attorney. Each state provides a template living will, some in greater detail than others, and there is space to add your own directions. You can find links to forms for all fifty states at the website of the National Hospice and Palliative Care Organization (www.caringinfo.org).

Experts say it is imperative that you add your own thorough instructions. "The forms are never specific enough," said Dr. Grimm. "Go into detail and avoid vague terms like 'I don't want to be a vegetable.'"

Also, keep your living will up to date as your condition and desires evolve. Otherwise, they could end up prescribing instructions that are the opposite of what you want now. "We see forms that were created ten years ago," said Dr. Grimm.

"The best ones reflect changes as the person moves through a disease."

In addition, living wills generally devote a page to granting medical power of attorney to a relative, close friend, or other individual you trust to make decisions for you if you are unable to do so. It's critical that you and that person—in my case, my wife, Carole—discuss your wishes thoroughly and agree completely on what would be done, and not done, for you.

Those conversations are never easy, even smoothed along with a glass of wine. You can get help on how to talk with loved ones at the Conversation Project (www.theconversationproject.org). The advice boils down to this: Start with what's most important to you. Be honest. And be specific.

Dr. Grimm recalled an active eighty-five-year-old who crashed his vehicle. He was on a breathing machine, with a serious head injury and a broken neck. Doctors said he would be a quadriplegic if he survived. But he had never talked with his family about end-of-life care. She said she tried to work with the family to figure out what he would have wanted, but sadly, their disagreements led to more conflict than resolution.

Sharp family disagreements about what to do next are all too common. One hospital chaplain said, "Sometimes, I'm not sure if I'm a spiritual adviser or a referee."

"Without the family conversation ahead of time," said Dr. Grimm, "end-of-life can become awfully difficult."

I agree with Dr. Grimm. In most cases, the family conversation eases end-of-life's emotional decisions. But to be honest, the conversation alone cannot fix fractured families.

At an elegant lunch in Beverly Hills, I was seated next to the wife of a prominent politician. Though I had never met her, when she heard I was writing a book about health care, she said:

"I killed my mother."

"How did you do that?" I asked.

"She was in pain, close to death, and didn't want to go on. One beautiful day last year, she called and said, 'Today's the day.' I drove over, made her as comfortable as possible, and put on her favorite classical music. I fed her the pills we had saved, just as we had planned, and then I sat with her as she slowly and peacefully fell asleep and faded away. She died with dignity; the way she wanted to die."

"What did your family think of her decision?" I asked.

"We didn't tell my sister," she said. "If we had told her, we knew she would have driven over and tried to stop it."

"How does your sister feel now?"

"I'm sure she's still upset," she said. "But we haven't talked since then."

A mother passes, and her two daughters part ways—perhaps forever.

THE PRICE OF HOPE

What would you do if you concluded that your conventional doctors could no longer help you? Would you accept a slow death? Or would you grasp at any therapies, no matter how implausible they might sound, as long as they offered what your current doctors no longer could—the hope of a cure?

Every day educated and intelligent people turn away from their conventional doctors—sometimes even when the physician offers an FDA-approved medicine that might give them another year or two, yet not a cure. Some choose to pay large amounts of money to alternative providers who hold out the hope of reversing their diseases, or even miraculously curing them overnight.

In one case I researched in 2016, a woman I'll call Jan from New Mexico was diagnosed with late-stage cancer in her liver, lymph nodes, and bones. Her oncologist urged her to start chemotherapy immediately. She refused. She said she had watched too many friends and family members waste away miserably on chemo and die anyway.

Instead, she checked into an out-of-state clinic run by a dietician who administered IVs of the essence of two common botanicals (plants), along with other so-called alternative therapies and medicines. The dietician told Jan that her proprietary therapies had "eradicated" malignant cells.

The cost of the treatment was $8,000 to $10,000 a day.

Jan might experience a miracle recovery. But three naturopathic professionals I interviewed doubt it. The officials enforce the standards for naturopathic physicians (NPs)—graduates of accredited naturopathic medical schools in two of the nineteen states that license NPs. Based on their years of supporting the naturopathic movement, the officials said details about the clinic raised a number of red flags that patients should weigh before they sign up for that type of costly alternative care.

The Provider Has Sketchy Credentials. The dietician running the clinic was not a member of the national organization that licenses naturopathic physicians, the American Association of Naturopathic Physicians (AANP). And there were no records of her having taken any of the AANP's licensing exams. In addition, she operates in one of the thirty-one states that do not require licensing for naturopaths; anyone there can call himself or herself a naturopath. Still, she claimed more than twenty specialties, from allergies to yeast syndrome, as well as oncology.

"If she is not a medical doctor," said Anne Walsh, director of Oregon's naturopathic licensing board, "she should not be treating someone with such a serious condition."

The Provider Demands Cash Up Front and Has High Fees. Walsh said that her "fraud antenna twitches" when an alternative provider wants even $500 up front. She called the clinic's $8,000-to-$10,000-a-day fees "ridiculous."

Rebecca Mitchell, who enforces California's naturopathic licensing, added that such "unprofessional fees" could be a sign that the provider is "preying on people who are desperate."

The Provider Claims to Have an Exclusive Medicine. The dietician said a nearby research company was making a medicine exclusively for her that could eradicate cancer cells. "There are no miracle cures," said Walsh.

The Provider Offers No Credible Data to Support Her Success. The dietician stated little more than that she has had "outstanding" results treating cancer.

Both Walsh and Mitchell said that if the clinic were operating in their states, which require strict licensing, they would send an investigator to it immediately and also refer the case to their state's attorney general's office, consumer fraud division. "I'd go after her for criminal prosecution," said Mitchell. "She appears to be practicing medicine without a license."

I'll call the other person looking for hope Giovanni of New Jersey. He has an autoimmune disease called inclusion body myositis (IBM) that degenerates muscle. By 2016, a few years after first experiencing weakness in his left arm, the former black belt struggled to lift five pounds, couldn't open a drawer with his left hand, and had begun using a walker after falling repeatedly. "If you looked at my thigh," he said, "you'd think I had polio."

Researchers have not found an effective treatment for IBM. Giovanni also could not find a clinical trial anywhere in the world that could help him. There have been reports of an experimental drug that might help, but it appeared to be a year or more away from seeking FDA approval.

"What can I do, just stay home and get weaker?" said Giovanni, who served as an infantryman in Korea. "I'm a fighter. I know I may be throwing away money. But I decided to give an alternative guy a shot."

Giovanni paid a New York doctor, who is a board-certified anesthesiologist, about $25,000 in 2015. In return, he got a series of oxygen, ultraviolet, and neural therapies, as well as vitamin supplements from Germany that he bought directly from the doctor at $400 a batch.

The doctor also injected him with potentially regenerative stem cells, but from a pig. "The injection hurt," Giovanni said. "I don't feel any stronger," he added. "And I've lost twenty pounds of what I think is muscle. I'm not going to see that doctor anymore."

Yet Giovanni refused to say that he had wasted his money.

"I'm not saying I'm sorry I tried it," he said. "One of my physical therapists said to me, 'You keep going to candy stores.' She's right. I keep going to candy stores because I need candy."

If I am ever in Giovanni's situation, or in Jan's, I am not sure what I would pay for the candy of hope. But I am determined not to pay a dime of my family money for the sweet high of false hope.

END OF LIFE

As hopes fade and energy wanes, choosing the care you want in your last months helps to determine how comfortable you will be. If you're like most people, including me, you will say you want medical care to the end, despite possible painful side effects and sometimes limited effectiveness. But do we really mean that?

Consider the drug Opdivo for patients with advanced non–small cell lung cancer. Perhaps you've seen its dramatic TV ad on the nightly news. The drug, which was approved by the FDA in 2015, lengthened the survival of its clinical trial patients an average of 3.2 months over prior therapies: 9.2 months versus 6 months. But 59 percent of the patients reported serious adverse reactions. The impression I got from the ad, however, was that the patients lived happily ever after. If you had terminal lung cancer, you might get the chance to decide whether the drug's additional twelve weeks of survival, perhaps with nasty side effects—and a reported cost of $12,500 per month—are actually worth it.

You Can Take a Different Path: Palliative Care. Many people mistakenly think that palliative care, also known as supportive care, is simply pain management. In reality, it is much more than that. Several studies show that palliative care in conjunction with medical treatment can extend survival and reduce costs during the last months of a patient's life.

"The idea is to look at patients holistically," said Vanstory, the oncology social worker. Besides managing pain, the care addresses side effects, emotional strains, and the quality of life. The care, which takes place in conjunction with standard treatment, can be especially helpful for someone on grueling chemotherapy regimens.

"You can have palliative care from the point of your diagnosis, regardless of your prognosis," explained Lisa Morgan, spokesperson for the Center to Advance Palliative Care (CAPC).

Studies suggest that around 40 percent of palliative patients are cured of such symptoms as nausea, fatigue, and depression, while not having to forgo more aggressive treatment or move on to hospice care with its life expectancy of six months or so. Palliative care can easily be blended into hospice care.

Although palliative care only became an approved medical specialty in 2007, by 2016 it was offered in more than two-thirds of the country's hospitals, including 90 percent of those with more than three hundred beds. Also, a few hundred hospitals, including New York's Mount Sinai, offer it as an outpatient service, since most patients want to be at home rather than hospitalized unless absolutely necessary.

If you want palliative care, you should ask your primary doctor—your quarterback—to help you get it, or discuss it with your hospital's social worker. Typically, a team of doctors, nurses, and social workers provide the care. The provider's bill for the care similarly to how they charge for other medical treatment.

Unfortunately, insurance reimbursement for it remains inconsistent. Medicare Part B will pay for some or all of palliative care under its hospice coverage, and more private insurers are offering coverage after becoming convinced that it can reduce overall costs. In addition, some hospitals now provide their versions of palliative care at no charge.

To learn more about palliative care, go to GetPalliative Care.org, sponsored by the CAPC.

Another Option Is Hospice Care. This service is available to people who are terminally ill with any disease. Medicare, for example, covers hospice care provided by approved teams once the patient's doctors certify that the individual has a life expectancy of six months or less.

Under original Medicare, the patient must then sign a release choosing hospice care over more heroic treatment, aside from palliative care to relieve discomfort. Once he or she signs up, Medicare covers the care fully, generally aside from a $5 copay for pain relief prescriptions.

While Medicare will also pay to treat the patient's other conditions, it no longer pays for standard care or for drugs to fight the patient's terminal illness. Nor will it pay for ambulance service, emergency room, or hospital care caused by the major illness.

Medicare Advantage or Medigap insurers might have different rules for hospice care. For example, in some cases, those insurers might cover so-called curative treatments for the terminal condition.

Original Medicare grants hospice care for only six months. But hospice specialists say that time limit is not hard and fast; it can be renewed.

Another plus is that hospice care is usually provided in the patient's home, which is where the overwhelming majority of people want to be in their last days. But while 70 percent of Americans say they want to die at home, in reality, 70 percent to 80 percent die in hospitals or other health care facilities. Dr. Grimm said she thinks many patients end up in facilities because they keep "waiting for a miracle" and don't turn to hospice care until it's too late.

Despite its positive aspects, hospice at home can put a significant strain on family caregivers, who might lack the time, money, skills, or basic energy to provide the support a dying loved one needs.

Medicare recognizes the problem—up to a point. The program allows the hospice team to send the patient to a hospital or other facility for a few days in order to give the family caregivers some relief. However, it pays only up to 5 percent of the "respite care" bills, which can easily be around $500 a day. So a three-day escape from the physical and emotional strain of caring for a dying loved one might end up wrenching the family's wallet by more than $1,400.

Still, with its pluses and minuses, Dr. Grimm strongly endorses hospice care: "It's quality living as you die."

SHOULD YOU JOIN A CLINICAL TRIAL?

As Pastor Rick Warren wrote in his book *The Purpose Driven Life: What on Earth Am I Here For?*, "It's not about you." A clinical trial is not about you and your disease. A clinical trial's purpose is to test a new drug, treatment, procedure, or device on human volunteers. The treatment being tested might help you, or it might not—or it might harm you. The harsh truth is that whatever happens to you is an incidental outcome of the research.

In addition, the odds of adults getting into a trial are extremely low, though experts estimate that 60 percent of children with cancer do get in. In all, though an estimated 40 percent of all cancer patients try to join clinical trials at one time or another to gain access to potentially lifesaving treatments, only around 5 percent of the group succeeds. Most fail to meet the exacting criteria that may include their precise condition and any medicines they may have taken. Researchers say the shortage of volunteers who end up qualifying is retarding medical advances.

Regardless of the hurdles, the benefits of joining can be considerable. You might get the attention of doctors and researchers at the top of their field, including medical experts who have spent their entire careers focused on your disease. If nothing more, you might be helped immeasurably by insights from these experts. Several studies have found that even participants in control groups who receive standard treatment rather than the experimental therapy being measured fare better than average patients. One reason is that all participants are observed closely and get first-rate follow-up care.

Beyond that, your treatment with cutting-edge medicines or therapies comes largely free of cost in National Institutes of Health trials, except for a few common expenses. For instance, your travel and other practical expenses might be covered, though hotel costs can sometimes become problematic.

In addition, you might be compensated for your time and inconvenience, particularly if you are a healthy volunteer sought for early-stage research. Although there is little government guidance, compensation is more commonly offered in asthma, HIV, diabetes, and dermatological trials, rather than in oncology and cardiovascular research.

Even more significantly, your doctor should not be compensated in any way for referring you to a trial. That is a conflict of interest. Your primary doctor may invite you to consider a trial because he believes what is being tested might benefit you, as well as advance medical science. And he may bill you for care you need related to the trial. That's fine. But if you ever feel you are being pressured into a trial, I would advise against participating. Walk away.

On the other hand, if you decide to participate, you automatically will be helping others. You will be making a contribution to medical science, whether you are healthy or ill. Assuming you are ill, for example, your study could break new ground, but the drug or procedure might not be effective for you. Or you might end up opting out early because of troubling side effects.

Who Conducts Clinical Trials?

Foremost among the many organizations conducting clinical trials is the National Institutes of Health, the world's largest source of funding for medical research, with twenty-seven centers across the country. Interestingly, an NIH-sponsored trial might cover as few as a single participant.

Other important federal medical research agencies include the Food and Drug Administration and the Centers for Disease Control and Prevention. In addition, thousands of clinical researchers are affiliated with hospitals or university medical programs as well as nonprofit organizations such as the American Cancer Society and my friends at the Multiple Myeloma Research Foundation.

Also, in recent years pharmaceutical companies have financed most of the drug trials in that industry's race to bring profitable new products to the global marketplace. The financial stakes are extraordinary. The investment needed to launch a new drug has been estimated into the billions. Whatever the number, clinical trials generally account for two-thirds of the cost. So, while business interests can push a drug forward, financial considerations can get in the way of scientific exploration.

A typical example of the power of the purse is the biopharmaceutical company Onconova Therapeutics. Its research into a drug to treat a rare bone-marrow disorder was halted early in 2015 as disappointing phase 3 results piled up and its principal investor, Baxter International, a diversified health care company, pulled out its funding. Some experts noted that Third

Point, an aggressive hedge fund, holds nearly 10 percent of Baxter's publicly traded stock and also holds Baxter's top executives responsible for delivering ever higher profits. Baxter had provided $50 million for the trial but might have had to put up another $515 million to keep it going. Still, when Baxter pulled the plug, its stock went down the drain, too.

On the other hand, the trial for Opdivo, which was funded by Bristol-Myers Squibb, was stopped two years ahead of its original deadline because the results were so positive. Opdivo beats back cancer that has recurred and spread. The FDA approved it for patients with melanomas that cannot be removed surgically or those with advanced conditions who have stopped responding to existing drugs. The FDA approved Opdivo for advanced (metastatic) non–small cell lung cancer in 2015. It's worth noting that the slick TV ads for Opdivo that blanketed the nightly news end by thanking the trial's clinicians and participants.

Phases of Trials

You've probably heard that trials are structured in distinct phases that hopefully lead to FDA approval. Generally, whatever is being tested must get through three phases before the FDA considers allowing it to be sold to the public. The FDA also monitors the product's safety and effectiveness once it's in the marketplace; that's phase 4. The laboratory phase, the one where, say, the drug is tested on mice rather than men, is sometimes called phase 0. Most trials, unfortunately, end at phase 2.

In phase 1, generally the first to involve humans, tests are conducted on as few as twenty often-healthy participants. The researchers might want healthy volunteers when they are trying to determine the effect of a drug on average people, including how it is metabolized and tolerated. Also, the goal might be to find the drug's best delivery option, such as by pill or injection. Or researchers might be trying to find the optimal dosage and frequency by giving participants steadily increased amounts to determine the highest level they can tolerate with the least side effects.

In phase 2, the researchers recruit anywhere from twenty-five to three hundred or so people with a certain disease or condition to gather data on the effectiveness of, again say, a drug. At this point, for instance, they might be measuring a cancer drug's effect on a tumor: Has it decreased in size or expanded? The researchers also are monitoring the impact on the patients: Has their quality of life been affected and, in extreme cases, their actual survival?

In phase 3, the last hurdle before the FDA considers approval, the trial might involve several thousand participants across the country and perhaps around the world. Researchers might be testing different dosages and frequencies as well as how effective the drug might be in combination with other drugs. Phase 3 trials also might compare the new treatment against the "standard of care," the currently accepted approach. Participants get one or the other. Financing aside, as I've noted, the research team decides whether to go forward or end the trial based on its own reasonable expectations of the treatment's benefits to society and science. Therefore, trial leaders have enormous responsibilities.

In phase 4, after FDA approval, the agency assigns an independent committee to monitor the long-term benefits or harmful effects of the product on people. The committee's studies measure the product's basic safety and effectiveness.

At times, the FDA has been slow to react to bad news in phase 4. For example, it took the agency years to step in after metal-on-metal hip replacements failed, sometimes soon after they were implanted in tens of thousands of patients. Among other issues, the metal in some replacements corroded, or flinty bits broke away. In a number of cases, the surrounding tissue became inflamed to the point of necrosis—the degradation and death of tissue cells. And some devices simply broke. By the time the FDA moved in forcefully in 2013, a half million Americans had been affected.

The problems had become widespread by 2012, when Johnson & Johnson's DePuy Orthopaedics paid $3 billion to three thousand people who had their defective hip devices. And the Stryker Corporation of Kalamazoo, Michigan, paid a $1.4 billion settlement to five thousand people in thirty-nine states in 2014, barely two years after similar devices it made were pulled from the market.

And in 2016 investigators for the US General Accountability Office, which polices government spending, said the FDA's phase 4 studies were "incomplete, outdated, and often contain inaccuracies."

The FDA also has been criticized for taking far too long to approve desperately needed drugs. FDA defenders argue that this country's standards for efficacy and safety must remain high, despite an explosion of significant clinical trials, from five thousand in 2000 to around twenty thousand to thirty thousand a year by 2016. Still, the Obama administration's Council of Advisors on Science and Technology estimates that it takes an average of fourteen years to bring a drug to market, eight years *longer* than it did fifteen years ago. Terminally ill people die every day for lack of access to new drugs, including drugs that are readily available in countries as near as Canada and as far away as Japan. In other words, around the globe.

In reaction, the agency has been wrestling with the issue of "expanded access" to drugs, at least since a thousand gay activists from the group ACT UP (AIDS Coalition to Unleash Power) demonstrated at the FDA's Bethesda, Maryland, headquarters in the mid-eighties. In 1986 the FDA allowed zidovudine, or AZT, the first effective drug against HIV II AIDS, to bypass the trial process.

Now under its compassionate care program, also known as expanded access, the FDA approves some drugs and other treatments for people who qualify as early as phase 1. The agency also has streamlined the application process from a hundred hours to forty-five minutes. And by 2016, it had granted expanded access—sometimes after one emergency phone call—to virtually every one of the thousand patients a year who requested it.

Yet critics insist the FDA can do better. Some point to Esbriet, a medicine that can significantly reduce deaths from a lung disease called idiopathic pulmonary fibrosis (IPF), which kills forty thousand Americans each year. The FDA finally approved the breakthrough drug in October 2014—nearly five years *after* an FDA advisory committee had recommended approval. By 2014, Esbriet, made by Swiss-based Roche, and retailing at over $90,000 a year, had been available in Canada for two years, in Europe for four years, and in Japan for seven years.

In frustration over what some critics still see as the FDA's glacial pace, a grassroots "Right to Try" movement championed by the libertarian Goldwater Institute has sprung up since 2014. Under the states' relaxed right-to-try regulations, terminal patients can get access to drugs that have passed only through a phase 1 trial, or they can go directly to pharmaceutical companies for drugs that have not been tested by independent sources at all.

Right-to-try laws existed in twenty-four states in 2015. California's progressive Democratic governor, Jerry Brown, vetoed his state's bill because he believes right to try mirrors the FDA's expanded access effort without meeting the agency's safety, research, and high patient protection standards.

In addition, the fact is that a number of pharmaceutical companies are reluctant to hand over an experimental drug to desperate patients for fear that the action would ultimately undermine the drug's marketability in two ways. First, bypassing FDA testing can complicate efforts to get the drugs approved. And the untested drugs might harm patients or even hasten their deaths.

Furthermore, right-to-try laws do not require insurance companies to cover the drug costs, and drug companies reserve the right to bill the patients directly for the drugs. Experts say that provision, which introduces a huge financial unknown into the process, has discouraged patients from pursuing right to try. In NIH trials, as I've noted, drug companies cannot bill patients for their drugs.

By 2016, independent experts said there was no documentation that anyone had been treated under right to try. Dr. Arthur Caplan, director of the Division of Medical Ethics at the New York University Langone Medical Center, who also serves on NYU's Working Group on Compassionate Use and Pre-Approval Access, said in 2015: "We haven't yet found a case where right-to-try laws have facilitated access to anything."

Caplan and others wrote in the journal *Health Affairs* that although the "laws have created an expectation that terminally ill patients will be able to quickly access potentially lifesaving treatments by being exempted" from FDA rules, "this expectation is, quite simply, false."

Protections for Participants

The sponsor of a trial, whether a government agency or a pharmaceutical company, must fully inform the participants about all aspects of its trial, including its purpose and how it might—or might not—benefit society and maybe you. For example, the trial leader must get the participant's "informed consent" about the very nature of the test. For instance, are placebos involved? That's very important, since placebos, though harmless, have no therapeutic value and merely help researchers measure the actual medicine's effectiveness. People in need of real treatment are barred from trials involving placebos. In addition, a participant must get an assigned medical professional whom he can contact at every stage of testing.

It might surprise you that the concept of informed consent dates back only to the 1970s, when a whistle-blower exposed the federal government's shameful Tuskegee syphilis experiment. The government's predecessor of the NIH traced the disease's progression for decades beginning in the Great Depression without warning the study's six hundred African American sharecroppers in Alabama that they had the disease and without treating them with the cure, penicillin. Many of the men died of syphilis; forty of their wives contracted it; and nearly twenty children were born with congenital syphilis.

On the heels of coast-to-coast headlines about the Tuskegee Study of Untreated Syphilis in the Negro Male, the US Congress passed sweeping regulations of clinical studies in 1974, including granting patients the right to informed consent, full disclosure of their diagnoses, and accurate test results.

Therefore, if you agree to join a trial, your protections will be contained in the informed consent agreements you'll be asked to sign. While this consent protects the sponsors, since you agree freely to participate, the extensive document spells out what the trial involves. For instance, it places responsibility on the research team to explain the trial design, or protocol, as well as its risks and benefits. The document must make it clear that a patient does not forfeit three key rights:

- **The Participant's Privacy Must Be Protected.** Patients are almost always identified by code, not name.
- **The Participant Can Opt Out Without Penalty.** The consent document is an agreement, not a contract, which means the participant has agreed in principle to the trial's conditions but is not obligated to complete it.
- **Above All, the Participant Does Not Surrender His or Her Legal Rights of Recourse.** Therefore, if the trial team is negligent or makes a grievous mistake, a volunteer can take legal action.

The Risks

Once you commit to a trial, you have effectively surrendered your choice of treatment. Remember, the trial is not about you. The researchers decide on treatments. In addition, not only might the drug, device, or treatment not help you, but it might harm you. Although extremely rare, there are cases where subjects have died. For instance, one volunteer was pronounced brain dead and five others hospitalized in a phase 1 clinical trial for an anxiety and pain medicine in 2016 in France that followed international regulations. The incident reminded some researchers that others died in early phase 1 trials of treatments for AIDS.

The risks are real. According to CenterWatch, a research information firm and website, about one in thirty participants in drug trials suffer a serious side effect and one in ten thousand die. But a meta-analysis shows that the odds of being affected by an adverse event drop to 0.31 percent—three in one thousand—in early noncancer trials.

Before you decide to participate, have a frank discussion with the trial leaders and your doctors about all possible side effects. You need to understand those risks, not just the possible benefits, to make an intelligent decision about whether to sign up. For example, a company spokesperson for a new oral form of the cancer drug Velcade said it produced peripheral neuropathy in 7 percent of trial patients. But since doctors blame Velcade's earlier intravenous version for causing my annoying peripheral neuropathy, which involves a loss of feeling in my fingers and feet, I'd be leery of joining a trial for that drug.

As I've said, treatment during an NIH trial is free, and most incidental expenses, including travel, are covered as well. But hotel costs can be a worry, if, for example, you are commuting a distance to the clinic and might regularly feel too weak to drive home. Sometimes private foundations step in and cover costs like that—but there are no guarantees.

Costs aside, these trials, which generally go on for months and often years, will surely have an impact on you and those close to you. Even if you do not travel far for the treatment, frequent visits to a doctor or clinic will become part of your schedule. That alone will put strains on your family, who might often choose to accompany you to and from the trial.

Trials also carry an emotional wallop, as participants swing from desperation to hope and too often to disappointment. For every story of a miracle cure, like the amazing one in the next chapter, there are countless others of patients who joined a trial full of hope and ended up sicker than before. If you decide to join a trial, you and your family should prepare for the worst but hope for the best.

Ask These Questions Before Signing Up

- Exactly what is being studied?
- Why do researchers believe the intervention (treatment, procedure, or device) being tested might be effective? Has it been tested before?
- Who will decide which intervention(s) I receive, and how will those decisions be made?
- Who will know which interventions I get? Will I be told beforehand about each during the trial?
- How do the possible risks, side effects, and benefits of this trial compare with my current treatment?
- Who will oversee my medical care while I am in the trial?
- How often will I have to visit the hospital or clinic?
- How long will the trial last?
- Will anyone pay for my participation?
- Will I be reimbursed for my expenses?
- What type of long-term follow-up care is part of this trial?
- If I benefit from an intervention, such as a drug, will I be allowed to keep getting it after the trial ends?
- What are my options if I am injured during the trial?

The NIH website is an excellent source about current trials. In addition, its ClinicalTrials.gov website provides answers to common questions, as well as a comprehensive glossary of terms, lists of trials and their locations, and explanations of participant protections. The Center Watch and

EmergingMed websites also list trials for numerous diseases and conditions.

In addition, you can find trials through nonprofit agencies that raise funds for research into specific diseases. Also, reach out to large research hospitals or university medical schools. Ask for the medical research department.

Good luck.

CHAPTER 20

Rules for Life

The Three Keys to Becoming a Health Care Detective and Getting Your Best Care—Now

As I've said, I got two of the phone calls Americans have learned to dread: "Sorry, you have cancer," and "Oops, we're cutting your health insurance benefits."

Then in August of 2015 I got the third call: "You've relapsed."

All in all, my wonder drug Revlimid had helped control my blood cancer for five years, which is about a year more than anyone can hope for. I knew I was on "borrowed time," as my father, Edmund, would have put it. As a fatalist who smoked "like a chimney" and lived to eighty-nine, he was an expert on the subject.

I had hoped Revlimid would work for another five years, but I knew better. For one thing, my shortness of breath had returned worse than ever. So I wasn't shocked when my oncologist Ray Pastore called and eased me into the bad news. My cancer markers tracking my dangerous excess proteins had risen sharply. They were still below the danger zone, but he sure didn't like the trajectory.

"You think I've relapsed," I said.

"I'm worried about that," he replied.

After consulting with Dr. Pastore, Dana-Farber's Dr. Kenneth Anderson prescribed Pomalyst, a new drug that is ten times more powerful than Revlimid. My markers plunged by 75 percent within a few months, and my doctor tells me my cancer should remain under control for years.

Still, after relapsing, I began looking for word of a breakthrough that might point to a cure. Fortunately, I was invited to a remarkable cancer research conference that highlighted both the inspiring progress researchers are making toward finding cures for various cancers as well as the dramatic stories of people who are learning to take charge and get the care they need despite our too often mindless and heartless health care system. Those people are becoming their own Health Care Detectives—and they are winning.

The conference in New York City's impressive Alexandria Center for Life Science complex was presented by the Multiple Myeloma Research Foundation, a privately funded organization that is helping to transform cancer research from a secretive activity dominated by pharmaceutical companies focused narrowly on their own products to an open and collaborative effort by a broad range of partners searching for cures.

The MMRF was created by Kathy Giusti, who ranks number nineteen on *Fortune* magazine's list of the World's 50 Greatest Leaders, next to the Pope, the Dalai Lama, and a few heads of countries. And she deserves the recognition. She was diagnosed with multiple myeloma back in 1996, when people with the disease were considered fortunate to live for more than three years. As the mother of two young children, she refused to accept that fate. Instead, she decided to use her Harvard Business School education and pharmaceutical company experience to overcome whatever forces were impeding the development of drugs for multiple myeloma and other cancers as well.

By 2016, her efforts had spurred the remarkable creation of ten multiple myeloma drugs over the previous seven years, including Velcade and Pomalyst, as well as the first proteasome inhibitor, ixazomib, which is taken in pill form, rather than by injection or intravenous drip.

Her MMRF is a major reason the median survival rate of multiple myeloma patients has tripled to nine years.

Along the way, Giusti has helped to revolutionize cancer research by fostering open collaboration between academic research centers and drugmakers. For too long, pharmaceutical companies and their academic allies have worked largely in secret to develop proprietary drugs. Once their scientists produce something promising in the lab, they organize trials with animals first and then patients to build evidence to convince the FDA that their drugs work better than anything else on the market.

Giusti is turning that model on its head.

The MMRF raised $40 million and recruited ninety academic research centers and four drugmakers to share everything they discover by monitoring one thousand newly diagnosed multiple myeloma patients in the years ahead. Instead of the traditional secretive silos of information, think of the MMRF's ongoing study as the creation of spigots of invaluable insights accessible to everyone interested in finding a cure for cancer. That is a revolutionary shift in cancer research and a great source of hope for families like mine.

At the conference, Giusti said repeatedly, "We are curing cancer—now."

EMIL PUSATERI'S STORY

After a string of inspirational presentations kicking off the MMRF conference, Dr. Samir Parekh, an associate professor at New York's Mount Sinai Hospital, tugged the audience back to the everyday realities of our frustrating health care system by introducing the story of Emil Pusateri.

Dr. Parekh said there was a drug called Mekinist on the shelf that he strongly believed would work for Emil, an exceptionally intelligent forty-eight-year-old father of three from Rockville Centre, New York. The drug was approved by the FDA for treating metastatic melanoma, skin cancer that has spread to other parts of the body, by attacking a particular mutation among melanoma patients called the BRAF mutation. Although Emil had myeloma, he is among the 6 percent of patients with that blood cancer who have the BRAF mutation. What's more, Mount Sinai's myeloma unit had used Mekinist successfully on seven myeloma patients like Emil.

In each of those cases, the insurers had covered the drug costs, in large part to avoid paying for a $250,000 stem-cell transplant if the patient's condition worsened without the drug.

Dr. Parekh's team requested the coverage from Emil's insurer, Independence Blue Cross of Philadelphia, stressing that they believed Mekinist could prolong Emil's life and perhaps even save him. But Independence refused to pay for the off-label use for Emil, despite the fact that more than half of all cancer patients receive at least one chemotherapy drug off-label.

Dr. Parekh appealed again and again by phone and in writing. But each time, the insurer said no. As weeks went by, Emil began declining, and the Mount Sinai doctors became increasingly concerned that his kidneys might fail.

Finally, Dr. Sundar Jagannath, director of Sinai's Multiple Myeloma Program, led a conference call to try to convince Independence's medical officers to approve Mekinist for Emil. "You could save this man's life," Dr. Jagannath told the insurance company doctors.

Still the insurer refused to cover the cost, partly because the use would have been off-label, and also because they thought Emil was too sick to be helped by it.

Dr. Jagannath told Emil's wife, Stacy: "You can fight the insurance company for reimbursement later. But if you want to keep your husband alive, buy the drug out of your own pocket."

It was a big decision. Like most of us, Emil and Stacy did not have tens of thousands of dollars lying around to spend. "I said

to Emil, 'I'd rather be poor with you than richer without you,'"
Stacy said.

The family put $10,000 on Emil's credit card and brought
home as much of the medicine as that got them: a three-week
supply. And as the Mount Sinai doctors expected, the Mekinist helped Emil immediately. His myeloma markers improved
within three days. But it was too late; Emil's kidney function
was collapsing.

Dr. Parekh decided that he had no choice but to perform
Emil's second stem-cell transplant, using the last of the patient's
own cells, which had been harvested years before when he was
healthier.

Instead of the insurer paying around $6,000 a month for
the Mekinist that might have stabilized Emil, Independence
Blue Cross shelled out around $200,000 for the second trans-
plant.

"We wasted weeks appealing to the insurance company while
he got sicker and sicker," Stacy told me. "If Emil had gotten the
Mekinist from the beginning, he would have avoided the second transplant—and maybe the drug would have saved him."

I asked Dr. Parekh what would happen if he went back to
the same insurer tomorrow with a similar case, but now armed
with the fact that the off-label Mekinist had helped Emil immediately. "They'd do the same thing. They'd say no," he said.
"Insurance companies are looking for reasons to deny coverage.
They are not looking for ways to help patients."

Late in 2015, the Pusateri family found a way to get Mekinist for Emil going forward at no cost. Stacy said a staffer at
Independence Blue Cross advised her that she would probably
have better luck appealing to the drug's manufacturer, Novartis, rather than the insurance company. With help from Mount
Sinai, Stacy applied for Novartis's Patient Assistance Now program and was approved quickly. "We submitted a few pay stubs
to verify our income," said Stacy, "and we got the drug right
away."

Although the cost of Emil's Mekinist was finally covered, medical bills keep pouring into the Pusateri home. "With Emil so sick, life is mentally and emotionally hard," Stacy said. "This is not the time for me to deal with bills. I'll get to them. But for the past months, I've just stuck them in a drawer, unopened."

She, of course, realized that someday the family would have to face the bills, and she imagined they would be paying down what they owe over ten to twelve years.

"You shouldn't have to sell your house to pay your medical bills. That isn't right. Someone needs to change that. But that's what could happen to us," Stacy said. "I told our kids that could be next."

Emil died surrounded by his loving family on February 18, 2016.

Lessons of the Pusateri Story

- **Do Not Waste Critical Time Appealing to a Recalcitrant Insurance Company.** If you have months to spare to go through the insurer's appeals process and perhaps take your case to an independent arbitrator or judge, by all means, continue the appeal. But if the delay is jeopardizing your health or a loved one's, as it did with Emil, turn your energy toward getting what you need another way—even if you have to put it on your credit card. As Mount Sinai's Dr. Jagannath told Stacy, you can resume your appeals to get reimbursed later, as she planned to do.

- **Ask the Drugmaker for Help.** The vast majority of drug manufacturers' patient assistance programs are a direct reflection of the makers' high prices. Drug executives know that many people can't pay these prices on their own, and also that some of those people have memorable stories that the executives would rather not read in the newspapers, like Emil's story. If the Pusateris had taken Emil's case to Novartis's Patient Assistance Now program earlier, they could have avoided spending $10,000 out of pocket for the Mekinist; instead, they would have gotten the drug for free from the drugmaker, as they eventually did.

- **Assume That You Are Eligible for Aid.** In sharp contrast to insurance company practices, many of the manufacturers' assistance teams want to find a way to approve worthy applications and get the drugs to you as quickly as possible—sometimes overnight. Eligibility rules vary, but it's not unusual for families to qualify with incomes of around $100,000. In many cases, you won't need to do much more than get a letter from your doctor saying the drug is medically necessary. And you'll have to verify your income, but probably not your assets. Drug companies do not want you to have to sell your car to buy a month's supply of one of their drugs.

- **Finally, Ask Yourself This Question.** As a nation, we stand at the edge of an age of tremendous medical advancement. The sum of medical knowledge is doubling every two years; by 2020, it will double in 73 *days*. But what good will those advances provide for most of us, including you, if you don't become a Health Care Detective prepared to pursue every sensible way to get your best care at an affordable price?

LORI ALF'S STORY

In addition to Emil's story, which holds lessons of how to deal with the hardships of our health care system, the audience at the MMRF conference met the remarkable Lori Alf, whose triumph over terminal cancer epitomizes the three key rules of this book:

- **She took charge.**
- **She kept searching for her best solutions.**
- **She never gave up, even with just weeks to live.**

Before Lori got very lucky with a clinical trial at the front line of cancer research, she was profoundly unlucky. The smart, speed-talking mother of three teenagers, who runs an Olympic-class ice rink in West Palm Beach, Florida, thought she had a worsening case of bronchitis back in 2009. She was getting ready for a workout one Friday morning when the phone rang. Her family doctor had her blood lab results, and he needed to see her—now. She drove right over in her black Lululemon outfit.

He got right to the point. Lori had multiple myeloma, an incurable blood cancer that rarely affects anyone so young. She was forty-three.

"I walked out to my car," she said, "slumped down onto the hood, and stayed there paralyzed, crying and crying in the middle of the parking lot."

Within a week, on a local oncologist's strong recommendation, she and her husband, Chris, flew to an Arkansas hospital that was reporting success with myeloma patients by performing two stem-cell transplants back-to-back, a harsh and costly treatment in vogue then.

Lori rejected it. "Suddenly I was in the Disneyland of cancer, surrounded by people who looked as if they walked out of the center of the sun, wan and bald," she said. "That wasn't me."

Furthermore, she would have had to stay there away from her children for six months. "No one can take me away from my kids that long," she said. "I'll be the hand reaching out of the ground for them."

She went home and took control like a Health Care Detective. And she remained in charge of every important medical decision throughout what became a seven-year ordeal to find a treatment to keep her particularly aggressive cancer in check.

While many myeloma patients find therapies that allow them to enjoy the semblance of normal health for years, Lori lurched from one ineffective treatment to another. In all, she and her specialists tried ten courses of treatment, but few helped her for more than months, rather than the years of relief others often get. "I have a really mean cancer," she said, "one of the worst my doctors had ever seen."

Stylish, blue-eyed Lori was down to eighty pounds with perhaps two weeks to live in 2014. She was facing a stem-cell transplant from her sister, who is not her twin and therefore not a perfect genetic match. She knew that rather than saving her, the transplant's graft-versus-host complications—in which the donor cells attack the patient's body—could kill her. "I was a lizard, surviving on blood transfusions," she said. "And now I was dying."

But she had done in-depth research and found one last option. Scouring the Internet, Lori and Chris, discovered that University of Pennsylvania researchers were organizing clinical trials of a "breakthrough" therapy to reprogram the immune systems of seriously ill myeloma patients like her. Instead of drugs from the outside to attack the cancer, these therapies unleash a patient's own immune system to kill specific cancer targets from within.

Lori was determined to get into the trial: "I told my sixteen-year-old daughter, 'If they reject me, you go into that doctor's office and cry your eyes out. Throw a scene until they change their minds.' We're not leaving without a yes.'"

Lori was accepted without the histrionics. But the trial itself was nothing but drama.

For one thing, the researchers were moving so fast to treat the seriously ill myeloma volunteers under expedited breakthrough status from the Food and Drug Administration that they did not stop to experiment, even on mice.

Lori was "the mouse model."

In a process similar to kidney dialysis, Lori was hooked up to a machine that collected white blood cells called T cells. Then the lab team "made my T cells very angry," as she put it. Actually, the team transformed her cells with a genetically engineered protein called chimeric antigen receptor (CAR) to create an army of CAR T hunters capable of recognizing her enemy myeloma cells and killing them with their claws and exploding tails.

On the twelfth day of her hospitalization, the doctors dripped a small bag of "red garlicky-smelling" CAR T cells into her veins. A day later, she sunk to what she called her "sickest state," feeling wired and twitchy and constantly nauseous. "I couldn't stop moving," she said, "and every time I moved, I got sick."

Which was more or less what the doctors had hoped. In their earlier successful clinical trials with leukemia patients, when the army truly devastated the enemy, the warfare commonly triggered high fevers, nausea, muscle pain, and sometimes serious neurologic symptoms such as hallucinations and outright delirium.

Lori was well enough to be discharged eight days later but continued to feel "jittery, itchy, twitchy, and miserable" for months. But her cancer decreased—and then disappeared.

Nearly two years after the immunotherapy, she was free of myeloma. Beyond that, she was convinced that the CAR T therapy had cured her cancer. "I'm sure it killed the mother cancer cells," she said, "not just the peripheral daughter cells." And more than one of her oncologists told me that they agreed with her.

At the presentation of Lori's story at the MMRF conference, Dr. Carl June, Penn's director of translational research, showed the before and after slides of Lori's bone marrow. In the before slide, her round liquid tumors clog 95 percent of her marrow, crowding out all but a whisper of healthy cells. The after slide is completely clear.

As he presented the slides, the disciplined clinician couldn't help but choke up, knowing that the breakthrough immunotherapy had not only saved Lori but had the potential to cure countless others with multiple myeloma, leukemia, and other cancers in the years ahead.

Then Lori, a petite but powerful force of nature, spoke: "I was supposed to die. But here I am. I feel as if I was placed into one of the lifeboats from the *Titanic*. And I will forever be grateful for that.

"But I can't help looking back and wishing that everyone on that ship could join me in this lifeboat of safety. And I will do all I can in my small way to help make that happen."

Lori is the mouse who roared.

Lessons of the Lori Alf Story

- **She Took Charge.** After she was diagnosed with multiple myeloma, she assembled a team of specialists, led by Dana-Farber's Dr. Kenneth Anderson, who has devoted his career to prolonging his patients' lives long enough for researchers to finally find a cure. At the same time, Lori learned enough about the disease to talk to her doctors as partners. "We made all the decisions about my care together," she said.

- **She Searched for Solutions.** When all the conventional therapies her doctors suggested no longer helped her, she and her husband searched the Internet until they found a clinical trial that held out hope for her. Then, with her doctors' support, she got into that experimental immunotherapy trial. And the treatment eradicated her cancer.

- **She Never Gave Up.** Even when Lori was down to eighty pounds and facing death, she didn't give up trying to get the care she needed. "What it came down to," she said, "was that I didn't want to die. I was determined to live. I have too much I want to do with my family in the life ahead of me."

Three Rules for Life

Lori Alf walked away from her seven-year journey with cancer to her miraculous recovery with three rules for life.

Learn Who You Are at Your Core. "I was the mother of three young children. That's what made me tick. There was no way I was going to let anything separate me from my kids without a fight. My children would come to me every night when I was in bed to make sure I'd taken my pills. And I'd tell them, 'Yes, I've taken the pills to help me get better.' And then they would kiss me good night. No matter how badly my treatment was going, they knew that Mommy was there for them, and she was going to get better."

Become Your Best Medical Advocate. "I learned everything I could about my cancer and then about my own case. That allowed me to have in-depth conversations with my doctors and other myeloma experts that led to informed decisions all along the way. Then after my aggressive cancer resisted every conventional treatment we tried, I became convinced that I needed an immunology breakthrough to defeat my cancer from within my body. When I spotted the announcement of my immunology trial on the Internet, some top myeloma experts didn't know about the trial. But I did. And that knowledge saved my life."

You Need Grit to Get Through It. "A fight against cancer takes an enormous toll on you, physically, emotionally, financially, and spiritually. You need grit to make it through the worst of it. I woke up one morning, and I didn't have the use of my right leg. But I kept going. I got down to eighty pounds. But I kept going. I said, 'God, if you allow me to live, I'll never ask for anything else.' To be honest, I still chirp to God about this or that for my kids. But I'm just chirping. I know my prayers have been answered."

The Health Care Detective
Glossary in Plain English

actuarial value—The percentage of total average costs that an insurance plan expects to pay for covered services. For example, if someone has a plan with an actuarial value of 80 percent, he or she could expect to personally pay, on average, 20 percent of the cost of covered medical services.

Affordable Care Act (ACA)—Comprehensive health reform law enacted in 2010. The ACA was intended to make health insurance accessible and affordable for previously uninsured Americans, to lower health care costs, and to eliminate industry practices such as denial of coverage due to a person's preexisting health condition. Also known as "Obamacare," the ACA was signed into law by President Barack Obama.

ambulatory patient service—Health care a person can get without being admitted to a hospital. Also called outpatient care.

balance billing—When a provider bills a patient for the difference between the amount that the provider charged and the amount allowed by the insurance plan. If the provider charges $150 for a service but the insurer pays only $100, the balance of the bill sent to the patient would be for the remaining $50.

beneficiary—Someone who derives benefits from a health plan; this can be either an enrollee or a dependent.

benefits—The medical services and supplies an insurer agrees to pay for.

billing code—A unique code assigned to a specific medical service. Billing codes are used to report every medical service to health insurance companies.

biopsy—The removal of cells or tissues for microscopic examination by a pathologist. Biopsies are performed to determine the presence or extent of a disease.

blood work—Term used for blood screening tests that patients might receive when they see their doctors for a physical exam and checkup. Blood work commonly includes complete blood count and kidney function tests, as well as cholesterol and triglyceride tests.

board certification—A credential that demonstrates a doctor's capability in a particular specialty. As opposed to a medical license, which is mandatory and indicates that a physician has met a minimum standard for competency, board certification is voluntary and indicates that the doctor has exceptional, specialized expertise.

Cadillac plan—A high-cost employer-provided health plan that costs $10,200 or more a year for individual coverage and $27,500 for family coverage. Cost of coverage includes total contributions paid by both employer and employee, but not cost-sharing amounts such as deductibles, coinsurance, and copays. Under the Affordable Care Act, the federal government will begin enforcing a high-cost-plan tax

(HCPT), or "Cadillac Tax," for Cadillac plans beginning in 2020.

candy store—A health care practitioner's practice that offers patients false hope based on its often alternative "cures," rather than on evidence-based medicine and data.

cardiologist—A doctor who specializes in finding, treating, and preventing medical conditions of the heart and blood vessels.

catastrophic coverage (Medicare)—Once Medicare enrollees and their insurers pay a certain amount out of pocket for their drug prescriptions in a given year ($4,850 in 2016), members get catastrophic coverage. With that coverage, they are charged 5 percent of the total cost of their covered drugs for the rest of the year. Depending on the cost of the drugs, catastrophic coverage can leave enrollees paying a large amount for their prescription drugs, sometimes topping $500 a month or more for $10,000 cancer drugs, for example.

catastrophic limit—A limit on the amount of money that a person must pay out of pocket for health care costs incurred by a catastrophic illness.

Centers for Medicare and Medicaid Services (CMS)—The government agency that manages the national health insurance programs Medicare and Medicaid.

chemotherapy—A drug treatment that uses powerful chemicals to fight fast-growing cells, most often cancer cells, in a person's body.

clinical breast exam—A hands-on physical breast exam performed by a health care provider to check for lumps or other abnormalities. Often conducted as part of a regular medical checkup.

clinical trial—A research study done on human subjects to test the safety and effectiveness of certain medical interventions.

COBRA (Consolidated Omnibus Budget Reconciliation Act) coverage—Temporary health coverage offered after someone loses job-based health coverage.

coinsurance—The percentage of the cost that a patient is required to pay for medical services after a deductible has been met. Coinsurance is always expressed as a percentage. For example, if the insurer pays 80 percent of the charge for a service, the patient would be asked to pay a 20 percent coinsurance.

colonoscopy—An exam used to find changes or abnormalities in the large intestine and rectum. A colonoscopy is performed by inserting a flexible viewing tube into the rectum; if abnormal areas are seen, sometimes a biopsy is performed through the hollow colonoscope.

consumer directed health plan (CDHP)—A friendly-sounding term for a high-deductible health plan paired with a health savings account (HSA), health reimbursement account (HRA), or other medical payment program.

convenient-care clinic—A facility—also called a walk-in clinic—usually in a store front, big-box store, or grocery chain, and often staffed by nurses who provide non-emergency medical care, like flu shots or over-the-counter medicine, usually without an appointment. Some, not all, of these clinics have doctors on staff.

copay—A fixed amount a patient pays for a health service covered by insurance, such as a visit to the doctor.

cost sharing—A provision of health plans requiring enrollees to pay a portion of the bills for their care. This term can refer to deductible amounts, coinsurance, or copays that the plan member is asked to pay.

Current Procedural Terminology (CPT) code—A set of 9,700 medical billing codes. Each unique CPT billing code corresponds to a specific medical service, and is used by providers to bill services of ambulatory patients outside of hospitals to health insurance companies. (See ICD codes on page 299 for the more precise sets of codes used for hospital services since 2015.)

deductible—The amount a health plan member pays for approved expenses before health insurance plans begin to cover the costs. A yearly deductible of $2,000 means the plan won't start covering costs until the plan member has paid $2,000 for covered expenses.

diagnostic test—A medical test performed to aid in the diagnosis of a disease, injury, or other medical condition. The same test can be considered either diagnostic or preventive, depending on what symptom or complaint motivated a provider to ask for it.

disability insurance—Insurance that supplies supplementary income to people if they have an illness or accident that causes a disability and prevents them from working.

discharge planning—The development of a plan for how an inpatient will be cared for after he or she is discharged from the hospital or another inpatient treatment center.

emergency care—Care administered to someone with a medical condition requiring immediate assistance.

emergency conditions—An emergency health issue that is considered life threatening. Any medical problem that appears to be life threatening should be addressed immediately by calling 911 and getting the patient to an emergency room. Conditions that are considered emergencies include severe chest pain, difficulty breathing, uncontrollable bleeding, convulsions, seizures, loss of consciousness, signs of a stroke or heart attack, severe abdominal pain, and suicidal or homicidal feelings.

employer mandate—As required by the Affordable Care Act, employers with fifty or more employees must provide them with health insurance that meets minimum value and affordability standards; otherwise the employers face a penalty of around $2,000 to $3,000 per worker a year in 2016.

essential health benefits—A set of ten health care services that individual and small-group plans are required to offer under the Affordable Care Act. These include outpatient services; emergency services; hospitalization; maternity and newborn care; mental health and substance abuse services; prescription drugs; rehabilitative and habilitative services; laboratory services; preventive and wellness services; and pediatric services, including oral and vision care.

evidence-based medicine—Clinical practice that adheres to the principle of treating a patient when there is evidence that treatment would benefit patients and not treating when there is evidence that treatment might not provide a benefit or cause harm.

explanation of benefits (EOB)—A statement sent by a health insurance company to a covered individual after he or she has received a health care service. The EOB explains the amount that the health insurance company paid for the service and the amount that the covered individual may be billed.

false positive—A test result that indicates a health threat is present when, in fact, it is not.

Family and Medical Leave Act (FMLA)—A federal law that allows eligible workers to take up to twelve weeks of protected leave from their jobs due to a serious illness, the birth or adoption of a child, or to care for a seriously ill relative. If workers take FMLA leaves, they remain eligible for job-based insurance plans and must be offered jobs equal to their old ones when they return.

fee-for-service—The predominant way that providers bill medical services they deliver. Generally, the doctors and providers bill separately for each medical service.

formulary—A list of the prescription drugs that a health plan will cover. A formulary usually covers at least one drug in each class of drugs, such as these common classes: glucocorticoids, anti-inflammatories, cholesterol absorption inhibitors, skeletal muscle relaxants, progestins, serotonin reuptake inhibitors, opioid analgesics, and tetracyclines.

formulary exception—A request to get a drug that isn't on a particular Medicare Plan D's approved drug list, or formulary. A doctor recommending that the insurer cover the omitted drug must state that it is necessary to treat an enrollee's condition because all the formulary drugs, from any tier, would not be as effective or would cause adverse effects.

generic drug—A prescription drug that has the same active-ingredient formula as a brand-name drug. According to the

FDA, on average, generic drugs cost 80 percent to 85 percent less than brand-name drugs.

genetic counseling—Counseling offered by specially trained professionals to help a person learn the chances of being affected by a generic condition—or of having a child with a genetic condition—and then to make informed decisions about treatment and testing.

genetic testing—Tests that map a person's genes and detect possible mutations in the person's chromosomes, genes, or proteins. The tests can cost more than $3,000, and not all health plans pay for them. Under the Affordable Care Act, most health plans must make genetic testing and counseling available, with no out-of-pocket cost, to women facing a higher-than-average risk of BRCA1 or BRCA2 gene mutations.

group health plan—An insurance plan that provides coverage to a select group of people. Group health plans often cost less for participants than individual plans do because the health risk is spread over an entire group. A group health plan is typically maintained by an employer or employee organization.

group number—A number that identifies a particular group of insured people among various member groups in a health plan. Commonly, a member needs to provide his or her group number to file claims.

habilitative services—Health care services that help someone retain or improve skills and function for everyday living. Typical services include physical therapy, occupational therapy, speech-language pathology, and other services for people with disabilities.

health care proxy—Someone who has been designated to make health care decisions for another person if he or she is no longer capable of making decisions for himself or herself.

health exchange—An online health insurance marketplace set up to facilitate the purchase of health insurance. On an online exchange, different plans usually can be compared side by side.

health savings account (HSA)—A tax-favored savings account for medical expenses. The pretax funds a person deposits into an HSA are not taxed, and at the end of the year, any balance rolls over tax free to the next year. Members must spend the money on qualified medical expenses or face stiff penalties. To be eligible for an HSA, a person must enroll in a high-deductible health plan. (See below.)

high-deductible health plan (HDHP)—A health care plan with a higher deductible but lower premium than traditional health insurance plans. HDHPs are often combined with a health savings account (HSA) that can be used to pay for out-of-pocket medical expenses. In 2015 HDHP plans had minimum deductibles of $1,300 for individuals and $2,600 for families.

high-risk pool—Some states have lumped uninsured people with health conditions into high-risk customer pools; private insurers can choose to insure the pool of customers.

hospice care—Medical care focused on providing people with relief from the symptoms, pain, and physical and emotional stress associated with terminal illnesses. Typically, hospice care is administered to people in the last six months of life, most often at home. Medicare considers someone eligible for hospice care if a hospice doctor and a regular doctor certify that the patient has less than six months to live.

ICD-10 code—A very precise set of around ninety-seven thousand medical codes used by providers to bill for services delivered in hospital settings. ICD-10 codes are used primarily for recording diagnoses, and ICD-10-PCS codes are used for inpatient procedures. Each unique code corresponds to a specific medical diagnosis or action.

informed consent—Informed consent is a process that providers follow to fully inform a patient about an upcoming treatment, procedure, or clinical trial and then get the patient's decision to proceed or not. For example, doctors must get informed consent from patients before risky procedures such as chemotherapies. In clinical studies, participants must give written consent. But trial participants retain the right to withdraw consent at any time, and they have the right to privacy and to legal recourse if a grievous mistake is made.

in-network—The doctors, hospitals, and other health care providers that are part of a network that an insurer has contracted with to provide services. Insured people typically pay less for services when they use in-network providers.

inpatient care—The care of a patient who has been admitted to a hospital or skilled nursing facility. Inpatient or outpatient status affects what he or she is charged for services and the insurance company reimbursement. Getting inpatient status usually requires at least one overnight in a hospital. In addition, inpatient hospital status is required for Medicare beneficiaries to get skilled nursing rehabilitation benefits following hospitalization. (See outpatient care on page 305.)

internist—A doctor who specializes in internal medicine for adults. Internists generally do not treat pediatric patients.

late-enrollment penalty—With certain exceptions, a penalty for people who did not enroll in Medicare Parts A, B, or D when they first became eligible. The penalties for enrolling late are stiff, amounting to 1 percent per month or more for life.

life event—A major event that allows people to become eligible for a special enrollment window to shop and buy Affordable Care Act insurance. Life events include losing health insurance at work, marriage, a birth or adoption, or a move to an area outside of an existing plan's coverage zone.

limited lump sum—Usually, an employer's onetime payment or annual payment to workers to help them purchase health insurance, as opposed to a series of payments made over time. For example, an employer might offer a limited lump sum to workers or retirees rather than continue to cover their entire monthly insurance premiums.

living will—Legal instructions regarding a person's preferences for medical care if he or she becomes incapable of making such decisions. The instructions usually address the medical treatments that the individuals state they would or would not want to undergo in order to be kept alive—for example, no chance of regaining consciousness.

Magnetic Resonance Imaging (MRI)—A procedure that uses a magnetic field and radio waves to create high-resolution images of organs, tissues, and the skeletal system. MRIs are used to diagnose a variety of medical problems.

maintenance drug—A medication taken on a regular and recurring basis to control a chronic condition.

mammogram—An X-ray image of the breast used to detect breast cancer. Radiologists, doctors, and specialists examine the X-rays for signs of breast cancer.

maternity coverage—Health insurance coverage for pregnancy, labor, delivery, and newborn baby care. Maternity care is one of the ten essential health benefits required by the Affordable Care Act.

Medicaid—Government health insurance program for low-income families and children, also including pregnant women, the elderly, and people with disabilities. The federal government provides some of the funding; states provide the rest and administer the programs. Medicaid benefits vary considerably by state.

medical power of attorney—A legal form that allows people to designate another person to make decisions about their health care and medical treatments if they become incapable of making rational decisions for themselves.

Medicare—Federal health insurance that is available to people aged sixty-five and older, people with certain disabilities, or anyone with end-stage renal disease.

Medicare Advantage plans—Health plans sold to Medicare customers by private carriers who sign contracts with the Centers for Medicare and Medicaid Services (CMS) (see page 293). The insurers promise to cover all original Medicare services, but their Advantage products do not have to cover every benefit in the same way. The plans receive federal subsidies for providing the insurance. With federal subsidies, the Medicare Advantage plans commonly feature low or no premiums and provide extras such as free gym classes. But their provider networks are often narrow and may be limited to one geographic area—sometimes as small as one county.

Medicare Part A—The part of Medicare that covers inpatient hospital care. Most people don't have to pay for Part A, beyond the annual deductible of $1,288 in 2016, because they paid for it already through payroll taxes while they were working.

Medicare Part B—The part of Medicare that helps to cover outpatient care, doctors' services, and some other medical services not covered by Part A. Most people pay a monthly premium for Part B of $104.90 in 2016. New 2016 enrollees pay $121.80, and households making $170,000 or higher pay much more.

Medicare Part D—Medicare's prescription drug program. On average in 2016, people pay around a $35 monthly premium for Part D coverage provided by various private health insurers.

Medicare Rights Center—A national nonprofit organization that helps older adults and people with disabilities understand their rights under Medicare, Medicaid, and other government health programs.

Medicare Savings Programs—Assistance programs that help eligible people of limited means to pay for their Medicare premiums, and sometimes their deductibles, coinsurance, and copayments as well.

Medigap plan—Medicare supplemental insurance sold by private insurance companies that pays for the typically 20 percent of health costs that original Medicare doesn't cover. A person must have Medicare Parts A and B to apply for a Medigap supplemental policy.

multiple myeloma—A treatable but not curable type of blood cancer affecting a hundred thousand Americans. Around eleven thousand die each year. Multiple myeloma can eat away at bones, reduce kidney function, and compromise the immune system's ability to fight infection.

navigator—A person trained by a health exchange to help applicants enrolling in an exchange health plan or Medicaid.

Obamacare—Colloquial and often disparaging term for the Affordable Care Act (ACA), a comprehensive health reform law enacted in 2010. (See Affordable Care Act on page 291.)

oncologist—A doctor who specializes in diagnosing and treating cancer.

open enrollment period—The once-yearly period, usually in the fall, when people can enroll in a health insurance plan or make changes to their current plan without penalties. Insurers require an open enrollment period for everyone—the sick and the healthy—to create predictable customer risk pools. Insurers then study the pools to figure out how to design and price their health plans for the coming year.

orphan drug—A drug intended for the treatment, diagnosis, or prevention of a rare disease. Traditionally, drugmakers ignored orphan drugs because so few patients needed the medicine. But some drug companies have been boosting orphan prices sharply and making large profits.

out of network—Doctors, hospitals, and other health care providers that do not have contracts to participate in an insurance plan. Depending on the health plan, the insurer will not cover the costs of services that plan members get from out-of-network providers, or may cover only a portion of those costs.

out-of-pocket costs—Costs people pay on their own for medical services that aren't covered by insurance. The expenses include deductibles, copays, and coinsurance for covered services, plus expenses for services that the insurance plan doesn't cover.

out-of-pocket limit—The maximum amount someone will have to pay for covered services in a policy period, which is typically a year. This includes deductibles, copays, and coinsurance. But it doesn't include premiums, out-of-network services, and services that the insurance plan deems nonessential.

outpatient care—Services provided to a patient who has not been admitted to a hospital as an inpatient. Someone might be designated as an outpatient even when he or she stayed overnight for a day or two in the hospital. A doctor must write an order for a person to be admitted as an inpatient. Inpatient versus outpatient status affects what patients get charged for services, certain benefits, and the amount insurance companies decide to pay. (See inpatient care on page 300.)

palliative care—Medical care focused on providing people with relief from the symptoms, pain, and physical and emotional stress associated with serious illness. Although the care is associated with terminal illnesses, one or more health care professionals can administer it at any stage of illness in a medical institution or at the patient's home.

patient advocate—A person or organization that helps patients find quality care at affordable prices. Patient advocates are hired by companies for their workers and by private individuals facing particular concerns, such as finding a more generous health plan or responding to a surprise hospital bill.

patient assistance program—A program created by a pharmaceutical or medical supply company to help needy customers get the medicine or equipment they can't afford on their own.

preexisting condition—A health problem someone developed before he or she sought health insurance coverage. The Affordable Care Act prohibits insurers from denying coverage to people with preexisting conditions, or charging them more than their healthy customers.

premium—The amount an insurance company charges for coverage. A premium is a periodic charge, often billed monthly.

prenatal care—Health care a woman receives while she is pregnant. The services include checkups and prenatal testing. Under the Affordable Care Act, prenatal care visits with an in-network provider are considered a preventive service that health care plans must cover at no cost.

prescription—An instruction written by a medical practitioner that authorizes a patient to get a certain medication or treatment. Prescription drug coverage is one of ten essential health care services that individual and small-group plans must provide under the Affordable Care Act. However, prices and coverage vary greatly from plan to plan, drug to drug, and year to year.

preventive services—Health care, including cancer screenings and checkups, for the early detection and prevention of diseases. Many preventive services are available free of charge.

preventive test—A medical test intended to detect medical problems before there are noticeable symptoms. The same test can be considered either diagnostic or preventive, depending on why the provider decided to request it.

primary care provider (PCP)—A physician, nurse practitioner, physician assistant, or other health care professional who provides care and coordinates a patient's overall health care services. Synonym: your health care quarterback.

prior authorization—Authorization granted to providers in advance by a health insurance plan that allows a patient to get a specific medical service or to fill a prescription. Where required, the insurance plan will not pay for the service without its prior approval.

private exchange—A private insurance marketplace created by employers seeking to shift health costs onto their workers. Often the workers must select a marketplace plan to get premium subsidies or a lump sum from their employer. With a private exchange, an employer can choose to make a limited monetary contribution toward an employee's health insurance rather than cover the workers' open-ended health costs, as employers do in traditional group health care plans.

provider network—A group of doctors, hospitals, and other health care providers that contract with a health insurer to deliver their services at set prices.

pulmonologist—A physician who specializes in the diagnosis and treatment of lung conditions and diseases.

rehabilitative services—Health care services that help a patient regain and retain function that was lost or impaired due to illness or injury. The services include physical therapy, occupational therapy, speech-language pathology, and psychiatric rehabilitation.

self-insured plan—Health insurance coverage usually provided by large corporations directly to their workers. Plan members pay their premiums directly to the company, which takes on the responsibility of paying the medical claims of enrollees and their dependents. Self-insured plans are commonly administered by third-party insurance companies.

special enrollment period—A period outside of the annual open-enrollment period when someone can sign up for health insurance without penalty. Under the Affordable Care Act, a person qualifies for a special enrollment period of up to sixty days after a life event, such as losing health coverage at work or a change in family size due to marriage, birth, or adoption.

specialty drugs—High-cost prescription drugs used to treat complex, chronic conditions such as cancer and multiple sclerosis. Specialty drugs often require special handling, administration, and monitoring. (*Synonym:* Wonder drugs.)

specialty pharmacy—A pharmaceutical delivery system that delivers high-cost specialty prescription drugs to customers with complex or chronic conditions such as cancer and multiple sclerosis.

standard of care—Treatment that is acknowledged by medical experts as appropriate for a particular condition and is widely delivered by health care providers.

step therapy—A method of drug treatment imposed by health plans that requires patients to try low-cost medications for a condition before turning to higher-cost medications. If a plan member buys the higher-cost medication before trying the cheaper alternatives, the plan might not pay for the costly medication.

supplemental health insurance—An insurance plan sold by a private company that can help cover costs that a person's primary plan doesn't cover. The insurance can be bought to supplement a marketplace plan, a job-based health plan, or a Medicare plan.

Supplemental Security Income (SSI)—A federal program that provides cash to elderly, blind, and disabled people who have little to no income to meet their basic needs. SSI is funded by general tax revenues, not by Social Security taxes.

tier drug coverage—The system where an insurer divides its lists of approved drugs—its formulary—into four or more cost levels, or tiers. Generally, the lower the tier, the less members must pay. For example, tier one might cover only generics with low copays, while the highest tier includes the high-priced specialty drugs requiring sizable coinsurance payments, sometimes up to 80 percent.

underinsured—People are considered underinsured when their health benefits don't adequately cover their health expenses, including when they spend more than 10 percent of their income on out-of-pocket medical expenses.

United States Preventative Services Task Force—An independent panel of experts in preventive services and primary care that makes recommendations about preventive services such as screenings, counseling services, and medications. Recommendations are based on peer-reviewed evidence and are intended to help doctors and health insurers decide whether or not a particular preventive service is right for a patient's needs.

unitized pricing—A type of insurance coverage that requires workers to pay for each dependent individually rather than being able to buy a less costly family group plan.

urgent care—Care provided for medical conditions that are not considered emergencies but typically require care within twenty-four hours. Urgent care is commonly provided at doctor-run urgent care centers as opposed to many nurse-run convenient-care clinics (see page 294). Urgent care facilities tend to stay open on days and hours when physicians' offices are normally closed. Some doctor-run urgent care centers are staffed by surgeons who perform planned operations at lower costs than patients may be billed for the same operations in hospitals.

utilization review—The process of reviewing medical services to determine their necessity, cost effectiveness, and quality. People trying to determine whether they were admitted to a hospital as an inpatient or properly treated as an outpatient sometimes contact the hospital's utilization review department for clarification.

wellness incentive—A reward given by an employer to an employee who takes certain steps—like starting a stress- or weight-management program, quitting smoking, or undergoing a health risk assessment—to improve his or her health. Some companies also penalize employees who fail to take these steps.

Easy-to-Find Resources

Organized by health care category with website and phone information as available.

Affordable Care Act (Obamacare)

For general information: https://www.medicaid.gov/affordable careact/affordable-care-act.html
To enroll or renew: https://www.healthcare.gov/, 1-800-318-2596
For tax benefits and penalties: https://www.irs.gov/Affordable -Care-Act

Caregiver Support

Cancer Care, support organization: cancercare.org, 800-813-4673
National Alliance for Caregiving: caregiving.org, 301-718-8444

Clinical Trials

CenterWatch, clinical trial directory for patients and professionals: centerwatch.com, 866-219-3440
EmergingMed, trial directory for patients: emergingmed.com, 877-601-8601
National Institutes of Health: comprehensive trial directory, https://clinicaltrials.gov/, 301-496-4000

Crowdfunding (for raising money from friends and the public to pay medical bills)

GiveForward.com
GoFundMe.com

Drug Discount Websites

Blink Health, predominantly for generic drugs sold online and picked up at local pharmacies: blinkhealth.com

Good Rx, drugs primarily offered with large discount coupons and for sale at national chain pharmacies: goodrx.com

Milligram, drugs often available with large discounts and for sale at national chain pharmacies and many independent pharmacies: milligram.biz

Prescription Blue Book, wholesale drug price directory (subscription required): prescriptionbluebook.com

Family Leave

Family and Medical Leave Act (FMLA): dol.gov/whd/fmla/

Health Care Advocates

Families USA, nonprofit advocate for quality, affordable health care: familiesusa.org

Lown Institute, nonprofit that promotes appropriate care for all Americans: www.lowninstitute.org

Pink Lotus Foundation, nonprofit that provides complete breast cancer treatment, including surgery, at no cost for eligible women: PinkLotusFoundation.org

Health Insurance Information

Kaiser Family Foundation, independent source of health policy research information: kff.org/private-insurance/
Long-Term Care Information, fact sheet: longtermcare.gov
Medline Plus, government source of up-to-date insurance information: nlm.nih.gov/medlineplus/healthinsurance.html

Medicare/Medicaid

Benefits CheckUp, website where people fifty-five and older can see if they qualify for benefits or assistance: www.benefitscheckup.org, 571-527-3900
Centers for Medicare & Medicaid Services, administrator of Medicare, Medicaid, and federal health insurance marketplace: cms.gov
Children's Health Insurance Program (CHIP): https://www.medicaid.gov/chip/chip-program-information.html
Medicaid, federal/state health insurance program for low-income people: medicaid.gov
Medicare, government health insurance program for the disabled and those sixty-five and older: www.medicare.gov, 800-MEDICARE (800-633-4227)
Medicare Home Health Compare, compares home health agencies, organized by community or zip code: medicare.gov/homehealthcompare
Medicare Hospital Compare, compares hospitals, organized by community or zip code: medicare.gov/hospitalcompare
Preventive medical services: cms.gov (type "preventive services chart" into the home page drop-down menu to see preventive services commonly available at no extra charge, complete with provider billing codes)

Medicare Beneficiary Advocates

Center for Medicare Advocacy, national nonprofit law advocate for Medicare beneficiaries: medicareadvocacy.org, 860-456-7790
Medicare Rights Center, national nonprofit consumer-advocate organization: www.medicarerights.org, 800-333-4114

Medical Procedure Billing Codes

Current Procedure Terminology (CPT) codes, for provider billing from the American Medical Association: ocm.ama-assn.org/OCM/CPTRelativeValueSearch.do?submitbutton=accept
HCPCS codes, for Medicare billing: findacode.com
ICD-10 codes, primarily for hospital billing: icd10data.com

Medical Procedure Cost Estimates

Clear Health Costs, cash prices for health care services by specific providers in major cities: www.clearhealthcosts.com
FAIR Health, price estimates for health care in local areas: fairhealthconsumer.org
Healthcare Bluebook, price comparisons presented by procedure and zip code: healthcarebluebook.com
Medicare Physician Fee Schedules, complex chart of Medicare's provider payments: https://www.cms.gov/apps/physician-fee-schedule/overview.aspx

Medical Travel

Companion Global Healthcare, coordinates overseas medical care and travel arrangements: companionglobalhealthcare.com, 800-906-7065
Patients Beyond Borders, directory of vetted foreign hospitals

by specialty and region: patientsbeyondborders.com, 919-924-0636

Multiple Myeloma Information

American Cancer Society, for general information on multiple myeloma, a treatable but not curable blood cancer: http://www.cancer.org/cancer/multiplemyeloma/

International Myeloma Foundation, nonprofit that provides research and patient support: myeloma.org

Multiple Myeloma Research Foundation, nonprofit with successful record of promoting the development of multiple myeloma medicines: themmrf.org

Palliative and Hospice Care

Center to Advance Palliative Care, general information about easing the pain and tourment of late-stage life, plus a provider directory: getpalliativecare.org

National Hospice and Palliative Care Organization, directives and information about end-of-life hospice and late-stage palliative care: caringinfo.org, 800-658-8898

The Conversation Project, advocates for end-of-life planning: theconversationproject.org

Patient Advocates

Alliance of Professional Healthcare Advocates: aphaadvocates.org

Med Bills Assist: medbillsassist.com, 203-569-7610

Medical Billing Advocates of America: billadvocates.com, 855-203-7058

Patient Care: www.patientcare4u.com, 414-271-1790

Stone Ortenberg Support: stoneortsupport.com, 650-323-0216

Prescription Cost Assistance

Good Days (formerly Chronic Disease Fund), drug cost assistance for chronic disease patients: gooddaysfromcdf.org, 972-608-7141

Healthwell Foundation, drug cost assistance for patients with certain diseases: healthwellfoundation.org, 800-675-8416

Needy Meds, list of drug assistance programs and low-cost clinics: needymeds.org, 800-503-6897

Partnership for Prescription Assistance, drug industry copay support: pparx.com

Patient Access Network Foundation, grants to cover prescription costs: panfoundation.org, 866-316-7263

Rx Assist, directory of drug assistance programs: rxassist.org

Social Security Health Care Benefits

Social Security Extra Help, for assistance with prescription costs: socialsecurity.gov/extrahelp, 800-772-1213

Social Security, information about disability benefits and Supplemental Security Income (SSI): ssa.gov, 800-772-1213 (or visit your local social security office)

Specialist Physicians' Credentials

American Board of Medical Specialties, medical profession source where patients can check physician qualifications: certificationmatters.org, 866-275-2267

Acknowledgments

This optimistic book was born out of my bad luck of being diagnosed with multiple myeloma, a blood cancer that I'd never heard of until it got me in 2008. My struggles to navigate our broken health care system as I dealt with my cancer inspired me to try to help others find affordable care. As much as I knew about how to get straight answers as a career journalist, and particularly as the former editor of *Money* magazine, time and again I was reduced to being just another confused consumer trying to deal with astronomical prices for the medicine I needed to live, my old employer's sudden decision to slash my drug benefits, double-talking health insurers, and lousy Medicare policies.

Yet with the help of more people than I can thank here, I figured out what it takes to get the affordable care that everyone deserves. I also came to realize that everything I was doing to become my own Health Care Detective, others could do as well.

My wife, Carole, was the first to tell me to get to work. While I was grappling with whether my cancer medicine would cost us $571 a day or maybe only $2, she said, "You should write about this mess." It was more of a command than a suggestion.

Without Carole, I would not have made health care my beat. I would not have written this book—and, truth is, I wouldn't have left Bogota, New Jersey, and had a fraction of the life I've had.

Of course, there would be no book without the doctors who

have kept me as healthy and productive as possible for years. I owe my life to them. Our internist, Dr. John Rodman, is the family doctor everyone deserves and only the fortunate few have: brilliant, caring, and accessible. John became the quarterback of my growing team of specialists.

John directed me to a wise young oncologist, Dr. Raymond Pastore. Ray has been at my side for every step of my treatment, and I am proud to count him as a friend.

I am also indebted to Dr. Kenneth Anderson, who has been a leader of myeloma research at Boston's Dana-Farber Cancer Institute for three decades. Carole and I were more than a little frightened that I had gotten a death sentence before we first visited Ken. He quickly reassured us that he could keep a lid on my cancer with drugs he had helped pioneer. "Forget what you've read," he said with his usual cheerful twinkle. "You'll probably die of whatever you were going to before you got this. So drive carefully." We took the train back to New York and shared a huge medium-rare-on-the-rare-side "cowboy" steak at our favorite Italian joint—and toasted Ken with an excellent Barolo.

In addition to my myeloma team, I have been awed by the many doctors and health professionals I met who are dedicating their lives to curing illness and by the extraordinary advances they are making, particularly with cancer. I would be remiss if I also didn't thank the physicians and other professionals who helped me personally: Gerard Abrahamsen, Dr. Sanjay Bakshi, Dr. Patrick O'Leary, Dr. Martin Post, Dr. Eric Rose, Dr. Gerald Smallberg, and Lori-Lynne Webb—as well as the Multiple Myeloma Research Foundation's founder Kathy Giusti, who is an inspiration to cancer patients everywhere.

And I offer my special gratitude to our close friend Dr. Gerald Imber for his pitch-perfect encouragement, beginning from when I was reeling from the diagnosis.

Our children also have sustained me. After their initial worry and fear, and some tears, they became leaders of the home team that believed I'd get well again after a rough summer of chemo. Before too long, our daughters, Nina and Carla, were back to the eye-rolling they'd perfected in middle school as I delivered yet another "Frank's talk" over cooling soup at family gatherings. That inner team includes Carla's accomplished husband, Fernando Music, who became our son long ago. Plus their loving boys, Leo and Cosmo, who are the stars on our family tree.

Once I committed to this project, a number of people guided me. My list begins with Bryan Fisher, who arranged the first of my three hundred interviews for this book when he was at Families USA. He then took countless calls from me over the years, made sense out of whatever I might be muttering, and always patiently steered me to knowledgeable sources.

In addition, *Money*'s brilliant former Washington, DC, bureau chief Teresa Tritch helped at an important point by putting the draft of my original Health Detective op-ed under the right noses at the *New York Times*, where she works now.

For the past several years, my principal publishing outlet has been *Parade* magazine. The talented editor in chief Maggie Murphy invited me in, and her wonderful successor, Anne Krueger, as well as Katie Neal, have been very generous to me.

My other creative home has been National Public Radio's Robin Hood Radio. I want to thank the irrepressible Jill Goodman for imploring me to speak my mind and the always professional Marshall Miles for helping me to sound as intelligent as I can be.

When I was doubting I could ever finish a book, my friend Beth Kobliner, author of *Get a Financial Life*, told me all I had to do was write five hundred words a day, and sooner or later I'd write the book. And the kid from Queens was right.

The respected Dr. Richard Levine, a pal since high school, took the time from his schedule as professor of obstetrics and gynecology at Columbia University College of Physicians and Surgeons to read an early draft and told me he learned a lot from it. Those kind words lifted my spirits more than he knows and helped convince me that this book could help health care providers as well as patients.

Not only did publishing pro Bob Asahina—another old friend—also take time to offer his support, he provided important insights about how I should create my Health Care Detective brand.

And then there is Steve Gelman, the last of the great *Life* magazine editors and my friend of forty years. Beyond his sharp pencil as he pored over my successive drafts, Steve offered one smart idea after another that improved this book enormously.

I also want to thank my quietly persistent agent Nat Sobel, who lured me in at lunch and then refused to accept anything short of my best work.

In addition, my publishing team at Touchstone Books has been outstanding, led by my incisive editor, Michelle Howry, who championed this project from day one, along with her ever-helpful assistant Lara Blackman.

Along the way, I've had the heartfelt support of many others, including more than one friend who also has multiple myeloma. Tom Brokaw was diagnosed after I was and went on to write *A Lucky Life Interrupted: A Memoir of Hope.* His book is at once frank, touching, and useful to others. It was important to me that we were able to compare notes about our recoveries and draw strength from each other.

I also owe a debt to Steven Brill, as does the public, for exposing how dysfunctional and costly our country's health care system has become, first in *Time* magazine and then in his bestseller *America's Bitter Pill: Money, Politics, Backroom Deals, and the Fight to Fix Our Broken Healthcare System.* As Steve and I have discussed, my practical guide picks up where his indictment of our system leads.

And then there is the circle of friends and family who rallied around me when I was down and cheered me on when I decided to tackle this project. I couldn't possibly name you all, but I trust that each of you knows that I am grateful to you. Here is a partial list: Pat Benson, Bina Bernard, Walter Bernard, Andrew Bergman, Alexandra Mayes Birnbaum, Peter Bonaventre, Gerald Chaleff, David Corvo, Tony Cook, Carlo Danese, Christina Danese, Renato Danese, Byron Dobell, John Di Blasio, Joyce Di Blasio, Helene Gaynor, Philip Gaynor, Myrna Greenberg, Steve Greenberg, Jeff Greenfield, Jane Hartley, Johanna Hecht, Louise Fay, Susan Friedland, Stephen Kelemen, Ellen Levine, Deborah Mason, Mary Murphy, Millie Myers, Donna Olshan, Murray Pepper, Richard Reeves, Vicki Reynolds, Paul Ritter, Richard Roth, Roberta Roth, James Seymore, Joyce Seymore, Ralph Schlosstein, Dena Sklar, Catherine Smith, Richard A. Smith, Ray Sokolov, Ciji Ware, Michele Willens, and Lloyd Ziff.

And allow me a final note about reporter extraordinaire Ron Bartizek. From spotting hidden legal quirks to conducting eye-opening interviews, every time I rang his bell, Ron delivered.

Index

AARP health care plans, 94, 98
AARP the Magazine, 10
AbbVie, 184, 194, 202
acetaminophen, 200
Ackman, William, 180–81
ACT UP, 272
Actavis, 185
Actonel, 185
"actuarial value," 56–60
Adderall, 207
ADHD, 207
Advance Beneficiary Notice (ABN), 113
ADVO Connection Directory, 251
advocates, patient, 230–31, 232, 244, 251–52, 290
Aetna, 82, 203, 257
Affordable Care Act (ACA)
    affordability of plans under, 50–54
    "employer mandate" of, 32, 61–66, 77–78
    exemptions from, 64
    goals/benefits of, 11, 31, 38, 39, 40–47, 53–54, 58, 60–61
    "individual mandate" of, 32–33, 34, 35, 64–65
    loopholes in, 77–78
    Obama's campaign for, 34, 53, 69
    penalties in, 77
    and pool of insured, 51–54
    as standard for all insurers, 39, 51
    standards of, 61–66
    Supreme Court rulings about, 34–36
    and uninsured, 31, 60–61
    See also Obamacare
African Americans: breast cancer screenings for, 119
age
    and annual examinations, 12–13, 169–70
    and breast cancer screenings, 116–17, 118, 119–21

"catastrophic" health plans and, 60
    and HSAs, 77, 143, 146
    Obamacare and, 32, 42, 44–45, 46–47, 51
    and shopping for health insurance, 60
    and waiting room waits, 16
AIDS, 13, 272, 276
AIDS Coalition to Unleash Power (ACT UP), 272
AIDS Healthcare Foundation, 187
Alabama: and reducing future bills, 258
Alexandria Center for Life Science, 280
Alexion Pharmaceuticals, 212
Alf, Chris, 286, 287, 289
Alf, Lori, 285–90
alprazolam, 202
alternative providers, 261–64
Alzheimer's disease, 202
ambulance services, 64, 236–38, 266
ambulatory patient care, 40
American Academy of Family Physicians, 165
American Association of Naturopathic Physicians (AANP), 262
American Board of Internal Medicine (ABIM) Foundation, 164
American Board of Medical Specialties, 219, 245
American Cancer Society (ACS), 105, 115–17, 118, 120, 121, 123, 195, 269
American Congress of Obstetricians and Gynecologists, 119
American Dental Association (ADA), 138–39, 140
American Enterprise Institute (AEI), 36
American Heart Association, 242
American Medical Association (AMA), 104, 111–12, 149
Americans with Disabilities Act (ADA), 49
America's Bitter Pill (Brill), 110

amphetamine, 207
amyotrophic lateral sclerosis, 98
Anderson, Kenneth, 22, 243, 279–80, 289
AndroGel, 194, 202
anesthesiologists, 223, 227, 263–64
Angell, Marcia, 175
annual examinations, 6, 12–14, 168–71
Anthem Blue Cross, 70, 232, 237
antibiotics, unnecessary, 163
Antos, Joseph, 36
Aon Hewitt, 48, 76, 77
Archibald, Joycelyn, 53–54
Arnold and Porter law firm, 62–63
arthritis, 88, 98, 184, 185, 200
Ashikari Breast Center (New York City),
    105, 117
aspirin, 44–45
assistance programs
    and bad news, 249–50, 253, 255
    cash, 250
    drug, 87, 89–90, 192–93, 194–95, 207,
        214–17, 253
    eligibility for, 285
    and income, 87, 89–90, 195, 207, 216–17,
        253, 283, 285
    and Medicare, 81, 87, 89–90
    and Obamacare, 33
    of pharmaceutical companies, 180,
        192–93, 207, 214–17, 253, 283–84
    and reducing future bills, 253, 255
    and saving money at hospitals, 229
    See also specific program
assistant surgeons, 223, 227
asthma: clinical trials for, 268
Atelvia, 185
atenolol, 208
atorvastatin, 202
autoimmune disorders, 176

Bach, Peter, 183
back pain, 164
bad news
    and alternative providers, 261–64
    assistance programs and, 249–50, 253, 255
    clinical trials and, 267–78
    and delays, 243–46
    end-of-life issues and, 240, 258–61,
        264–67
    and family, 240, 241, 246–47, 260–61, 267
    and finding right care, 240, 242–46
    initial feelings about, 240–42
    and patient's core personality, 241
    and paying bills, 240, 250–52

    questions people face when given, 239–40
    and reducing future bills, 252–58
    as scary, 240–42
    and support, 242, 246–48
    telling people about, 240, 246–50
    and tests, 21
    and work obligations, 240, 248–50
Baker, Joe, 81, 86
balance billing, 150–51
bankruptcy, 58, 76
Baxter International, 269–70
BenefitsCheckUp, 89
Benicar, 200
Bennett, Roni, 202
Berwick, Donald, 107
Beth Israel Medical Center (New York), 124
BGA Insurance Group, 98
Big Pharma. See pharmaceutical companies;
    specific corporation
bills
    bad news and, 240, 250–58
    and balance billing, 150–51
    and becoming a Health Care Detective, 6
    and dental insurance, 137–40
    errors in, 228, 230–32, 251, 252
    false, 62–63
    and finding specialists, 244
    and fund-raising, 252
    guarding against surprise, 137–40
    ignoring, 251
    informing patients about, 137–39
    and Medicare, 84, 87–88, 103, 104–7,
        108–9, 111, 112, 256, 257, 258
    and Medicare Advantage plans, 256
    and Obamacare, 255–56
    paying, 240, 250–52
    reducing future, 252–58
    and saving money at hospitals, 230
    and sneaky fees, 158
    See also codes; billing; negotiations; type
        of bill
biopsy, 8, 122, 126, 128, 219–20
Blackwelder, Reid, 165, 166, 168
Blakely, Russ, 48, 79
Blink Health, 198, 206
blood pressure, 170, 208
blood tests, 21–22, 44, 123, 163, 166–67, 225,
    253, 254
Blue Cross Blue Shield, 52, 226
Blue Cross Blue Shield of Massachusetts,
    126, 127
board certification, 219, 221, 244–45
body mass index (BMI), 170

Boeing, 75
Boistard, Philippe, 205
bone cancer, Pasquini's, 239–40
bone-density scans, 164
bone-marrow disorder: clinical trials for,
    269–70
Boolbol, Susan, 124–25
Booth, Bruce, 179
Boothe, Sareatha, 151, 236
Boston Globe, 10, 126, 127
Boughton, Kathryn, 99–102
Bowie, David, 248
BRAF mutation, 282
brand-name drugs, 5, 88, 174, 201–2. *See also*
    specific drug
BRCA gene, 123–24, 126, 129
breast cancer
    and ACA benefits, 44
    beginning of screenings for, 116–17, 118,
        119–21
    billing codes for, 103, 104–5, 108
    biopsies for, 122, 126, 219–20
    and clinical breast exams, 117, 119, 121
    and CPM, 126, 128
    DCIS and, 125–26, 129
    double mastectomy and, 124, 129, 130
    early detection of, 118, 120
    false positives and, 115, 117, 118, 121–23
    and family history, 116–17, 120, 122,
        123–25, 126, 128, 129, 131
    free treatment for, 132–33
    genetic testing and, 123–25
    guidelines for screening for, 115–19
    and LCIS, 129
    and media, 127
    and Murphy case, 128–31
    Obamacare and, 125
    in only one breast, 126–28
    overtreatment for, 115, 116, 118, 121–22,
        125
    prevalence of, 116
    and reconstruction, 126
    routine annual screenings for, 115–19
    stopping examinations for, 121
    valuable lessons about, 131
Brill, Steven, 110
Bristol-Myers Squibb, 187, 194, 270
Brown, Jerry, 273
Brown, Sherrod, 190
Burwell, Sylvia Mathews, 109
Burwell v. Hobby Lobby Stores Inc. (2014), 34
Butcher, Candace, 231
Butterfield, G.K. Jr., 31

Cacchione, Joseph, 75–76
California
    disciplinary actions against doctors in, 245
    dispensing physicians in, 200
    drugs as political issue in, 187, 188
    and keeping favorite doctors and hospitals,
        71
    naturopathic licensing in, 262
    Obamacare in, 71
    right-to-try laws in, 273
    and saving money at hospitals, 229
    See also Covered California
California Pacific Medical Center (CPMC),
    232
Canada: drugs in, 188, 212, 272, 273
cancer
    and alternative providers, 261–62, 263
    children's, 267
    clinical trials for, 267–68, 270, 287–88
    cost of screening for, 154
    drugs for, 5, 88, 173, 175, 176, 276
    and MEC plans, 64
    medical travel for, 255
    and MMRF conference, 280–89
    and Obamacare, 31
    paying bills for, 250–51
    as preexisting condition, 98
    and reducing future bills, 255
    research progress on, 280, 281
    and shopping for health insurance, 64
    specialty drugs for, 211, 213–14
    and work obligations, 248
    See also type of cancer or specific person
Cancer Care, 242
Caplan, Arthur, 274
caps
    and ACA benefits, 41
    and dental insurance, 135, 136
    on doctor fees, 41
    on drug prices, 41, 45, 46, 50, 187–88, 214,
        216–17
    and employer health insurance, 37, 47, 48,
        76, 78–79
    on hospital bills, 41
    and Medicare Advantage plans, 257
    and Obamacare, 30, 38, 217
    and out-of-network providers, 41
    on out-of-pocket costs, 41, 45, 46
    reimbursement and, 78–79
    and saving money at hospitals, 228–29
    and shopping for health insurance, 60,
        78–79
cardio stress tests, 162

cardiovascular disease, 45, 268
Caremark plan. *See* CVS
Carson, Ben, 187, 188–89
cash, 112, 153–54, 206–7, 222–23, 250, 262
Castle Connolly Medical, 245
"catastrophic" health plans, 46, 60
Celgene, 194, 215, 253
Center for Medicare Advocacy (CMA), 93, 94, 105
Center to Advance Palliative Care (CAPC), 265
Centers for Disease Control and Prevention, U.S. (CDC), 154, 269
Centers for Medicare and Medicaid Services (CMS), 63, 90, 94, 95–96, 97, 107, 109
CenterWatch, 276, 277–78
cervical cancer, 164
child health care, 46–47, 64, 66, 258
childbirth/prenatal care, 41–42, 60
Children's Health Insurance Program (CHIP), 66, 258
chimeric antigen receptor (CAR), 287–88
cholesterol, 45, 163, 200, 202
chronic conditions, 44–45, 53, 110, 145, 199, 255. *See also* preexisting conditions
Chronic Disease Fund, 216
Cigna, 69, 98, 238
Clear Health Costs, 48, 87–88, 108, 111, 152, 154
Cleveland Clinic, 74, 75–76, 255
clinical trials
    and Alf's story, 287–88, 289
    and bad news, 267–78
    benefits of joining, 268
    for cancer, 28, 287–88, 289
    commonly offered, 268
    control groups in, 268
    doctor referrals for, 268
    and end-of-life issues, 264–65
    exacting criteria for, 267–68
    expenses for, 268, 276
    and follow-up care, 268
    and free drugs, 274
    and informed consent, 274–75
    laws about, 275
    for multiple myeloma, 287–88, 289
    odds of getting into, 267–68
    opting out of, 275
    and pharmaceutical industry-academic collaboration, 281
    phases of, 270–74
    placebos in, 274
    protections for participants in, 274–75
    purpose of, 267, 274
    questions about, 277
    and recourse rights, 275
    and "Right to Try" movement, 273–74
    risks of, 275–77
    searching for, 277–78, 287, 289
    and side effects of drugs, 269, 276
    who conducts, 269–70
ClinicalTrials.gov, 277
Clinton, Bill, 242
Clinton, Hillary, 182, 187–88
COBRA, 80–81, 130, 131
Cochrane Collaboration, 168
codes, billing
    and costly procedures, 224, 225
    CPT, 87–88, 104, 105–7, 110, 111–12, 113–14
    dental, 136, 138–39
    and doctor fees, 149, 151
    and drive-by doctoring, 224, 225
    and exaggeration of care provided by doctors, 224
    HCPCS, 112
    and hospital billing, 230
    ICD, 87, 104, 110, 112
    importance of, 103–12, 113–14
    lessons about, 109–12
    and Medicare, 87–88
    online, 111–12
    and preventive care, 108
    up-, 224
Cohan, Phuli, 127–28
coinsurance
    and ACA benefits, 43, 45
    and becoming a Health Care Detective, 8
    breast cancer screenings and, 119
    and colonoscopies/polyps, 45
    costly procedures and, 221
    and drug prices, 175, 214
    Medicare and, 86, 87
    Obamacare and, 8
    and rehabilitative/habilitative services, 43
    and scheduling doctor visits, 148
    and shopping for health insurance, 58
Collins, Sara, 145
colon cancer, 13, 45, 239–40
colonoscopy, 13, 20, 45, 155
Commonwealth Fund, 145
Companion Global Healthcare, 75
"compassionate care" programs, 253, 272
comprehensive coverage: and affordability of ACA plans, 51
concierge doctors, 154

congenital toxoplasmosis, 29
Congress, U.S.
  and breast cancer screenings, 118–19
  and clinical trial regulations, 275
  drug lobbying of, 190
  Gilead investigation by, 177
  and Medicare Advantage plans, 94
  and Obamacare, 31
  pharmaceutical investigations by, 185
Connecticut
  Medicare Advantage plans in, 94
  and reducing future bills, 258
  and saving money at hospitals, 229
  United HealthCare networks in, 70
Connolly, John J., 245, 246
conservatives: and Obamacare, 34, 35
"consumer-directed health plan," 49–50
Consumer Reports magazine, 57
Consumer Watchdog, 76
consumers
  as absorbing drug price increases, 175, 185
  as buying drugs abroad, 188, 190
  shifting of health care costs to, 76
  and what you can do about drug prices,
    194–96
  See also patients; specific topic
Consumers Union, 57
"continuity of care rules," 94
contraceptives, 34
"contracted rates" of insurance companies,
    220
Conversation Project, 260
Cooper, Jane, 79, 231, 238, 244
copayments
  and ACA benefits, 40, 43, 44
  assistance programs and, 192
  and becoming a Health Care Detective, 8
  breast cancer screenings and, 119
  drug prices and, 173, 175, 203, 216, 253
  and end-of-life issues, 266
  hospital stays and, 258
  independent physician networks and, 78
  Medicare and, 86, 87, 238, 258
  and Medicare for All, 191–92
  and Medigap plans, 97
  Obamacare and, 8
  and outpatient care, 40
  and reducing future bills, 258
  rehabilitative/habilitatitive services and, 43
  and scheduling doctor visits, 148
  and shopping for health insurance, 58
  testing and, 44
  transportation services and, 238

Corwin, Howard A., 224
Costco, 207, 208
costly procedures, 19, 218–27, 254–55
cough medicine, 164
Council of Advisors on Science and
    Technology, 272
counseling services, 44
Court, Jamie, 76
Covered California, 38
CPAP machine, 234
CPM (contralateral prophylactic
    mastectomy), 126, 128
CPT (Current Procedural Terminology)
    codes, 87–88, 104, 105–7, 110, 111–12,
    113–14
Crestor, 200
crowdfunding, 252
CT scans, 162, 164
Cuomo, Andrew, 233
Cuprimine, 179
curative treatments, 266
CVS/Caremark, 72, 203, 204, 205, 208
cyclobenzaprine, 200
cycloserine, 185
Cyr, Patricia, 16–17
Cystic Fibrosis Foundation, 195, 216

Daiichi-Sankyo, 187
Dana-Farber Cancer Institute (Boston), 22,
    233, 243, 250, 279, 289
Danese, Carole, 241
Daraprim, 181–83
Darien, Connecticut: emergency/ambulance
    service in, 237
date of discovery law, 233
Davis, Elizabeth, 206–7
DCIS (ductal carcinoma in situ), 125–26,
    129
Deadly Spin (Potter), 69
death. See end-of-life issues
deductibles
  and affordability of ACA plans, 52–53
  bad news and, 250, 255, 256, 257
  and becoming a Health Care Detective,
    6, 8
  and breast cancer screenings, 119
  and costly procedures, 222
  drug prices and, 173, 175, 183, 206
  and employer health insurance, 37, 49–50,
    76, 77
  HSAs and, 77, 141–45, 146
  increase in, 250
  and medical travel abroad, 74

deductibles (*cont.*)
  and Medicare, 86, 87, 88
  and Medicare for All, 192
  and Medicare Part A, 229, 256
  for Medicare Part B, 238, 256
  for Medicare Part F, 257
  negotiating with doctors and, 24
  for Obamacare, 6, 8, 255
  and reducing future bills, 255, 256, 257
  scheduling doctor visits and, 148
  and shopping for health insurance, 57, 58,
    60, 61, 74, 76, 77
  transportation services and, 238
  and underinsurance, 61
delays
  and bad news, 243–46
  in getting medical records, 25–26
  in getting test results, 21
  and waiting for doctor appointments,
    14–15
Delta Dental, 135
Democrats, 42–43, 94
Demser, 179
dental care, 46–47, 64, 134–40, 192, 257
depression, 41, 42, 202, 209
DePuy Orthopaedics, 272
dermatology: clinical trials for, 268
Devlin, Robert, 226
dextroamphetamine, 207
diabetes, 64, 98, 179, 199–200, 202, 268
diagnostic testing, 44
Diane (alias), 103, 104–5, 106, 107, 108,
  109, 113
disability insurance, 249–50
disciplinary actions: against doctors, 245–46
discounts, 23–25, 151–53, 201–2, 214, 229,
  254
dispensing physicians, 200
"Doctor John" letters, 26–27
doctors
  as accepting new patients, 52
  and affordability of ACA plans, 52
  appointments with, 14–15, 95–96, 147–55
  balance billing by, 150–51
  and becoming a Health Care Detective,
    7, 8
  and billing codes, 104, 106, 110, 112
  board certification of, 219, 221, 244–45
  breaking up with, 26–27
  chatting with, 234–35
  and clinical breast exams, 117
  and clinical trial referrals, 268
  concierge, 154

  and costly procedures, 223–25
  credentials of, 219, 221, 244–46, 262
  and diagnostic exams, 158
  disciplinary actions against, 245–46
  drugs and, 147–48, 199–203, 216
  earnings of, 190
  and emergency care, 14, 15, 151
  exaggeration of care provided by, 224
  face time with, 18–19
  and finding right care, 242–43
  follow-up by, 20–22, 158
  home phone/email address of, 22–23
  hospital affiliations of, 151, 245
  keeping favorite, 69–82
  kickbacks to, 185–86
  lack of knowledge about patients of, 7–8
  "last appointment" with, 27
  lawsuits against, 166
  limits on visits to, 71
  and MEC plans, 64
  and Medicaid, 23–24
  and Medicare Advantage plans, 93–94
  Medicare participation of, 14, 23–24, 93,
    95–96, 256
  in network, 149–51
  out-of-network, 151
  overbooking by, 15, 16
  and patient medical history, 19
  patient relationship with, 7, 8, 11–28, 121,
    147, 165–67, 169–70, 244, 289
  and preventive care, 154–55, 158
  "problem-based evaluation" by, 157
  provider contracts of, 7
  and saving money at hospitals, 234–35
  self-certification of, 245
  and shared decisions, 8, 165–67, 169–70,
    219, 225, 234
  and shopping for health insurance, 69–82
  and standard of care for patients, 12–28
  as "taking" your insurance, 150–51
  thank-you notes to, 27
  and unnecessary care/services, 14, 19, 20,
    158–64, 165–66
  use of medical terms by, 165
  waiting room waits for, 15–18
  See also doctors, fees of; naturopathic
    physicians (NPs); network providers;
    out-of-network providers; Part B,
    Medicare; primary care doctors
doctors, fees of
  and billing codes, 149, 151, 224
  caps on, 41
  and colonoscopies/polyps, 45

and discounts, 23–25, 151–53, 166
and emergency care, 151
and Medicare, 7, 23–24, 25, 148, 149,
    152–53, 154, 157
negotiating about, 5, 7, 8, 24–25, 148–55,
    222–23, 251
and patients' inability to pay, 166
paying cash to, 153–54, 222–23
and preventive care, 154–55
sneaky, 156–71
variation in, 7, 104
domestic violence, 42
dosage: and saving money on drugs, 197–98,
    199–200, 202, 209
doxycycline, 23, 185
Drier, Peter, 223, 224–25
"drive-by doctoring," 223–27
drugmakers. *See* pharmaceutical companies;
    specific company
drugs
    and ACA benefits, 44, 45–46
    approved, 71, 80, 81–82
    and bringing own medicines to hospitals,
        234
    clinical trials for, 196, 269–74
    desperately needed, 272
    directions for taking, 209–10
    and doctor-patient relationship, 147–48
    and end-of-life issues, 266, 273–74
    "expanded access" to, 272–73
    foreign countries as source of, 188, 190
    mail-order, 205
    marketing/advertising of, 184, 213
    and Medicare Advantage plans, 82, 92, 94
    off-label, 282, 283
    preventive, 44
    R&D programs for, 178–80, 184–85, 213
    reduction in coverage of, 175
    and "right-to-try" laws, 273–74
    and scheduling doctor visits, 147–48
    and shopping for health insurance, 64, 71,
        80, 81–82
    side effects of, 276
    for terminal patients, 273–74
    unnecessary, 19
    See also brand-name drugs; drugs, price of;
        generic drugs; over-the-counter drugs;
        Part D, Medicare; pharmaceutical
        companies; specialty drugs; *specific drug,*
        type of drug, or company
drugs, price of
    and ACA benefits, 41, 45–46
    and affordability of ACA plans, 50, 52

and Americans as paying more, 173–86
and assistance programs, 192–93, 194–95,
    207, 214–17, 253
bad news and, 250, 252, 253
and being a Health Care Detective, 4, 5,
    6–7
Big Pharma and, 175, 184, 185, 186, 187
caps on, 41, 45, 46, 50, 187–88, 214,
    216–17
and cash, 206–7
coinsurance and, 175, 214
copayments and, 173, 175, 203, 216, 253
and criticism of pharmaceutical industry,
    253
deals on new, 195–96
and deductibles, 173, 175, 183, 206
discounts for, 201–2, 214
and doctor-patient relationship, 147–48
and employer health insurance, 46, 173,
    175, 185, 197, 215
and FDA, 176, 184, 185, 194, 202, 208
14-day prescriptions and, 203
and free drugs, 5, 7, 172, 196, 201
and free-market system, 174–75, 181,
    182
generic, 172–73, 174, 181–83, 186, 193,
    194, 198, 200, 201, 208–9
increase in, 29, 175, 185, 253
and kickbacks to doctors, 185–86
lose-lose proposition concerning, 196
Medicaid and, 177, 180, 183, 185, 189
Medicare Advantage plans and, 92, 94
Medicare and, 183, 185, 187, 188, 189,
    212, 214, 266
and national health insurance plans,
    173–74, 212
Obamacare and, 29, 38, 214
obscure, 177–81
as political issue, 187–91
profiteering from, 188
public anger about, 173, 180, 181–86
and Pusateri's story, 281–85
R&D programs for, 178–80, 213
and reducing future bills, 252, 253
and rising health care costs, 50
and shopping for health insurance, 79
for speciality drugs, 3, 38, 79, 81–82, 173,
    175, 211–17
variation in, 3–4
ways to save money on, 197–210
what consumers can do about, 194–96
See also Part D, Medicare
drugstores, 91, 203–4, 205–7

Duke University, 250
durable power of attorney, 259, 260

EKGs, 163, 225
elections of 2016: health care as issue in, 187–91
Elmore, Joann G., 220
Emanuel, Ezekiel J., 168
EmblemHealth, 150
emergency care
　ACA benefits and, 40
　ambulance services and, 236–38
　and appointments with doctors, 14, 15
　billing and, 110, 151
　cost of, 237
　and dental insurance, 135
　and doctor fees, 151
　end-of-life issues and, 266
　and MEC plans, 64
　Medicare Advantage plans and, 93
　Medicare and, 238, 266
　out-of-network providers for, 40, 151, 224, 225–26
　patients' rights and, 226
　questionable procedures and, 113
　and shopping for health insurance, 60, 64
　uninsured and, 227
EmergingMed, 278
employer health insurance
　actuarial value of, 59
　bad news and, 249, 255
　and becoming a Health Care Detective, 6, 8
　breast cancer and, 118, 131
　and caps, 37, 47, 48, 76, 78–79
　and colonoscopies/polyps, 45
　complexity of, 54
　as "credible," 66
　decrease in, 3, 5, 37
　deductibles and, 37, 49–50, 76, 77
　and disability insurance, 249
　drugs and, 46, 173, 175, 185, 196, 197, 214, 215
　"employer mandate" of, 32, 61–66, 77–78
　as exempt from ACA, 64
　and federal government goals, 39
　flu shots and, 171
　and how to shop for health care, 73–79
　HSAs and, 77, 141–45, 146
　and MEC plans, 64–65
　and medical travel, 73–75
　motivation for, 37
　and network providers, 62

Obamacare and, 31, 32, 36, 37, 78
and out-of-network providers, 48
and pediatric care, 46–47
penalties for, 65, 77
and physician networks, 78
premiums for, 37, 48–49, 61
and "private exchanges," 76
questionnaires for, 48, 49
and same-sex marriage, 79
and shifting of costs to employees, 47–50, 76
and shopping for health insurance, 59, 61–66, 76
standards for acceptable, 61–66
tax deductions for, 36
and underinsurance, 61
and wellness incentives, 48–49
and work obligations, 249
"employer mandate," 32, 61–66, 77–78
employers
　and Medicare for All, 192
　See also work
end-of-life issues, 100, 258–61, 264–67, 273–74
end-stage renal disease (ESRD), 98
Ephron, Nora, 212
Epzicom, 200
equipment, medical, 43, 234
Esbriet, 273
"evidence-based medicine," 161–62
exchanges, Obamacare, 32, 33, 35, 38
"expanded access": to drugs, 272–73
Express Scripts, 205
Extra Help through Social Security, 89
eye care, 46–47, 257

Fair Health, 111, 152
False Claims Act (1863), 62, 63
Families USA, 36–37, 38, 58
family
　and bad news, 240, 241, 246–47, 260–61, 267
　as caregivers, 267
　and clinical trials, 276, 277
　end-of-life issues and, 260–61, 267
　and shopping for health insurance, 79
　and "unitized pricing," 47–48
　See also family history
Family and Medical Leave Act (FMLA), 249
family history
　and annual checkups, 169
　and breast cancer, 116–17, 120, 122, 123–25, 126, 128, 129, 131

Fay, Louise, 241
Federal Bureau of Investigation (FBI), 183
fees. *See specific provider or service*
Find-A-Code, 112
finding right care: and bad news, 240, 242–46
Fine, Michael, 13, 14, 15, 19, 20, 21, 24–25
Flonase, 200–201
Florida: Obamacare in, 80
flu shots, 155, 171
Follistim AQ, 207
follow-up care, 20–22, 158
Food and Drug Administration, U.S. (FDA)
    clinical trials of, 269
    compassionate care program of, 272
    and Crestor, 200
    criticisms of, 272, 273
    and drug prices, 176, 184, 185, 194, 202, 208
    and "expanded access" to drugs, 272–73
    generic drugs and, 194, 200
    and Giovanni's IBM, 263
    hip replacement approval by, 271
    and Mekinist, 282
    and myeloma research, 287
    Ninlaro approval by, 195–96
    and Opdivo, 264, 270
    and pharmaceutical industry-academic collaboration, 281
    and phases of clinical trials, 270, 271–72
    and R&D drug programs, 184–85
    and terminally ill patients, 274
food stamps, 250
foreign countries
    buying drugs from, 188, 190
    medical travel to, 73–75
foundations
    and assistance with drugs, 195
    See also specific foundation
fraud: in health insurance industry, 62–63
Fred Meyer stores, 207
free drug samples, 201
free drug trials, 196
free-market system: drug prices and, 174–75, 181, 182
fund-raising: and paying bills, 252
Funk, Andy, 132–33
Funk, Kristi, 120, 121, 122–23, 125–26, 132, 133

Gadd, Michele, 128
Geer Skilled Nursing and Rehabilitation Center (New Canaan, Connecticut), 99–100, 101

Geisinger Health System, 240
gender issues: and Obamacare, 30, 32
General Accountability Office, U.S. (GAO), 272
General Dynamics, 109
General Electric, 49
generic drugs
    and becoming a Health Care Detective, 5
    and Medicare, 88
    and patient-aid programs, 193, 194
    price of, 172–73, 174, 181–83, 186, 193, 194, 198, 200, 201, 208–9
    and saving money on drugs, 198
    and specialty drugs, 212
    for Viagra, 198
    and ways to save money on drugs, 200, 201, 208–9
    See also specific drug
"generosity": of health insurance plans, 57–58, 59
genetic testing, 123–25
George magazine: Lalli as editor of, 243
Georgetown University, 90
GetPalliativeCare.org, 266
Gilead Science, 176, 177
Giovanni (case), 263–64
Giusti, Kathy, 280–81
GiveForward, 252
Glassman, Harry, 17
Gleevec, 89, 186
Glumetza, 179
Goencz, Katalin, 150, 231
GoFundMe, 252
Goldwater Institute, 273
Good Days, 216
Good Samaritan Hospital (Los Angeles), 179
GoodRx, 198, 199, 202, 205–7
Grimm, Katie, 13, 246, 259, 260, 267
grit: importance of, 290
group purchasing organizations, 175
Gudis, Greg, 98–99

Harvard Medical School, 40
Harvoni, 176–77, 204
Haynes, Jordan, 177–78
Health Access (California), 51, 64, 65
Health Affairs journal, 274
Health and Human Services (HHS), U.S. Department of, 42, 86, 94, 109, 174, 204
health care
    advances in knowledge about, 285
    and becoming a Health Care Detective, 5–8, 10

332 INDEX

health care (*cont.*)
  cost of, 12, 37, 50, 69–70, 80
  earnings in, 190
  overutilization of, 12
  underutilization of, 11–12
  See also specific topic
Health Care Cost Institute, 174
Health Care Detective
  and Alf's story, 285–89
  benefits of being a, 10
  importance of being a, 5
  keys to becoming a, 279–90
  Lalli's articles/research about being a,
    4, 10
  and never giving up, 285–89, 290
  and Pusateri's story, 281–85
  and search for best solutions, 285–89, 290
  skills/tools for becoming a, 5–8, 10
  and taking charge, 285–89, 290
health care proxy, 259
Health Department, Idaho, 167
Health Department, New York State, 161,
    162
health insurance
  "actuarial value" of, 56–60
  and end-of-life issues, 266
  fraud and abuse in, 62–63
  "generosity" of, 57–58, 59
  how to shop for, 73–82
  mistakes concerning, 56
  national, 173–74, 212
  phony, 66–68
  and pre-signing activities, 71–73
  and reducing future bills, 252, 255–56
  shopping for, 55–68, 69–82
  and underinsurance, 60–66
  See also specific type, insurer, or topic
Health Insurance Portability and
    Accountability Act (HIPAA) (1996), 25
Health Net, 52
Health Savings Accounts (HSAs), 77,
    141–46, 188–89
Health Well Foundation, 252
Healthcare Bluebook, 87–88, 111, 152
Healthcare Foundation, 187
HealthCare.gov, 32, 65, 78, 80, 256
HealthPocket, 255
HealthWell Foundation, 195, 216, 253
hearing aids, 113
heart problems, 98, 255. *See also*
    cardiovascular disease
Henry J. Kaiser Family Foundation. *See*
    Kaiser Family Foundation

hepatitis C, 88, 89, 176–77
Hewitt, Aon, 48
hip replacement, 254–55, 271–72
Hirsch, Doug, 205–6
HIV, 13, 200, 268, 272
Holmes, Ariel, 126–27
Holzman, Tami, 107
home health care, 40, 96–97, 100–102, 265,
    267–68
Honeywell International, 49
Horizontal Pharma, 185
hospice care, 40, 99–102, 265, 266–67
hospitals
  and ACA benefits, 40–41, 42
  and amount of care, 234
  assistance programs of, 216, 229
  average cost per day in, 234
  billing by, 41, 104, 110, 228, 230–32, 258
  bringing own medicines to, 234
  and clinical trials, 269, 278
  and costly procedures, 222, 223–27
  discharge from, 235, 236
  and discounts, 229
  doctors' affiliations with, 151, 245
  double operations at, 235
  and eligibility for skilled nursing care, 96,
    99
  and end-of-life issues, 265, 266, 267
  finding the right, 112
  and health care advocates, 230–31, 232
  in-network, 224–27
  keeping favorite, 69–82
  keeping records while in, 235
  maternity/newborn care at, 41–42
  and MEC plans, 64
  and medical travel abroad, 73–75
  Medicare Advantage plans and, 93–94, 258
  Medicare and, 91, 93, 95, 223, 258, 266
  and "Medicare equivalency," 228–29
  negotiations with, 222–23, 229, 251
  out-of-network staff at, 151, 224, 225–27
  and "out-patient observation status,"
    91–92
  paying cash to, 222
  pharmacies at, 234
  saving money at, 228–38
  scheduling surgery at, 235
  and shopping for health insurance, 69–82
  spending a night in, 91–92
  suing, 232–34
  travel to, 75–76, 236–38
  See also emergency care; Part A, Medicare
HSA. *See* Health Savings Accounts

Huff, John G., 119, 120, 121, 122, 123
Humana, 82, 226, 257
Humira, 184, 200
hydrocodone, 200

ICD codes, 87, 104, 110, 112
idiopathic pulmonary fibrosis (IPF), 273
Illinois
    dispensing physicians in, 200
    and saving money at hospitals, 229
imaging
    unnecessary, 164
    See also type of imaging
immune system: drugs for disorders of, 212
immunotherapy, 287–88, 289
incentives, wellness, 48–49
inclusion body myositis (IBM), 55–56,
    263–64
income
    and annual checkups, 171
    assistance programs and, 87, 89–90, 195,
        207, 216–17, 253, 283, 285
    Medicaid and, 53
    Medicare and, 81, 86–87, 89, 256
    Obamacare and, 33, 37–38, 255
    and patients' inability to pay for needed
        care, 166
    and reducing future bills, 253, 255, 256,
        258
    and saving money at hospitals, 228, 229
    and shopping for health insurance, 65–66
Independence Blue Cross of Philadelphia,
    282, 283
"individual mandate," ACA, 32–33, 34, 35,
    64–65
informed consent, 274–75
insurance companies
    appeals to recalcitrant, 282–84
    "contracted rates" of, 220
    doctor fees and, 148
    and Medicare Advantage plans, 92–95
    "Right to Try" laws and, 273
    as selling insurance across state lines, 36
    and ways to save money on drugs, 203–5
    See also specific company or type of insurance
Internal Revenue Service (IRS), 65, 229
Isuprel, 179
ixazomib, 280

Jackson, Michael, 160
Jagannath, Sundar, 282, 283, 284
Jan (case), 261–62, 264
Jazz Pharmaceuticals, 177–78

Johns Hopkins Hospital, 75, 76, 117
Johnson & Johnson, 187, 271–72
Joint Commission on Accreditation of
    Healthcare Organizations (JCAHO), 74
Jolie, Angelina, 120, 124, 125, 132
*Journal of the American Medical Association
    (JAMA)*, 128, 219
journals, hospital, 235
JPMorgan Chase & Co., 49
Jublia, 192
June, Carl, 288
Justice Department, U.S. (DOJ), 62, 63, 180

Kaiser Family Foundation, 37, 49, 50, 53, 65,
    88–89, 90, 175, 187
Kale, Minal, 163
Kaletra, 200
Keck Hospital, USC, 158
Kelemen, Pond, 117–18, 120, 121
Kennedy, John F. Jr., 243
King v. Burwell (2015), 35–36
Kings County Hospital (New York), 233
Kmart, 199
Kroger, 207
Kyl, Jon, 42

laboratory services
    and ACA benefits, 44
    See also tests; *type of test*
laid-off workers, 80–81
Lalli, Ann (mother), 5
Lalli, Carole (wife), 2, 3, 4, 8, 16, 18, 153,
    154, 241, 242, 243, 260
Lalli, Edmund (father), 279
Lalli, Frank
    and affordability of ACA plans, 52–53
    and annual checkups, 170
    assistance programs and, 194, 253
    back surgery for, 5, 152–53, 162, 220–21
    bad news for, 240–43, 247, 248, 255
    and billing codes, 109
    blood tests of, 21–22
    core personality of, 241–42
    dental insurance for, 135–41
    and doctor follow-up, 21–22
    drugs for, 3–4, 5, 21–23, 50, 72, 194, 199,
        210, 211, 213, 214, 215, 276, 279–80
    and end-of-life issues, 258–59
    and home phone/email addresses of
        doctors, 22–23
    insurance plans for, 47, 50, 255, 256, 257
    and marketing of Medicare Advantage
        Plans, 66–68

Lalli, Frank (*cont.*)
   multiple myeloma/cancer of, 1, 2–3, 10,
     153, 170, 199, 211, 213, 240–43, 279
   and negotiating prices with doctors, 152–53
   professional background of, 1–2, 4, 10
   relapse of, 279–80
   and saving money at hospitals, 235, 236
   and taking care of yourself, 5
   tests for, 21–22
Lalli, Josephine (aunt), 5
Landman, Anne, 156, 157, 158, 165, 168
Langone Medical Center (New York
   University), 274
Lavern's Law, 233
lawsuits: against hospitals, 232–34
lawyers, 62–63, 259
LCIS (lobular carcinoma in situ), 129
Lee, Patrick, 13, 15, 18, 19, 27, 246
Lenox Hill Hospital (New York City),
   224–25, 232–33
leukemia, 89
Leukemia & Lymphoma Society, 216
Lipitor, 202
Lipschutz, David, 94
liver disease, 176–77
living will, 259–60
long-term nursing care, 192. *See also* home
   health care; skilled nursing facilities
Lowe's, 75–76
Lown, Bernard, 12
Lown Institute (Massachusetts), 11, 12–13,
   15, 16, 18–19, 20, 22, 24, 25, 184
lung cancer/disease, 264–65, 270, 273
lupus, 98
Luthra, Rita, 185
Lynn Community Health Center
   (Massachusetts), 13, 246
Lyrica, 203, 210

mail-order drugs, 205
mammograms, 48, 116, 118, 120, 155
marketing: and shopping for health
   insurance, 66–68
marriage, same-sex, 79
Maryland
   assistance programs in, 250
   and saving money at hospitals, 229
Massachusetts
   and preexisting conditions, 98
   Valeant case in, 180
Massachusetts General Hospital, 128
maternity care, 41–42, 64, 66. *See also*
   childbirth/prenatal care

Mayo Clinic, 75, 76, 124, 255
McAndrew, Claire, 38
McCain, John, 190
McMahon, Elissa, 232–33
MEC (minimum essential coverage) plans,
   64–65
MedbillsAssist, 231
media
   and breast cancer, 127
   soliciting of donations by, 252
Medicaid
   Carson's views about, 188
   and doctor appointments, 14, 95–96
   and doctor fees, 7, 23–24, 25, 148, 152
   drug prices and, 177, 180, 183, 185, 189
   and drugs as political issue, 187
   and "employer mandate," 77–78
   end-of-life issues and, 100
   and enrolling in Medicare, 87
   enrollment in, 31–32
   expansion of, 53–54
   income and, 53
   and reducing future bills, 258
   and shopping for health insurance, 66,
     77–78
   specialty drugs and, 213
   Supreme Court rulings about, 34–35
   taxes for, 183
Medi-Cal, 187
medical benefit managers, 175
Medical Billing Advocates of America, 231,
   252
medical records, 25–26, 27
medical travel, 73–76, 222, 254–55
Medicare
   ABN of, 113
   approved payment amounts from, 93,
     108, 112
   and bad news, 240
   and becoming a Health Care Detective, 6
   Carson's views about, 188
   and copays, 86, 87, 238, 258
   cost of, 86–87, 256
   coverage by, 66, 257
   and decline in employer health care plans,
     37
   and deductibles, 86, 87, 88
   denials and appeals of, 84
   doctor participation in, 93, 95–96
   "donut hole" of, 88
   enrollment in, 32, 84–86
   and finding right providers, 112
   fraud and abuse of, 63

helpline for, 81, 82, 87, 89, 90, 95–96, 105–6, 107, 108, 109, 238
and "Hospital Compare" page, 112
hospital participation in, 93
HSAs and, 143–44
income and, 81, 86–87, 89, 256
lack of understanding of, 83–84
mistakes to avoid with, 83–99
and Obamacare, 66
open enrollment period for, 84, 87, 90, 94–95
penalties of, 84–85
Plan Annual Notice of Change for, 95
and questionable procedures, 113
schedule of charges of, 238
and shopping for health insurance, 66, 81–82
and Social Security, 81, 84, 85, 86, 89, 256
"special enrollment period" for, 85
transitions into, 84–86
type of questions asked about, 84
See also Medicare Advantage plans; Medicare for All; Part A; Part B; Part D; specific topic
Medicare Advantage plans
and ABNs, 113
and caps, 257
cautions concerning, 92–95
cost of, 258
coverage for, 82
dental care and, 257
drugs and, 82, 92, 94
emergency care and, 93
end-of-life issues and, 266
eye care and, 257
and hospital coverage, 258
and keeping favorite doctors and hospitals, 94
marketing of, 66–67
and network providers, 82, 92, 94, 97, 258
and nursing home coverage, 97
and out-of-network providers, 258
Part B and, 92, 257
and preexisting conditions, 98
premiums for, 82, 92, 257
promises of, 93–94
and questionable procedures, 113
questions asked about, 84
and reducing future bills, 256, 257, 258
and shopping for health insurance, 66, 82
and subsidies, 92, 98
and surprise bills, 256

"Medicare equivalency," 228–29
Medicare for All, 54, 187, 191–92
Medicare Plan Finder, 90, 94–95, 257
Medicare Rights Center, 81, 83, 84, 85, 86, 105
Medicare Savings Program, 81, 87, 89
Medicare.gov, 82, 90, 97, 108, 109, 112, 257
medications. See brand-name drugs; drugs; drugs, price of; generic drugs; over-the-counter drugs; specific drug or type of drug
Medigap plans, 66, 97–99, 257, 258, 266. See also Part F supplement plan
Mekinist, 281–85
melanomas, 270
meloxicam, 208
memantine, 202
Memorial Sloan Kettering Cancer Center (New York City), 183
menopause, 121
mental/behavioral health, 42–43, 64
Mercer Insurance Group, 76
Merck & Co., 174
metformin, 199–200, 202
Metropolitan Life Insurance Company (MetLife), 135–40
milk ducts: growths in, 125–26
Milligram, 198, 206, 212
Milliman Medical Index, 37
minimum essential coverage (MEC) plans, 64–65
Minnesota
and affordability of ACA plans, 52
and preexisting conditions, 98
Minnesota Board of Medical Practice, 245
Mitchell, Rebecca, 262, 263
Money magazine, 4, 10, 242
Morgan, Lisa, 265
mortality. See end-of-life issues
Mount Sinai Hospital (New York City), 160, 163, 265, 281–83, 284
Mr. S (case), 84–85
MRIs, 24–25, 44, 48, 64, 103, 104–5, 113, 164, 253, 254
Ms. F (case), 83
multiple myeloma
Alf's story about, 285–90
drugs for, 280, 281–85
Giusti's work on, 280–81
of Lalli, 1, 2–3, 10, 153, 170, 199, 211, 213, 240–43, 279
and Pusateri's story, 281–85
and reducing future bills, 253–54
survival rate for, 281

Multiple Myeloma Research Foundation
  and clinical trials, 269
  conference by, 280–89
multiple sclerosis, 43, 88, 89, 176, 184
Munger, Charlie, 179
Murphy, Maggie, 15, 128–31, 219, 220
Mutual of Omaha, 98
myeloid leukemia, 212

Namenda, 202
Nasacort, 200–201
Nasonex, 201
National Alliance for Caregiving, 248
National Comprehensive Cancer Network
  (NCCN), 116, 119, 121
National Council on Aging, 89
National Federation of Independent Businesses v.
  Sebelius, 34–35
national health insurance plans, 173–74, 212
National Hospice and Palliative Care
  Organization, 259
National Institutes of Health (NIH), 268,
  269, 274, 276, 277
naturopathic physicians (NPs), 261–64
navigators: for Obamacare, 65
NeedyMeds, 216
negotiations
  and becoming a Health Care Detective,
    5, 6–7, 8
  with doctors, 5, 7, 8, 24–25, 148–55,
    222–23, 251
  with hospitals, 251
  See also advocates, patient
network providers
  and affordability of ACA plans, 51
  and ambulance services, 237
  and balance billing, 150–51
  churning of, 69
  costly procedures and, 219, 221, 223–24,
    225, 226
  and drive-by doctoring, 223–24, 225
  employer health insurance and, 62
  and finding right providers, 112
  independent, 78
  and keeping favorite doctors and hospitals,
    69–73
  and Medicare Advantage plans, 82, 92, 94,
    97, 258
  negotiating price with, 149–50
  and Obamacare, 58
  as primary care doctor, 244
  and shopping for health insurance, 58, 62,
    69–73, 78, 80

and shopping for Medicare plans, 91
  as specialists, 244
Neurontin, 241
neuropathy, 203, 276
never-give-up attitude, 289, 290
New England Journal of Medicine, 175
New Hampshire: Obamacare in, 70
New Jersey: and saving money at hospitals,
  229
New York City: scheduling specialist
  appointments in, 96
NewYork-Presbyterian Hospital (New York
  City), 23, 150, 226
New York State
  and affordability of ACA plans, 52–53
  and balance billing, 151
  date of discovery law in, 233
  emergency care law in, 226, 227
  and keeping favorite doctors and hospitals,
    70
  maternity/newborn care in, 42
  Obamacare in, 70
  patients' rights in, 226
  Valeant case in, 180
New York Times, 4, 10, 35, 107, 109, 124, 167,
  223, 224
Ninlaro, 195–96
nitrofurantoin, 199
Nitropress, 179
Norvir, 200
Novartis, 175, 186, 283, 284–85
nursing homes, 91, 96–97, 99–102, 238. *See*
  also skilled nursing facilities

Obama (Barack) administration
  and drug prices, 177
  and FDA approval for drugs, 272
  Lalli prediction about, 1
  and Obamacare, 31, 34, 53, 69
Obamacare (Affordable Care Act)
  actuarial value of, 59
  affordability of, 50–54
  and age, 32, 42, 44–45, 46–47, 51
  and bad news, 255–56
  and caps, 30, 38, 217
  Carson's views about, 188
  and copays, 8
  criticisms of, 34–38, 51, 53
  deductibles for, 6, 8, 255
  as election of 2016 issue, 187
  and employer health insurance, 78
  enrollment in, 32, 66, 255
  and enrollment in Medicare, 85–86

essential health benefits of, 30, 31–38
and exchanges, 32, 33, 35, 38
and gender issues, 30, 32
"gold plans" in, 53
and health coverage as right, 32
helpline for, 65, 256
income and, 33, 37–38, 255
influence of, 28
and keeping favorite doctors and hospitals,
    70
and Medicare, 66
navigators for, 65
overview about, 29–38
penalties/fines concerning, 32–33
platinum plan of, 70
and pool of insured, 51–54
and premiums, 6, 30, 33, 36, 61, 70, 80,
    255
and religion, 34
"shared-responsibility payment" of, 32–33
and shopping for health insurance, 58, 59,
    62, 64, 69, 70–71, 77–78, 80–81
"silver plans" in, 52–53
"special enrollment" for, 255–56
subsidies for, 33, 35–36, 37–38, 52, 61, 65,
    80, 81, 255
and underutilization of health care system,
    11
and uninsured, 31
yearly renewal of, 30
See also specific topic
obesity screening, 45
off-label drugs, 282, 283
Office of the Inspector General (OIG), 62
Ohio
    dispensing physicians in, 200
    drugs as political issue in, 187
Oklahoma: and affordability of ACA plans,
    52
O'Leary, Patrick, 162
omeprazole, 201
oncology: clinical trials for, 268
Onconova Therapeutics, 269–70
One to One, 78
Opdivo drug, 264–65, 270
operations. See surgery
Oregon: and affordability of ACA plans, 52
Organization for Economic Cooperation
    and Development (OECD), 173
Orrange, Sharon, 158–59
out-of-network providers
    and ACA benefits, 41
    and affordability of ACA plans, 53

ambulance services and, 237
and blood work, 167, 224–25
caps and, 41
cost of, 220–21
costly procedures and, 220, 223–24,
    225–26
emergency care and, 40, 151, 224, 225–26
employer health insurance and, 48
Medicare Advantage plans and, 93, 258
Obamacare and, 70–71
and saving money at hospitals, 232
and shopping for health insurance, 70–71
specialists as, 244
"usual and customary" rates for, 220
out-of-pocket expenses
    and ACA benefits, 41, 45, 46
    and bad news, 250
    and booking visits with doctors, 148
    for cancer patients, 250
    employer health insurance and, 49–50
    high-deductible plans and, 49–50
    and keeping favorite doctors and hospitals,
        70
    for Lalli, 3–4
    Obamacare and, 38, 71
    and shopping for health insurance, 60,
        70, 71
    See also caps
"out-patient observation status," 91–92
outpatient care, 40
ovarian cancer, 123–25
over-the-counter drugs, 200–201

palliative care, 265–66
Palmer, Pat, 231, 252
Pap smears, 44, 164
Parade magazine, 10, 128, 130, 218
Parekh, Samir, 281, 282, 283
Parkinson's disease, 98
paroxetine, 209
Part A, Medicare, 84, 85, 86, 87, 91–92, 96,
    229, 256
Part B, Medicare, 81, 84, 85, 86, 87, 91–92,
    238, 256, 257, 266
Part D, Medicare
    and ACA benefits, 46
    caps and, 46
    "catastrophic" care of, 46, 88–89, 213, 215
    cost of, 256
    coverage of, 256
    and drug prices, 88–89, 90, 189
    and enrolling in Medicare, 84
    formulary for, 204

Part D, Medicare (*cont.*)
  mistakes to avoid with, 83, 88–89, 90–91, 95
  premiums for, 90
  renewal of, 95
  and saving money on drugs, 197, 204, 215
  and shopping for health insurance, 81–82, 90–91
  and specialty drugs, 211, 213, 215
  yearly planning for, 90–91
Part F supplement plan, Medicare, 256, 257
Partnership for Prescription Assistance (PPA), 194, 216
Pasquini, Frank, 239–40, 243–44, 247, 252
Pastore, Raymond, 2, 22, 279
Patient Access Network (PAN) Foundation, 89–90, 195, 216
patient-aid programs. *See* assistance programs
Patient Assistance Now, 283, 284
Patient Care, 79, 151, 153, 231, 244
patients
  core personality of, 241–42, 289–90
  demand for unnecessary services by, 165–66
  guidelines for, 11–28
  health history of, 19
  questionnaires for, 19
  and shared decisions, 8, 165–67, 169–70, 219, 225, 234
  standard of care for, 12–28
  and unnecessary care, 20
  See also consumers; doctors; *specific person or topic*
Patients Beyond Borders, 74
A Patient's Perspective (Cyr), 16
Patton, Steve, 198, 208
Paxil, 202
Pearson, J. Michael, 178–80
pediatric care. *See* child health care
Pennsylvania: Valeant case in, 180
PepsiCo, 76
Pershing Square Capital Management, 179, 180
persistent symptoms: and annual checkups, 170–71
personality, core, 241–42, 289–90
Pfizer, 174, 175, 187, 198
pharmaceutical companies
  academic collaboration with, 281
  assistance programs of, 180, 192–93, 207, 214–17, 253, 283–84
  clinical trials of, 269–70, 273

"compassionate care" programs of, 253
congressional investigations of, 185
criticisms of, 253
and drug prices, 175, 176–81, 184, 185, 186, 187, 190, 214–15
and drugs as political issue, 187
and drugs for terminal patients, 273
and reducing future bills, 253
and revolution in cancer research, 281
and specialty drugs, 213
See also specific company
Pharmaceutical Research and Manufacturers of America, 184
pharmacies
  hospital, 234
  See also drugstores; pharmacists
pharmacists, 171, 205–7, 208–10, 216
Philidor RX Services, 180, 192–93
physical examinations
  length of time for, 18
  See also annual examinations
pill organizers, 210
pill splitting, 197–98, 202
Pinder, Jeanne, 107–8, 154
Pink Lotus Breast Center (Beverly Hills), 120, 132, 133
Pink Lotus Foundation, 120, 132–33
Plan Annual Notice of Change, Medicare, 95
Plan Finder, 82
political issue: drugs as, 187–91
Pollack, Ron, 36–37, 58
Pomalyst, 21, 199, 279–80
Popitz, Lisa, 243
Potter, Wendell, 69, 134
pravastatin, 200
preexisting conditions, 30, 32, 36, 66, 97–99, 249, 255. *See also* chronic illness
"preferred" drugstores, 203–4
premiums
  and affordability of ACA plans, 51–52, 53
  and drug prices, 183
  and employers health insurance, 37, 48–49, 61
  HSAs and, 144
  importance of, 54
  and keeping favorite doctors and hospitals, 70, 72–73
  MEC plans and, 64
  for Medicare Advantage plans, 82, 92, 257
  no-, 57
  and Obamacare, 6, 30, 33, 36, 61, 70, 80, 255
  for Part D Medicare, 90

for Part F Medicare, 257
and preexisting conditions, 98
and reducing future bills, 255, 257
and shopping for health insurance, 55–56,
57–59, 61, 64, 70, 72–73, 80
and specialty drugs, 211
prenatal care. *See* childbirth/prenatal care;
maternity care
PrescriptionBlueBook, 198, 208
preventive care
and ACA benefits, 44–45
and affordability of ACA plans, 53
annual checkups and, 13, 170
billing codes and, 108, 109
breast cancer screenings as, 116, 118, 119,
120
cost of, 154–55
and dental insurance, 135, 136
doctor visits and, 154–55, 158
double mastectomy as, 124
and HSAs, 145
and laboratory services, 44
Medicare Part B and, 256
and rising cost of health care, 50
and shopping for health insurance, 57
Prilosec, 201
primary care doctors
appointments with, 14–15
and bad news, 243–44, 246, 265
and clinical trials, 268
and end-of-life issues, 265
as network doctors, 244
patients' relationship with, 246
referrals by, 14–15
privacy issues, 275
"private exchanges," 76
private insurance, 118–19, 266. *See also*
employer health insurance
"problem-based evaluations," 157
procedures
and reducing future bills, 252
See also costly procedures; routine
procedures
propofol, 160
prostate cancer, 44, 89, 108, 239–40
providers
finding right, 112
See also network providers; out-of-network
providers
Publix chain stores, 208
Pulmicort, 173
Purdue Pharma, 187
The Purpose Driven Life (Warren), 267

Pusateri, Emil, 205, 281–85
Pusateri, Stacy, 282, 283–84

questionable procedures, 113–14
questionnaires
for employer health insurance, 48, 49
for patients, 19
questions
about clinical trials, 277
about Medicare, 84
and keeping favorite doctors and hospitals,
71
and shopping for health insurance, 71
Quillen College of Medicine, 165
Quincy, Lynn, 57

R&D programs: for drugs, 178–80, 184–85,
213
Ralphs stores, 207
Reader's Digest magazine, 1, 10, 66–67, 173,
240, 243, 248
"referenced-based pricing," 48
rehabilitative/habilitative services, 43. *See
also* skilled nursing facilities
Reichel, W. Carl, 185–86
religion: and Obamacare, 34
Republicans
and ACA benefits, 43
and Medicare Advantage plans, 94
and Obamacare, 31, 34, 35–36
"respite care," 267
Retin-A, 207
Revatio, 198
Revlimid, 3–4, 22–23, 72, 88–89, 194, 199,
212, 215, 253, 279, 280
rheumatoid arthritis, 98, 184, 200
Rhinocort Aqua, 201
"Right to Try" laws, 273–74
right(s)
and clinical trials, 275
health coverage as, 32, 34
patients', 226, 275
and work obligations after bad news, 249
risks
of clinical trials, 274–77
and "evidence-based medicine," 162
and patients' demands for unnecessary
services, 166
of routine procedures, 159–61
and shopping for health insurance, 76
Rite Aid, 207
Rivers, Joan, 159–61
Rivers, Melissa, 160–61

Roberts, John, 34–35
Roche, 273
Rockefeller, Nelson, 189
Rodelis Therapeutics, 185
Rodman, John, 22–23
routine procedures: risks of, 159–61
rules for life, 289–90
RxAssist, 216

Sacks, Oliver, 19
Safeway, 207
Sage, Sybil, 17
Saini, Vikas, 16, 18, 19, 184, 185
same-sex marriage, 79
Sanders, Bernie, 54, 190, 191–92
Savoy, Hannah, 115, 117
Scalia, Antonin, 35
scans
    and reducing future bills, 253
    See also type of scan
Schanfield family, 29–30
second opinions, 131, 218–20
self-certification of doctors, 245
Sequoia Fund, 179
sertraline, 202
Shandling, Gary, 170–71
"shared-responsibility payment," 32–33
Shkreli, Martin, 181–83, 184, 185, 186, 216.
    See also Turing Pharmaceuticals
Shockney, Lillie, 117
Shyla (case), 232
sildenahl, 198
skilled nursing facilities, 40–41, 91, 96–97, 99–102
skin cancer, 282
sneaky fees, 156–71. *See also specific fee or service*
Social Security, 81, 249–50, 256
    and Medicare, 84, 85, 86, 89, 256
Social Security Disability Insurance (SSDI), 249–50
Soliris, 212
Solodyn, 192
South Carolina: assistance programs in, 250
Southern Investigative Reporting Foundation, 193
Sovaldi, 176–77
specialists
    and ACA benefits, 40
    appointments with, 14–15, 95
    board-certified, 244–45
    earnings of, 190

finding, 244, 245–46
    and Medicare Advantage plans, 258
    as network/out-of-network doctors, 244
    and outpatient care, 40
    patients' relationship with, 246
    referrals to, 14–15
specialty drugs
    and ACA benefits, 45–46
    cost of, 45–46
    effectiveness of, 211
    exceptions/appeals concerning, 204–5
    and generic drugs, 212
    Medicare and, 88
    Obamacare and, 38, 217
    and preexisting conditions, 98
    price of, 3, 38, 79, 81–82, 173, 175, 211–17
    R&D programs for, 213
    and reducing future bills, 253
    reduction in coverage of, 175
    and shopping for health insurance, 79, 81–82
    and ways to save money on drugs, 204–5
    what to do about, 214–17
speech therapy, 43
St. Francis Hospital and Medical Center (Hartford, Connecticut), 104, 105, 107
Stabenow, Debbie, 42
State Pharmaceutical Assistance Programs (SPAP), 253
statins, 163
Stein, Judith, 93, 94
stem-cell transplants, 282, 283, 286, 287
"step therapy," 79
stocks, health care, 190
Stone Ortenberg Support, 231
Stone, Patty, 231, 238
strokes, 98
Stryker Corporation, 272
subsidies
    for Medicare Advantage plans, 92, 98
    and Obamacare, 33, 35–36, 37–38, 52, 61, 65, 80, 81, 255
    and preexisting conditions, 98
    and reducing future bills, 255
    and shopping for health insurance, 65, 66
    See also assistance programs
substance abuse, 42–43
succinylcholine, 160
Supplemental Nutrition Assistance Program (SNAP), 250
Supplemental Security Income (SSI), 249–50
support: and bad news, 242, 246–48
Supreme Court, U.S., 34–36, 64, 79

surgeons: earnings of, 190
surgery
    double, 235
    scheduling of, 235
Susan G. Komen Foundation, 119, 132
Syprine, 179

Takeda Pharmaceuticals, 195, 196
"taking" your insurance: doctors as,
    150–51
TapeACall, 235
Target, 207, 208
taxes
    employer health insurance and, 36
    HSAs and, 143, 144, 145, 146
    Medicare and Medicaid and, 183
    Medicare for All and, 191
    Obamacare and, 33
Teel, Allan "Chip," 11, 19, 22
Tennessee: and affordability of ACA plans, 52
terminal patients
    drugs for, 273–74
    See also end-of-life issues
tests
    and ACA benefits, 44
    accuracy of, 19
    and bad news, 21
    copies of results of, 235
    delays in, 21
    diagnostic, 44
    downside/risks of, 159
    duplication of, 161
    follow-up on, 21
    patient checks on results of, 21
    unnecessary, 19, 162–64
    See also type of test
Texas
    emergency care in, 226
    and reducing future bills, 258
thank-you notes: to doctors, 27
Third Point (hedge fund), 269–70
Thompson-Westra, Kyle, 167
Thorne, Gary, 253–54
Thuronyi, Victor, 259
tier-four drugs. See specialty drugs
Time Inc., 3, 50, 135, 243, 255
Timoney, Susan, 172, 208
Today show (NBC-TV), 129
top-tier drugs. See specialty drugs
tramadol, 200
transportation
    for medical care, 236–38
    See also ambulance service

travel, medical. See medical travel
tretinoin, 207
Trump, Donald, 253
Truven Health Analytics, 145
Turing Pharmaceuticals, 182, 183, 185, 216.
    See also Shkreli, Martin
Tuskegee syphilis experiment, 274–75

underinsurance: and shopping for health
    insurance, 60–66
uninsured
    colonoscopies/polyps and, 45
    costly procedures and, 222, 226–27
    and doctor fees, 24–25, 148
    and expansion of Medicaid, 54
    "Medicare equivalency" laws and,
        228–29
    and negotiating with doctors, 24–25
    Obamacare and, 31, 60–61
    and reducing future bills, 254
    and saving money at hospitals, 228–29
    and shopping for health insurance,
        60–61
United HealthCare, 70, 80, 94, 149–50,
    226, 257
United Nations, 124
United States Preventive Services Task
    Force (USPSTF), 44–45, 116, 118, 119,
    121, 168
"unitized pricing," 47–48
university medical programs
    and clinical trials, 269, 278
    and revolution in cancer research, 281
    See also specific university or hospital
University of Minnesota, 29
University of Pennsylvania, 287–88
University of Southern California Hospital,
    158–59
unnecessary care/services
    and annual examinations, 14, 168–71
    common, 162–64
    and costly procedures, 219–20
    and doctor-patient relationship, 14, 19,
        20
    and doctor-patient shared decisions,
        165–67
    of doctors, 14, 19, 20, 158–64, 165–66
    fees for, 158–64
    patients' demand for, 165–66
    risk of, 166
up-front information, 104, 109, 157
urinalysis, 164, 167
"usual and customary" rates, 220, 221

Utah
   and benefits of ACA, 43
   mental health coverage in, 43

vaccinations, 154
Valeant Pharmaceuticals International,
   178–81, 185, 186, 192–93
Vanderbilt-Ingram Cancer Center, 119,
   120
Vanstory, Carol, 240, 242, 249, 265
Velcade, 195–96, 276, 280
Veramyst, 201
Veterans Administration (VA), 32, 188
Viagra, 197–98, 204
Vicodin, 200
Vimovo, 185
vitamin supplements, 64
Vladeck, Bruce, 107, 113–14

waiting periods
   for benefits, 135–36
   for dental insurance, 135–36
   and Medigap, 258
waits
   for appointments, 14–15
   in waiting rooms, 15–18
Walgreens, 203, 205, 207
walk-in clinics, 40, 171
Wallace, DeWitt, 1
Walmart, 75, 199, 205, 208
Walsh, Anne, 262, 263
Warmbier, Fred, 141
Warner Chilcott, 185–86
Warren, Rick, 267
Washington, DC: and reducing future bills,
   258

websites
   fund-raising on, 252
   See also specific organization or website
Wellbutrin XL, 193
wellness incentives, 48–49
wellness visits, 44–45, 170
Wells Fargo, 49
WeRx, 206
whistle-blowers, 63
Wilkinson, Lavern, 233
Wisconsin: and preexisting conditions,
   98
Wohlfert, Frances B., 99–102
Woodman, Josef, 74–75
work
   and bad news, 240, 248–50
   and disability insurance, 249–50
   and laid-off workers, 80–81
   See also employer health insurance
Working Group on Compassionate Use and
   Pre-Approval Access (NYU), 274
World War II, 191
Wright, Anthony, 51
Wright, Wayne, 74

x-rays, 46, 64, 164, 254
Xanax, 202
Xyrem, 177–78

Yale University Medical Group, 70, 94

Zarfos, Kristen, 104, 105, 106–7
Zetia, 200
zidovudine (AZT), 272
Zoloft, 202
Zytiga, 89

About the Author

Frank Lalli became The Health Care Detective by discovering how to find affordable health care to treat his own blood cancer, multiple myeloma. With skills honed over his award-winning journalistic career, he has made health care his beat. In addition to writing this book, he is health correspondent for *Parade* magazine and National Public Radio's Robin Hood Radio.

Lalli has been a passionate consumer advocate since his early days as an investigative reporter at *Forbes*. His sharp consumer focus has helped him become the acclaimed editor of *Money*, *Reader's Digest International*, the *Sunday Daily News*, and *George*, where he succeeded founder John F. Kennedy Jr.

Lalli was named one of the top hundred business journalists of the twentieth century by media critic TJFR, after winning the three most prestigious prizes for excellence in financial journalism: the John Hancock, the University of Missouri, and the Gerald Loeb awards. *Adweek* also named him Editor of the Year.

In addition, Lalli wrote the first code of ethics for magazine editors while he was president of the American Society of Magazine Editors, and he was the Magazine Publishers Association's first Champion of Diversity.

Visit Frank at www.healthcaredetective.us.